Common Myths of Culture
An Introduction to
Cultural Anthropology

Common Myths of Culture

An Introduction to Cultural Anthropology

Nancy P. McKee

Linda Stone
Washington State University

2016
Sloan Publishing
Cornwall on Hudson, NY 12520

Library of Congress Cataloging-in-Publication Data

Names: McKee, Nancy Patricia, 1944-. | Stone, Linda, 1947-
Title: Common myths of culture : an introduction to cultural anthropology /
Nancy P. McKee, Linda Stone.
Description: Cornwall-on-Hudson, NY : Sloan Publishing, [2016] | Includes
bibliographical references and index.
Identifiers: LCCN 2015046321 | ISBN 9781597380591
Subjects: LCSH: Ethnology.
Classification: LCC GN316 .M43 2016 | DDC 305.8--dc23
LC record available at http://lccn.loc.gov/2015046321

Cover photo: Erik Lafforgue
Cover design by K&M Design

Sloan Publishing, LLC
220 Maple Road
Cornwall-on-Hudson, NY 12520

Printed in the United States of America

10 9 8 7 6 5 4 3 2 1

ISBN-10:   1-59738-059-8
ISBN-13:   978-1-59738-059-1

For Jorge and Rosario Vásquez, my first and best teachers of anthropology.

—NPM

For Harihar and Romila Acharya, with thanks.

—LS

Contents

Preface

This book introduces readers to cultural anthropology; it is designed for use in introductory, undergraduate courses. Because it is intended for students with no background in the subject, we begin by presenting the historical matrix in which anthropology developed as a field of study. We also provide a brief exploration of the biological basis for culture—the evolutionary underpinnings that allowed culture to develop. We do this to make clear that neither culture nor the study of culture arose spontaneously; they developed as the result of earlier environmental, biological, intellectual, and social phenomena.

At one time anthropologists concentrated exclusively on "exotic" cultural systems that were very different from those of the anthropologists. Today this is far less true. Anthropologists now come from a wider variety of cultural backgrounds, and they study culture anywhere in the world, including their own back yards. This book discusses cultural phenomena, the familiar and the unfamiliar, as they exist throughout the world and have existed throughout time. Ultimately, our goal is to illuminate and explore the overarching lesson of anthropology: that people are both dramatically different when it comes to many of their specific practices and profoundly the same in terms of their basic human needs and goals.

Among the social sciences anthropology is probably the least well understood by the general pubic; indeed, many people have ideas about anthropology and about culture that are misleading at best. Possibly this has come about over the years through various popularizations of the discipline as an exotic adventure. And today, while there is greater general interest than in previous decades in concepts such as "culture" and "ethnicity," often these constructs are bandied about loosely and with mistaken connotations and implications. In writing this text, we decided to focus directly on these misconceptions and correct (or at the least strongly challenge) them. Hence this book is titled and organized around *Common Myths of Culture*. We have listed a few of the most important misconceptions about anthropology and its subject—culture—at the beginning of each chapter, to alert readers to keep them in mind as they progress through the chapters. At the end of each chapter the refutations of these myths are summarized, with reference to material discussed in the chapter.

Aside from correcting common misconceptions, we have found a second advantage to structuring this book around "myths" of culture: This organization gives the book a clear and coherent focus. It gives students a framework to hang onto throughout the entire text and through a wide range of information and ideas. Too often our own undergraduate students in the past complained that their texts in introductory anthropology, while comprehensive and often beautifully illustrated, were too heavy, covered too much, and left many students feeling adrift in a sea of concepts and ideas. By contrast, this short book takes students over the full range of cultural anthropology through a constant thread of correcting or challenging popular ideas. While writing the book we were ourselves surprised to see how much of the field of cultural anthropology could be effectively covered by focusing on these myths and misconceptions.

This book, like most introductory texts, cuts its subject matter into manageable pieces and labels them with conventional terms like "kinship," "subsistence," and "religion." It is not that these categories are experienced as separate entities, or that they do not intertwine with each other. Rather, these labels are a heuristic device that make it easier for us, as observers, to make sense of other cultures and our own and to compare them. As students read through the book from chapter to chapter, it will become increasingly clear that each labeled category segues into the next, as it influences and is influenced by it.

Contrary to expectations for a book like this, there is no separate chapter entitled "Gender." This may seem particularly odd since both the authors of this text have focused a good part of their academic energy in writing about gender. Indeed we together wrote a previous book, *Gender and Culture in America* (2007, Sloan Publishing). We decided, however, that an understanding of gender in this book would best be served by *not* having a separate gender chapter, but by inserting discussions of gender into all the chapters. We have in this way illustrated the integration of gender into all aspects of culture.

Each chapter provides at the end several "Questions for Thought and Discussion." These questions have been carefully constructed to encourage students to explore the material, the ideas, and the implications of the content of each chapter. Whether students answer the questions as part of class discussion or in written form, instructors can effectively use these questions to help students approach topics critically and comprehensively.

We have tried to keep the use of anthropological jargon to a minimum in this book. On the other hand, as with any introductory text, there are inevitably plenty of new terms to learn and old terms that may have specialized new meanings when used by anthropologists. There are also some names of persons and places that are important for students of anthropology. The first time we use an unfamiliar word or expression it appears in bold type. This indicates that the term appears in the glossary.

With regard to the discussion questions and the glossary, we close here with two suggestions we strongly offer to students. First, pay close attention to the discussion questions. Try to provide your answers in a framework of clear general statements; give specific evidence that supports those statements and provide a coherent summary of your ideas. In the end, if you address the questions, either on paper or with others in your class, you will probably surprise yourself by knowing more about the material covered in the chapter than you did simply by reading it, no matter how carefully. Second, *use* the glossary! It will help you get more out of the class and your book. Even if the term does not appear in bold type, check the glossary. You may have missed the term the first time it appeared.

The German romantic poet Novalis (1772–1801, whose real name was Georg Philipp Friedrich von Hardenberg) advocated approaching life so as to make "the strange familiar and the familiar strange," which is a good way of thinking about anthropology. We hope that this book will help students in the endeavor, and that they will enjoy the effort.

ACKNOWLEGMENTS

Many individuals helped us bring this book to completion. Peter Castro (Syracuse University), Leslie G. Cecil (Stephen F. Austin State University), Jon McGee (Texas State University, San Marcos), and Ricci Grossman read various drafts of the book and made many helpful suggestions. Special thanks go to Paul F. Lurquin, who spent many hours in on-line research to provide the book with useful illustrations. We are also grateful to Casey L. Walle, a graduate student in anthropology, who produced many of the book's figures, and to Gilberto Guerrero Garza, a talented amateur cartoonist, who created the cartoon in Chapter 5. Last, but by no means least, we are grateful to generations of our undergraduate students at Washington State University who gave us valuable feedback on our ideas for the book and shared their educational preferences and perspectives with us.

Nancy P. McKee
Linda Stone

The Mouth of Truth is a marble scupture of a man-like face located in the portico of the church of Santa Maria in Cosmedin in Rome, Italy. The sculpture is thought to be part of a first-century ancient Roman fountain, or perhaps a manhole cover, portraying one of several possible pagan gods, probably Oceanus. Most Romans believe that it represents the ancient god of the river Tiber.

CHAPTER 1

ANTHROPOLOGY AND THE CONCEPT OF CULTURE

The nature and scope of anthropology and the role of culture within it

The ancient Greek scholar **Herodotus** (484–425 B.C.E.) traveled to distant lands, recording habits of different peoples, comparing these customs to one another and to those of his own society. Remarkably for his time, he provided fairly objective descriptions and commentary. He also made the following apt observation which he recorded in his *Histories*, Book 3; chapter 38): "If anyone… were given the chance to choose from among all nations the set of beliefs which he thought best, he would inevitably choose—after careful consideration of their relative merits—that of his own country." With justification, Herodotus is widely considered a Father of Anthropology. In broad terms anthropology is the study of cultural similarities and differences. It seeks to determine what is true of all human groups (what themes tie us together as a species) and what differs among groups in time and space (or what are the variations on these themes). It strives also to account for the similarities and variations. It attempts to answer the following kinds of questions.

1. Do all human groups have religion? If so, why?
2. Have all human cultures engaged in warfare?
3. Are any human groups truly egalitarian?
4. What is the origin of human socioeconomic inequality?

5. How varied are human practices in religion, marriage, sex, or artistic expression and what accounts for the variation?

Anthropology raises these and other interesting questions, even though anthropologists may not always agree on the answers.

Culture guides human behavior and thought, often in ways that seem mysterious or about which we are entirely unaware. Anthropology seeks to unlock this mystery, to make explicit what has been hidden. Anthropologists often say that through encounters with another culture we see our own culture thrown into relief; we become aware of how our culture influences us. For many North Americans, it is only when they encounter cultures where humans eat dogs or horses that they become fully and acutely aware of their own cultural attitudes towards these animals. It is only when they see the strong respect shown to elders in other cultures that they become sharply aware of the attitudes and practices concerning the elderly in their own society. Through systematic exposure to different cultures, anthropology can bring about a new sort of self-knowledge or self-awareness.

For a long stretch of human history, a heightened sense of cross-cultural awareness or skills of cross-cultural understanding were not so important for our individual or social well-being. This is no longer the case. With modern transportation, migration, and communication the world has shrunk. Today, our families, our neighborhoods, our schools, and our places of work, leisure, and worship are becoming more and more multicultural. Our negotiating this world and finding our place within it depend on our comprehending cultures other than our own. Increasingly, our jobs, careers, and success in other life opportunities depend on our ability to communicate effectively across cultural boundaries.

And yet, while the relevance of cultural and cross-cultural knowledge increases, so too do popular misperceptions of what culture is and how it works. These common misconceptions considerably impede our ability to appreciate and navigate the multicultural world around us. To counter this trend, this book introduces the field of cultural anthropology through focusing directly on these popular "myths of human culture." Each chapter lays out a set of common myths at the beginning, addresses these within the body of the chapter and then returns to them in the chapter summaries. As students learn about the field of anthropology and its subject, culture, the myths are dispelled.

This opening chapter of the book is an overview of the field of anthropology and the concept of culture. It pays special attention to the following myths:

Common Myths of Culture
Myth #1 Anthropology is the study of "exotic" cultures.
Myth #2 Because the word "culture" can refer to elite forms of expression, art, and entertainment (like ballet and classical music), not all human groups have culture.
Myth #3 There are no characteristics shared by all human groups, and so no way of making general statements about human culture.
Myth #4 Some cultures are superior to others.

Among academic disciplines on college and university campuses, anthropology is probably one of the least understood. Most people know what history and psychology are, and they have an idea about what chemists do, even though they may not know much chemistry. The term "anthropology" might conjure up visions of lone adventurers traipsing through jungles, dodging cannibals, or finding hidden temples of gold, but these images are hardly realistic. Anthropology *is* an exciting field and sometimes full of adventure, but what is it really all about? What is it that anthropologists actually do?

Anthropology Defined

Some anthropologists think of themselves as scientists, while others align themselves more with the humanities.[1] Yet most anthropologists will agree that whether they focus on child-rearing practices, language change, religious ritual, or the manufacture of stone tools, they use many of the techniques and approaches of science. These include a systematic approach to collecting and analyzing information; the construction and testing of **hypotheses** (provisional statements about the ways in which specific causes and effects are related); and a consensus about standards for assessing the validity of conclusions. There are many other valuable and legitimate ways of exploring the world other than science, of course. Poets, novelists, painters, sculptors, and philosophers, for example, all have distinctive ways of seeing humans and their situations. But anthropologists have carved out their own corner of the intellectual world, and in general it differs considerably from that of artists and more resembles that of scientists.

Anthropology is usually classified as a *social science*, along with sociology, political science, psychology, and history. What all of these disciplines have in common is that they are systematic attempts to understand humans, or the human condition. The focus of each one, however, is different. To understand the focus of anthropology, it is helpful to construct a more precise definition of the discipline. There are almost as many of these definitions as there are anthropologists, and those of us who teach anthropology usually start our introductory courses with our own definitions. Here is the one that we will use in this text:

> **Anthropology is the empirically based, comparative study of humans through time and space, focusing on the central concept of culture and informed by the principle of cultural relativism.**

This definition is useful only if all the terms are clearly understood. So let us consider the most important terms and phrases one by one, and explore what they mean.

1. empirically based Anthropological information is based on direct experience, rather than on speculation. Thus, instead of speculating as to what *might* be true about other peoples' ways of life, anthropologists go into the **field** (the communities of the people they wish to study) to find out how these people *actually* live (or used to live, in the case of archaeologists). An example involves the **!Kung** people (also called the **Ju/'hoansi**), hunters and foragers of the Kalahari Desert in Botswana and Namibia. Instead of speculating on what life *might* be like for them, anthropologists like Richard B. Lee and Marjorie Shostak, to name just two, have told us what life is *actually* like for them. These anthropologists were able to do this because they, themselves, lived with the !Kung people, and participated in their daily lives. Lee is well known to students of anthropology for his comprehensive **ethnography**, or cultural description, of the !Kung, while Shostak has fascinated thousands of readers with her life history, *Nisa, Autobiography of a !Kung Woman* (the symbols, "/," "'," and "!," represent consonants in the !Kung language). Without works like these on the !Kung, we might still believe, as the English philosopher, Thomas Hobbes, did in the seventeenth century, that before the advent of urban-based society, there were "No arts, no letters, no society; and which is worst of all, continual fear and danger of violent death; and the life of man, solitary, poor, nasty, brutish, and short" (Hobbes, 1958 [1651]). This book covers anthropological accounts of the lives of hunter-gatherers in Chapters 4 and 5, where quite a different picture is presented.

2. comparative   To determine what characteristics are universal to humans and what characteristics are distinctive to certain cultural groups, it is essential to *compare* different systems. This is what anthropologists refer to as "cross-cultural" comparison. Because of cross-cultural comparison, we know, for example, that not all peoples of the world live in nuclear families, with mother, father, and their young children together in one house. We know about groups in highland New Guinea where women and their children live in their own houses and are visited by their husbands (who may have several wives), while their husbands, as well as their adolescent sons, live together with other men in a men's house.

While showing us this kind of variation, cross-cultural comparison has also taught us that there are virtually no societies in the world that do not have some system of marriage. This is important, because a few centuries ago Europeans thought that some people elsewhere in the world were too "primitive" to have the institution of marriage. But thanks to cross-cultural comparative studies, we now know that whether a group believes marriage involves only one man and one woman (at a time), one man and several women, one woman and several men, several men and several women, two men, or two women, *every group* has a marriage system, and all these systems have specific rules. In some societies, under some circumstances, women may take other women as spouses, and men may take other men as spouses. This, in fact, is increasingly true in the United States. Without the comparative approach fostered by anthropology, we would have a very limited and unrealistic notion of what is considered acceptable or "normal" within human societies, or even what systems actually exist.

3. human   Anthropologists look at *all* human groups. All organisms designated *Homo sapiens* are human, and anthropology examines humans with both a cultural focus (see below for a definition of this) and a biological one. Thus, in addition to considering the language a human group speaks, its religious convictions, and its prehistory, anthropology also examines the distinctive biological characteristics of a group's members. Though there are numerous biological traits by which individual human groups vary, including hair form, blood type, and skin color, it is clear that, like any other species, *Homo sapiens* is marked by far more biological uniformity than diversity. Anthropologists examine not only biologically modern humans, but also their extinct ancestors and their living cousins, the nonhuman primates, to provide information about how humans evolved into what they are today.

4. through time and space Anthropology covers all human groups in all places and at all times. Obviously, no single anthropologist can be equally expert about all times and places, but every anthropologist contributes to the fund of knowledge upon which we all draw. Usually, cultural anthropologists (whom we will discuss shortly) concentrate on one geographical location, or on two or three, at most. And archaeologists (whom we will also discuss in a few pages) are likely to concentrate not only on a particular geographical location, but on a general time period, as well.

When anthropology began in the nineteenth century, the general focus was on exotic cultures that were little known to the Europeans and Euro-Americans who were the first anthropologists. Although part of the reason for this early research was to facilitate colonialism, these early anthropological studies did provide valuable information about hitherto unknown or poorly understood human groups. In addition, these early anthropologists often developed an appreciation for the groups they studied and a sense of responsibility toward them.

Today, anthropologists also examine groups who may be more familiar to them, including participants in their own culture. This is increasingly the case for cultural anthropologists and archaeologists. So, for example, although many archaeologists from the United States still labor in the shadows of the Egyptian pyramids, others explore the garbage discarded by contemporary people. One such study asks an important question: in times of economic recession, how do middle class Americans *actually* modify their consumption? Archaeologists can give us an idea, by examining the contents of contemporary garbage cans, as archaeologist William Rathje and his students did in Tucson, Arizona (Rathje, 2001). In the end, what is important about anthropology is not where the work is done, or who the objects of study are, but whether the studies are carried out according to anthropological concepts and concerns. What defines anthropology is the questions it asks and the way its work is done.

5. culture We will explore the idea of culture in greater detail as this chapter goes on. But because culture is so central to anthropology, we need to get a jump start with a working definition. Basically, anthropologists use the term "culture" to refer both to the rules and beliefs that organize the way people behave, as well as to their practices. So we can say that one's culture determines how many spouses to whom anyone can be married at one time, or whether men must tie strips of colored cloth around their necks when they engage in formal activities. Within any cultural system, some cultural rules are explicit, or clearly and formally laid out, while others are implicit, or simply generally understood and taken for granted. American culture explicitly says that a person can have only one spouse at a time; in fact, the United States has codified laws governing this behavior. But in many other situations our culture has only *implicit* rules about acceptable behavior, for example about when men need to tie those strips of cloth around their necks. While there are no necktie laws on the books, we seem to be able to guess which situations warrant the donning of this piece of symbolic clothing. If we guess wrong, mostly we just feel foolish, but occasionally a fancy restaurant will make us wear one of their spares. And of course, this implicit rule applies only to men.

6. cultural relativism   Cultural relativism is the idea that it is intellectually unproductive and unsound to make value judgments about cultural systems and practices simply because they differ from one's own. Thus, anthropologists, whether female or male, do not make negative value judgments about the veiling and seclusion of women in conservative Islamic societies, or about the arranged marriages of children in a variety of African and Asian societies. It is not the task of the anthropologist to judge cultures, but to study them. Anthropology is an attempt to understand a culture in the context of the ideas, beliefs, and values of *that* culture; to observe cultural practices integrated into a cultural system that allows its participants to live and reproduce; and to analyze the perspectives of that system. We will return to the concept of cultural relativism and some issues it raises at the end of this chapter.

Having now defined anthropology, it is important also to note a particular characteristic of the field that distinguishes it from other social sciences. Anthropology is a discipline that takes a **holistic** approach in its study of humans. This means that it looks at all aspects of the lives of humans; it is inclusive. Anthropology's holistic approach draws from a wide variety of techniques and bodies of knowledge which it attempts to organize into an integrated whole. And though individual anthropologists usually concentrate on one aspect of human experience at a time (economic, religious, political, and so on), they take pains to demonstrate how the aspect they focus on is related to other aspects of life.

THE SUBDISCIPLINES OF ANTHROPOLOGY IN NORTH AMERICA

As colleges and universities vary from country to country, so do academic disciplines, and anthropology is no exception. What anthropologists in North

America consider subdivisions of anthropology are in some other countries housed in separate academic departments and maintain separate identities. But in North America, anthropology is considered to be made up of four **subdisciplines.** These are **cultural anthropology, linguistics, physical anthropology,** and **archaeology.** Many North American anthropologists, including the authors of this text, would also include **applied anthropology** as a subdiscipline of anthropology. The authors of this text are both cultural anthropologists; McKee is also a linguist, and Stone has worked as an applied anthropologist. Although this book is primarily focused on cultural anthropology, this subdiscipline is best understood in terms of its place within the whole of anthropology.

Cultural Anthropology

Cultural anthropology is also referred to as socio-cultural anthropology, social anthropology (especially in Britain), and **ethnology**. Its focus is on existing cultural systems, their similarities and differences, the ways in which cultural traits are related within and across societies, and the kinds of circumstances in which certain cultural traits develop and change. To acquire this information, cultural anthropologists usually collect data through a distinctive anthropological technique called participant observation (see Chapter 2). This process involves anthropologists living in the communities they are studying and participating as much as possible in the community's daily activities.

Through participant observation and other methods of collecting information about communities, anthropologists put together a description and analysis of the cultural system that organizes the community they are studying. To build this picture, anthropologists usually break the cultural system into several constituent parts. This process helps to make the resulting **ethnography**, or cultural description, easier to compare with other ethnographies. Some of the traditional categories cultural anthropologists use for their ethnographies include the following:

Subsistence (how people make a living)

Social organization (how people organize themselves to take care of necessary tasks and allocate power and authority)

Kinship (how people calculate the ways in which they are related to each other and decide what rights and obligations these relationships entail)

Marriage (how people decide whom to marry, when to marry, how many people to marry, and what rights and obligations marriage entails)

Gender (how people assess human identity based on maleness, femaleness, or a combination of these qualities)

Religion (how people understand the spiritual world and interact with it)

Art (how people create, use, and define—or do not define—the specialized activities, skills, and creation of visual, verbal, and musical productions according to culturally-approved patterns)

If you examine the table of contents of this book, you will see that the chapters cover all of these categories of cultural anthropology except gender. In this book gender is a category discussed within several chapters.

Linguistics

Linguistics is a subdiscipline that, even in the United States, is likely to exist either as part of another academic department (such as English, foreign languages, or education), or as a separate department altogether. Linguistics covers a variety of endeavors, including the study of the properties of language; analysis of the social, symbolic, and psychological roles of language; the study of the "genetic" relationships among languages; and the study of the development of language over time. Chapter 7 of this text discusses those aspects of linguistics that are most closely related to other aspects of cultural anthropology.

Physical Anthropology

Physical anthropology is the study of humans as biological creatures. To do this, physical anthropologists study living human groups to determine the biological adaptations they have developed to cope with their surroundings. For example, the trait that produces sickle cell anemia, a serious disease that can kill those who have it, also provides limited protection from malaria, a very widespread disease that can also kill those who suffer from it. How do these two disorders interact, and how do they affect the survival of the people who have them? Physical anthropologists as well as medical doctors are involved in this research.

Virtually all contemporary anthropologists base their understanding of humans along with their productions and capabilities on the results of biological evolution—that is, the development of one species from another as a result of natural selection. Natural selection is the principle that those organisms best suited to their environments are likely to survive in larger numbers and more likely to pass their genetic characteristics on to their offspring than organisms that are less well adapted. These adaptive traits are thus transmitted to succeeding generations, whereas maladaptive traits are likely to be reproduced in smaller numbers or to die out altogether.

Some physical anthropologists, as noted earlier, examine the fossil remains of our evolutionary ancestors to study human evolution (see Chapter 3). Others (primatologists) observe our existing cousins. Today's monkeys and apes are not our ancestors, but they are *descended from our ancestors*, and they can tell us a great deal about how our ancestors behaved and what their physical bodies were like. To study human evolution, observation of our living cousins can be combined with information, especially fossilized bones, derived directly from creatures who actually *were* our ancient ancestors and other relatives.

Archaeology

Archaeology is the study of past societies and their cultural characteristics through the systematic examination of the material remains their participants have left behind. Another way to think about it is to say that archaeology is the cultural anthropology of dead people. Because the people are dead, we cannot participate in their societies or observe their subsistence activities or religious rituals. Instead, we have to look at what is left after the participants in the culture have died, and their culture, itself, has radically changed or even become extinct. The material remnants of a culture include buildings, tools, cooking and storage pots, grave goods, animal and human bones, and even remnants of animal and vegetable foodstuffs.

Many archaeologists focus on societies that did not have a written language, but this is not always the case. Most of us are familiar with archaeology done in Egypt, Mesopotamia, and elsewhere in the Near East, Europe, and Asia. Many of these societies *did* have written language, although some of the writing systems could not at first be decoded. Even after many of these writing systems have been deciphered, archaeology continues to be a rich source of information about the lives of ancient peoples.

There are some groups, like the Maya of southern Mexico, Guatemala, and Belize, whose carved inscriptions were not believed by many scholars to be genuine writing systems until after World War II. But since that time, archaeologists from several countries, including the United States and the former Soviet Union, have come to realize that the Maya in fact *did* have a full-fledged system of writing, and their inscriptions can now be read. Other groups, like the ancient residents of the Indus Valley in what is now Pakistan, or the Etruscans, northern neighbors of the ancient Romans, had writing systems that have never been deciphered. We must therefore rely almost exclusively on traditional archaeological remains for our information about these peoples.

There is also a special division of archaeology referred to as "historical archaeology." This study focuses on the material remains of contemporary or relatively recent societies, aiming to determine what these remains can tell us about human culture that written records do not. Historical archaeology can tell us, for example, how the early Pilgrims actually lived in the Plymouth Colony in what is now Massachusetts.

Finally, there are two aspects of archaeology that make it a bit different from cultural anthropology, in addition to the fact that its informants are things rather than people. One is the focus on technical methods necessary to extract as much information as possible from the silent stones, bones, and artifacts (human-made items) that are the primary sources of archaeological information. The second is the great time depth that archaeology can cover. This time depth permits archaeologists to make comprehensive statements about regularities in the development of cultural systems.

One final category of anthropology is **applied anthropology,** which is covered in the last chapter of this book. It is the application, or use, of the principles and findings of anthropology whether these are in cultural anthropology, physical anthropology, archaeology or linguistics. Applied anthropologists work in a variety of contexts, including criminal investigation, global health, government policy, and institutional planning. While the findings of academic anthropology form the basis of applied anthropology, insights from the practical work of applied anthropology have also enriched academic anthropology.

THE CONCEPT OF CULTURE

As noted earlier, anthropology draws from a broad range of intellectual and methodological traditions. But however varied the interests of anthropologists, and however divergent the subdisciplinary paths they follow, most anthropologists would agree that the single most important concept that binds us all together and unifies anthropology as a discipline is the concept of **culture**.

The term "culture" is derived from the Latin word *cultura,* which referred to the "cultivated" lifeways or practices of a group of people. It was not a technical or learned term for the Romans, and people did not worry much about defining it. As the word developed in English and other modern Western languages, it was increasingly used, as it had been by the Romans, to distinguish the practices of one's own group from those of others. Distinctions were (and often still are) made between people like *us* (whoever *we* may be), who are cultured or have culture, and people like *them* (whoever *they* may be), who are uncultured or have no culture. This is *not* what anthropologists mean when they use the term "culture." Of course, we now know that *all* people have culture. It is one of the consequences of the biological makeup of modern humans (*Homo sapiens sapiens*), and of our human and protohuman ancestors for several million years.

Another common use of the term "culture" has to do with the activities of high-status groups or elite individuals. According to this usage, ballet, classical music, Renaissance paintings, and novels whose authors win prizes are part of "culture," but dancing in clubs, hip hop music, graffiti, and romance novels are not. To distinguish this way of using the term "culture" from the way anthropologists use it, some people prefer to talk about "high" culture when they are discussing high status artistic endeavors.

Figure 1.1 (left): Luciano Pavarotti (1935–2007). A renowned Italian operatic tenor, Pavarotti's dress and demeanor demonstrate and reinforce the appeal of opera as a primarily high status musical form.   (right): Singers in the rock band Kiss. Their appearance is calculated to critique conventional cultural norms and appeal to young people.

Having spent some time discussing what anthropologists do *not* mean by the term "culture," let us now turn to an exploration of what they *do* mean. As you can well imagine for a term of such central importance to the discipline of anthropology, there have been many definitions proposed. In 1952 Alfred L. Kroeber and another distinguished anthropologist, Clyde Kluckhohn, published a critical review of 166 definitions of "culture," and of course, other definitions have been developed in the half century since then. But the definition that has been the most influential, and that continues to provide an excellent jumping-off point for a discussion of culture is the definition devised by British anthropologist E. B. Tylor in his 1871 book, *The Origins of Culture*. Many anthropologists writing and teaching today learned Tylor's definition while they were in school, and many of us can still recite the definition word for word. Tylor's first-ever anthropological definition of culture stated that culture is

> that complex whole which includes knowledge, belief, art, morals, law, custom, and any other capabilities and habits acquired by man as a member of society.

There are two noteworthy elements of Tylor's definition. First, it refers to culture as a "complex whole," or in today's terminology, an integrated system. That is, Tylor viewed the various aspects of culture as encompassing all the beliefs and practices of a particular social group, and as being related to each other, rather than merely happening to occur together. Second, Tylor tells us that the elements of culture are "acquired by man as a member of society." That

Figure 1.2   Edward B. Tylor (1832–1917). English anthropologist.

is, culture is *learned*, rather than "naturally" or genetically encoded. Humans acquire particular cultural practices and beliefs as a result of growing up in a society with those practices and beliefs, a process referred to as **encultura-tion**. Through enculturation Navajo children learn that it is rude to look people in the face when speaking to them, and Euro-American children learn that it is polite to do so. Enculturation allows women in some parts of Mali (Africa) to walk comfortably around their villages as they do daily chores, dressed in an ankle length skirt with no blouse. These same women would never dream of displaying their legs, like American women, whose enculturation has allowed them to go to class or the supermarket in shorts, but prevents them from displaying their naked breasts in public. People do *not* develop these specific traits simply because they are biologically Navajo, Euro-American, or Malian.

Figure 1.3 (left) Tahitian woman in long skirt. Her uncovered breasts but covered legs illustrates a conception of modesty different from that in contemporary metropolitan societies. Painting by John Webber (1751–1793). (right) Miniskirt. Note that her uncovered legs but covered breasts conform to contemporary metropolitan notions of female modesty (as long as the legs are not too uncovered).

Author: Ed Uthman. Wikipedia CC by –SA 2.0

They develop the traits because they are **encultured** to particular beliefs and practices; they acquire them as members of their societies.

Today, especially in an age of transnational adoptions, the notion that culture is learned rather than genetically encoded does not seem strange to most of us. But in Tylor's time most Europeans and Euro-Americans believed that there was some "natural" tendency for people to develop into practitioners of their native culture, regardless of how they were raised. So, according to this line of reasoning, a Euro-American baby girl kidnapped in a raid by "savage" Indians and raised with other tribal children to adulthood (something that did occasionally occur), was believed by many people to retain her "natural" sense of "civilized" decorum and physical "modesty." And an infant from a non-European group who was raised to adulthood as a European (something that happened more frequently) was believed to retain something of his or her original "primitive" culture, though she or he had never had any contact with it.

These beliefs are completely false, though they were once staples of popular fiction. The belief that specific cultural traits were biologically encoded in individuals was for centuries quite strong. It was not uncommon for people to talk unselfconsciously about the lazy, drunken Irish, for example, or the money-loving Jews, to mention just two Western ethnic groups. Such beliefs were once so strong that many people also believed that some cultural traits were genetically encoded into the members of **subcultural** groups (distinctive divisions that exist within a single, complex culture) based on such phenomena as wealth, occupation, or social class. There was also at one time considerable discussion, especially in the nineteenth century, of "criminal culture," which was often believed to be genetically transmitted from generation to generation. This kind of erroneous thinking, which has sometimes been accompanied by pseudoscientific "evidence," is part of what gave rise to genocidal atrocities such as those of the Nazis.

It is easy to see, then, that Tylor's statement that culture is "acquired by man as a member of society" was very important, even revolutionary, at the time in which it first appeared. And if it disturbs us in the twenty-first century that Tylor said "man" instead of "humans," we should remember that *he* was a member of *his* own culture, which by today's standards was seriously male-oriented and male-dominant.

Tylor's statement that culture is *learned*, not *biologically encoded,* actually took many decades to be generally accepted, even by scholars. However educated they were, and however they appreciated universal qualities inherent in all humans, many anthropologists in the nineteenth and early twentieth centuries, simply could not shake off their value judgments, and never quite lost the belief that there was something inherently superior about their own culture that was linked to some (usually unspecified) feature of biological superiority.

Culture as Abstraction

Most anthropologists tend to think of culture, itself, as an abstraction. According to this view, concrete material culture, religious rituals, and so on are perceptible expressions of culture, but culture itself is abstract. This abstraction is a complex web of conscious, semiconscious, and unconscious rules that all normal adults carry around in their heads to direct their actions and their interpretations. Infants start out with none of these rules, but they begin very quickly to acquire them. As children, we are all enculturated to the rules of our own societies, sometimes simply by example (whom to smile at and when, for example), and at other times by explicit teaching (how to milk a goat or weave clothes, or when to wear a necktie). Still other cultural lessons are absorbed in a variety of ways that may be less specific.

Anthropologists talk about the **worldview**, or *Weltanschauung* (the German word for the same term) that participants in a society absorb as an important part of their culture. In the United States, for example, it is generally believed that the universe is a relatively predictable place (and in some people's view, governed by a loving and all-powerful god). Most middle class Americans are oriented toward the future and change rather than the past and tradition. They tend to see themselves as apart from and in command over nature. They believe that, with effort, all people can better their socioeconomic situation. And they feel deeply that the interests and aspirations of the individual should take precedence over those of the group as a whole. How do people in the United States acquire this worldview? It is the result of conscious teaching on the part of parents and other elders; it is the result of the stories in books, movies, and even the songs of popular culture; and it results from being rewarded for "good" behavior and punished for "bad" by parents and others who share this particular worldview.

Of course, culture is enacted slightly differently by all of its practitioners. For example, women may have some different beliefs, practices and perspectives on life from those of men, and generally in any culture, older people have views somewhat different from those of young people. But however much variation there is within each group, what transcends these differences to bind the group together and provide its members with a coherent, integrated, and meaningful view of the universe is their culture. North Americans go through their daily lives in particular ways and understand the significance of their activities and those of others because of the cultural blueprint they carry around in their heads, just as residents of New Guinea do, only the blueprints are different. And though these blueprints result in concrete phenomena—from what to eat and what not to eat, to structures built to house religious rituals, and to whom one should and should not marry—the complete set of blueprints for any society, that is, the complete cultural system, is an abstraction.

The idea that culture is an abstraction may make some people uncomfortable, as though if culture is an abstraction, it cannot then be "real." But flash yourself back through time to your high school geometry class. Remember all those theorems that had to do with circles and triangles, and all those postulates and axioms having to do with the nature of a point (which has position but no length or breadth) or of a line (which has length but no breadth). What **Euclid,** the Greek mathematician-philosopher who developed geometry, was talking about was a whole collection of *abstractions.* In actual practice, no one can generate a point that has no length or breadth, any more than someone can produce a line that has no breadth. But these abstractions are necessary to build Euclid's system of geometry. With this geometry, we can understand some aspects of the universe into which we would otherwise have no insight. In addition, an understanding of geometry is essential to engage in a lot of practical activities, like building a temple that does not fall down or a surveying a field accurately.

There are many cultural rules that are as likely not to be followed as they are to be followed, but the participants in the culture still consider them rules, as do anthropologists. This is rather like the point and the line, which in real life actually *do* have dimensions their abstract definitions say they do not have. Take, for example, the cultural rule in many Arab societies that says that people should marry their **patrilateral parallel cousins** (that is, their father's brother's child). This is an example of what is called "preferential marriage," (discussed in Chapter 6). Like most preferential marriage patterns, the Arab system is followed in under half of all Arab marriages for a variety of reasons, mostly the lack of an appropriate candidate. But even when a person does not marry a patrilateral parallel cousin, he or she is likely to marry another close patrilateral relative about whom the family is well informed. This will ensure that the bride can expect good care from her husband, the husband can expect a virtuous wife who will protect his honor and that of his family, and the family's property will not be broken up. The point here is that whether or not a specific cultural rule is followed in the same way by all of a society's participants, the construction of a generalized pattern of a culture—in effect, an abstraction—is meaningful to participants and can illuminate important cultural principles and patterns to anthropologists. Without this process of abstraction, it would be difficult to see the significant structural outlines of a culture, just as without Euclid's abstract definitions of geometric elements and shapes it would have been difficult or impossible to create the philosophy (as the Greeks called it) of geometry.

Culture, like a Euclidean line or a perfect isosceles triangle, is an abstraction. But does this mean it is unreal? No more than those Euclidean geometric figures can be said to be unreal. Though they may not exist in their pristine forms in everyday life, their **heuristic** (illuminating or teaching) value is inestimable. One might almost say that they are *more* real that what occurs in nature. Similarly, though no specific culture exists in its "classic" or "perfect" form, the blueprints that participants of every culture carry around in their heads (and that anthropologists describe) may seem to members of a culture to be *more* real than the actual human institutions and behaviors.

The Emic/Etic Distinction

In its analysis of cultural systems, one of the more valuable of anthropology's contributions to this endeavor is the distinction between **emic** and **etic** perspectives. *Emic* refers to the view of a culture from within—that is, how a particular culture's practices, customs, beliefs and so on look from the perspective of its inside members. *Etic* refers to the perspective of an outside observer and analyst of the culture; etic is (or seeks to be) a scientific perspective. This emic/etic distinction in cultural anthropology was introduced by linguist Kenneth Pike (1967), who drew a comparison between culture and language. The term phon*etic* refers to the full range of speech sounds that humans make in their languages. There is a limited number of these sounds (in all, around 107 basic consonants and vowels, along with some modifications) and they can be scientifically described and measured according to how they are made (see Chapter 7). Each particular language uses only a subset of these sounds to form its words. The term phon*emic* refers to those sounds relevant within a particular language (and to rules governing their occurrence). So, for example, the French language uses a particular "u" sound (as in "*rue*" [street]) not found in English. We would say, then, that this phonetic "u" sound is phonemically relevant in French but phonemically irrelevant in English (it has no use in creating meaning within the English language). A reverse example of a phonetic unit that is phonemically relevant in English but not in French would be the "th" sound (as in the word "those").

The extension of this distinction from linguistics to the realm of culture was ingenious on Pike's part and useful to anthropologists (although, as we will see, it carries some problems of its own). Examples are endless. Medical science classifies and diagnoses human ailments scientifically; this is etic. Cultural groups whose members suffer from these very same afflictions might classify and diagnose them in a different way—along with ideas compatible with a belief system they may understand these afflictions in terms of, say, witchcraft, or bad air. This is emic. All human groups recognize relatives (etic) but the way in which they understand, classify and relate to these relationships varies considerably cross-culturally (emic). Indeed, even the simplest acts or gestures can reveal an emic/ etic distinction. For example, a public hug (an etically describable act) between an unrelated man and woman is in some cultures (as in North America) understood emically as an affectionate greeting or farewell gesture. In some other cultures (for example among Orthodox Jewish people in Israel) the same act would be interpreted emically as a flagrantly sexual encounter or possibly a sexual assault of the women by the man.

Thus emic refers to the internal interpretation or meaning of any element within a cultural system; and it is a strong tenet among many anthropologists that to truly understand another culture, one must try to understand it emically, from within. Emic and etic refer to different angles from which to understand phenomena—internal and external. They are different perspectives and not necessarily in conflict. They can both provide explanations of phenomena. An emic explanation of a cultural practice is the reason given for it by cultural members (e.g. "we do this to please our ancestors"). An etic explanation may invoke economic or ecological considerations, psychosocial motives or any number of other factors to give an explanation of human cultural behavior and throught, often referring to factors of which inside culture members are unaware. Both kinds of explanation may be simultaneously relevant.

One value of the emic/etic distinction is that it helps us to avoid unwarranted misinterpretations of others' cultural beliefs and practices. Most people will easily misinterpret another's cultural belief or practice by naively assuming that their own emic view of a situation (the view from within *their* own culture) is a credible etic (scientific) view. For example, a North American observer might see in a particular culture (in Nepal or Mexico for example) a man take a broom and strike his wife with it. This observer might quickly, as a gut reaction, interpret the situation as a clear case of domestic abuse because that is what it would be in the observer's own culture, that is, from the observer's emic perspective. But after a few discussions with local people this outsider would learn that emically in the observed culture the man with the broom is trying to "sweep out" an illness in his wife (using a broom infused with healing properties by a local healer). The man is trying to cure his wife, not punish or hurt her. In this case the outside observer has elevated his or her emic view to an etic level, holding that his or her own cultural view is the correct, real, or scientific one.

Of course, the analogy between culture and language is imperfect. We can very well classify and precisely define every possible human speech sound in linguistics, but we cannot know the full range of possible human cultural behaviors and beliefs. We can also see exactly how different human speech sounds operate inside languages, but we cannot always know so well what different cultural behaviors and ideas really mean inside a culture. In addition to this, some anthropologists contend that a true etic level does not exist because, they maintain, science itself is a cultural construction, an emic in its own right. They claim that scientific objectivity is not possible in the study of culture, or, for some, the study of anything. These issues aside, the emic/etic distinction in anthropology is a handy tool with which to begin a fresh, new look at human culture and the distinction between an insider's view of a cultural practice or perspective and an outsider's view, as will be apparent throughout this book.

ETHNOCENTRISM

Earlier in this chapter we placed the principle of cultural relativism within our definition of anthropology. **Ethnocentrism** is the reverse of cultural relativism. It is the notion that one's own culture is the correct one, the normal one, the yardstick by which all other cultures should be judged. Ethnocentrism is the viewing of another culture through the lens of one's own cultural system. Ethnocentric observers are inclined to consider other cultures as "weird" or "disgusting." Ethnocentric people usually find it hard to believe that members of other societies actually *like* their cultural systems, and they tend to believe that *if* people in other societies *do* like their own cultures, it is only because they "don't know any better."

All societies, from the largest to the smallest, are ethnocentric to some extent. We are all aware of offensive terms that some people in our own society apply to other ethnic groups. We can see the same phenomenon when we observe that many tribal peoples refer to themselves alone as "people," while they attach another, sometimes pejorative, term to outsiders. The group Euro-Americans call "Navajo" refer to themselves as *Dine,* which means "people," while all other people can be referred to as *anaa,* or "enemy." Many examples of ethnocentric thinking concern food practices. So, for example, Americans generally believe it is wrong, cruel, and disgusting to eat dog, while South Asian Hindus, especially high **caste** Hindus (those who have the highest status and condition of ritual purity) believe it is immoral to eat cattle. Some Americans used to refer to Germans as "krauts" (cabbages), because of a supposed German fondness for eating cabbages. French people were sometimes referred to as "frogs," from a real or imagined French liking for frogs' legs. And Catholics were sometimes called "mackerel snappers" because until the 1960s they were required to avoid eating meat on Fridays.

It is easy enough to understand ethnocentrism (and to counter it with cultural relativism) when the specific examples have to do with food or names for groups. But other more far-reaching issues concern fundamental morality or universal human decency. If we look, for example, at issues of crime and punishment, especially capital punishment and torture, we see an illustration of the complexity of ethnocentrism and its power to involve the deepest human emotions.

Today, in the early twenty-first century, there is probably more diversity of cultural opinion about crime and punishment than at any time in the recent past. Most significantly, people in the United States have split with their European cousins over the issue of capital punishment. Though 14 states and the District of Columbia do not practice execution of criminals, 36 states do. This stands in sharp contrast to countries that are members of the European Union (and some others, like Mexico), all of which are opposed to capital punishment and will not even extradite criminal suspects to countries (like the United States) where they may be liable to execution. There is a striking difference between the cultural outlook of those countries that permit capital punishment and those that do not. On the one hand there is the widespread belief within the United States that capital punishment is sometimes morally justified (or even required); that it is beneficial to society as a whole; and that the vengeance it offers the survivors of murder victims is a legitimate function of the penalty.

On the other hand, there is the belief among the members of the European Union that capital punishment is simply immoral and unacceptable. And yet even people in the United States who accept capital punishment can be appalled at the way the penalty is carried out in some conservative Islamic countries, where beheading and stoning are employed, and for behaviors, like adultery or homosexual activity, that in the United States not only would not merit capital punishment, but are not even considered criminal. What is common to people from all cultures when it comes to such deeply felt issues as crime and punishment is that the majority of them believe their own cultural practices are not only appropriate for themselves, but profoundly correct for the whole of humanity. People, as Herodotus noted, are generally convinced that the way they do things is the right way to do them, but only with respect to some issues is this felt so deeply and with such strong moral force.

Since the nineteenth century, anthropologists in the United States have felt a particular obligation to struggle against ethnocentrism. Part of this was undoubtedly due to the character of early American anthropologists, especially Franz Boas, a German Jewish immigrant who advocated cultural relativity and who is considered the founder of American anthropology. Part of it was due to the fact that some early anthropologists, like Boas, had experienced ethnic prejudice, themselves. Another reason is that many early American anthropologists worked closely with American Indian peoples for whom they developed empathy. These anthropologists often had a marked sense of the moral difficulty of their situation as members of the group that now controlled former Indian lands. All of these factors may have moderated ethnocentric tendencies among these researchers, but eventually, these anthropologists simply came to realize that ethnocentrism got in the way of "doing anthropology." That is, they came to see that if anthropologists haul along with them the idea that the assumptions, practices, and institutions of their own culture are the "normal," "natural," "correct," or intellectually or psychologically most "advanced" ones, they would blind themselves to the cultural realities of the very societies they aimed to explore and understand.

Anthropology offers the perspective of cultural relativism as a pathway to countering ethnocentrism. But, one may ask, are there *no* limits to cultural relativism? Perhaps we can agree not to make negative judgments about groups who advocate hallucinogenic religious rituals, like the Yanomamo people of the Amazon basin, or others who required men to practice **subincision**, which involves slicing the underside of the penis lengthwise, as some Australian Aborigines used to do. After all, it is *their* brains and *their* penises. But do we also have to agree that if a culture says that entire ethnic groups should be destroyed, this is fine if it works for the people who practice it? This is actually a good question, and a hard one to answer.

What about, then, the cultural practice of genocide, the destruction of a particular category of people simply because its members belong to that group? To most of us the best known example of genocide occurred in the 1930s and 1940s, when Adolf Hitler preached the destruction of Jews, Gypsies, Slavs, and other groups (including homosexuals and the handicapped) on the grounds that they were intrinsically, "naturally," evil and/or genetically inferior. According to Hitler's argument, the Jews' inherent evil had resulted in numerous economic and political disasters in Germany, and the salvation of the country was to a great extent dependent upon the total annihilation of the Jewish people. Because Germany had been humiliated by its defeat in the First World War and was still paying the economic price for this disaster, many Germans eagerly sought a scapegoat, some easily identifiable group to blame for their loss.

Yes, there are limits to cultural relativism, and genocide is certainly one of them. But, then, is there a difference between Hitler's genocide (and there have certainly been others) and the practice of arranged child marriage in India? Most anthropologists would say yes to this question. On the other hand, were we to ask about female genital mutilation as practiced in some societies (and which threatens the health and reproductive abilities of women) we would see a divergence of opinion among anthropologists. Though the general principle of cultural relativism is important and should be preserved, there are limits beyond which cultural relativism ceases to be tolerance of variation and

Figure 1.4 The limits of cultural relativity: Nazi concentration camp. Prisoners in Mauthausen concentration camp (Austria, 1945), liberated by US troops.
Source: National Archives and Records Administration.

becomes intolerable inhumanity. The dividing line, however, may be blurry and subject to disagreement.

Of course, anthropologists are not the only people who have ever had the idea that understanding other peoples requires a certain amount of energy in suspending the application of one's own values, expectations, and behaviors. We all know the saying "When in Rome, do as the Romans do." Another relevant quote we might consider is far less well known. It comes, ironically, from an involuntary immigrant to ancient Rome. Publius Terentius Afer (ca. 190–158 B.C.E.), whom we know today as **Terence**, was a North African slave whose brilliance as a playwright won him his freedom at an early age. Though few people read Terence's plays today, a single one of his quotations is widely remembered: "*Homo sum; humani nil a me alienum puto*" (I am a man; I think nothing human foreign to me). It is an insightful thought, and one that should be engraved over the entrance to every anthropology department!

SUMMARY

Anthropology is the empirical study of humans, both living and dead, both contemporary and extinct. Whatever the subdiscipline of anthropology (physical anthropology, archaeology, linguistics, cultural anthropology, or applied anthropology), the central unifying focus is the concept of culture. Having discussed the discipline of anthropology and the nature of culture, we are now in a position to review the five myths that began this chapter.

Myth #1   Anthropology is the study of "exotic" cultures.

As we have seen from the examples cited in this chapter, anthropology examines all kinds of cultures. Certainly, anthropology began as the study of nonwestern societies. But in the more than a century and a half in which anthropology has existed, it has come to be distinguished not only by the groups it studies, but even more by the way in which it studies communities, and the kinds of questions it asks. As we have seen, anthropology is now as likely to turn its eye to communities in London or New York as to societies in the South Pacific, Africa, or Asia. And not only does anthropology examine communities all over the world, it also compares the information from all of these societies.

Myth #2 Because the word "culture" can refer to elite forms of expression, art, and entertainment (like ballet and classical music), not all human groups have culture.

While it is true that activities like ballet and classical music are part of Western culture, so are rap music, professional football, and, in the United States, having a turkey dinner on Thanksgiving. The problem with the term stems primarily from the fact that the word "culture" is used in different ways by different people and in different circumstances. When anthropologists use the term "culture," it refers to the whole collection of values, beliefs, and practices that a society shares. Culture is a characteristic of all human groups. No human society is devoid of culture, however different its beliefs and practices may be from those of another group. Though humans are not *born* with culture, they are all born with the capacity to create and participate in it.

Myth #3 There are no characteristics shared by all human groups, and so no way of making general statements about human cultural systems.

Certainly, human societies display a tremendous amount of variation. Some permit men to have multiple wives at a time, while others do not. Some believe that women who display their breasts in public are immoral, while others assume that this is a perfectly sensible way to dress. But all societies have rules about whom one can and should marry, and all societies have rules about what kind of presentation of oneself is decent. The more we come to know about different societies as we meet them in subsequent chapters of this book, the more we will not only come to understand why certain cultural practices exist in particular societies, but also we will come to understand that many apparently very different practices have powerful underlying similarities. We will ultimately come to understand the organizing principle of anthropology, that though cultural systems are different everywhere, the people whose lives they guide are profoundly the same.

Myth #4 Some cultures are inherently superior to others.

After going through a lengthy discussion of cultural relativism, it seems unlikely that any reader of this text would try to argue for the inherent superiority of any one culture over others. The only exceptions to this anthropological principle are societies in which there is systematic cruelty practiced against a specific segment of the populations simply because they belong to that category. In considering this issue, we need to remember to distinguish those actions and institutions that make us uncomfortable or that we would find painful to live with, from those that are simply and obviously cruel by any standard external to the societies that practices them. People in other societies may find comfort, meaning, and security in practices that outsiders would find intolerable, but no slave or member of a persecuted category would defend slavery or persecution.

QUESTIONS FOR THOUGHT AND REFLECTION

1. Sometimes anthropologists (including the authors of this book) become a little sloppy with their language and use the words "culture" and "society" interchangeably. But there is an important difference between the two. How would you describe the distinction?

2. We state in this chapter that culture is an abstraction rather than a concrete set of behaviors, institutions, or artifacts. Not all anthropologists find the notion of culture as an abstraction to be particularly useful. What do you think? Construct an argument for culture as an abstraction and then for culture as a concrete phenomenon. What do you see as the strengths and weaknesses of each approach?

3. Suppose that the move to extend the school year and school day in the United States gained steam, and politicians and school administrators across the country decided to lengthen daily instruction by two hours a day and the months of instruction by six weeks a year. This is an example of culture change to which there would be very strong reactions. Describe the responses to this change, both pro and con. What groups would be in favor of the change and why? What groups would be opposed to the change, and why? What basic cultural values would this change be based on, and what basic cultural values would it disrupt?

4. Select from a society other than your own a cultural practice about which most people in the United States would feel very uncomfortable. Describe it, and explain why these North Americans would be uncomfortable about it. How do you think a member of the society that has this cultural practice would defend it?

5. In most societies there are distinct differences of opinion between young people and old about some cultural practices. In some societies these differences are expressed fairly straightforwardly, as they are in the United States In other societies, the differences are much more repressed, as young people must always acknowledge the superior authority of their elders. Why do you think these differences of opinion are so likely to exist? Can you make a general statement about the nature of these intergenerational disagreements? What are two or three intergenerational cultural disagreements that persist in the United States? What do you think accounts for them?

6. What was your idea of anthropology before you began this class? How has it changed since you learned more about the discipline? In most colleges and universities there are fewer anthropologists than there are professors in other social sciences. Why do you think this is true?

ENDNOTES

[1]At the same time, by the 1990s anthropology, like many other disciplines, had become engulfed in a wave of postmodernism. For the social sciences, postmodernism is an intellectual movement that asserts that objective knowledge of the world is not possible. It opposes itself to the "modernist" vision that, since the Enlightenment, has been governed by notions of scientific detachment and rationalism, which were considered capable of bringing forth progress and, ultimately, the betterment of humanity.

By contrast, postmodernism rejects all claims to truth and, in its more extreme forms, is anti-science. Because with postmodernism, claims to objectivity and knowledge are not possible, no one mode of knowing, or subjectivity, has any claim to superiority over another. The postmodern movement continues to inspire strong debate within anthropology. For a critique of postmodernism in anthropology see D'Andrade (2000).

REFERENCES CITED

D'Andrade, Roy
  2000 The Sad Story of Anthropology 1950-1999. *Cross-Cultural Research* 34(3):219–232.

Herodotus
  1929 *The Histories.* English translation by Arthur Dennis Godley. Cambridge: Harvard University Press.

Hobbes, Thomas
  2012 [1651] *Leviathan,* Noel Malcolm, ed. Oxford: Claarendon Press.

Kroeber, A.L. and Clyde Kluckhhohn
  1952 *Culture: A Critical Review of Concepts and Definitions.* Papers of the Peabody Museum of Archaeology and Ethnology. Harvard University, Vol XVLII, No 1. Cambridge, MA: Peabody Museum.

Lee, Richard B.
  2012 *The Dobe Ju/"hoansi,* 4th edition. Beverly, MA: Wadsworth Publishing.

Pike, Kenneth L.
  1967 *Language in Relation to a Unified Theory of the Structure of Human Behavior.* 2nd ed. The Hague: Mouton & Co. (1st edition published in 1954 by the Summer Institute of Linguistics, Glendale, CA).

Rathje, William L.
  2001 *Rubbish: The Archaeology of Garbage.* Tucson: University of Arizona Press.

Shostak, Marjorie
  2000 *Nisa: The Life and Words of a !Kung Woman.* Cambridge, MA: Harvard University Press.

Tylor, Edward Burnett
  1958 [1871] *Primitive Culture.* New York: Harper and Row.

CHAPTER 2

FIELDWORK

How cultural anthropologists collect their information

Cultural anthropologists collect data primarily through fieldwork—a period of residence in a community where they use a variety of strategies and techniques to gather information. This chapter discusses the fieldwork process and some of the research methods cultural anthropologists use. Anthropological fieldwork is often a personally intense and challenging experience. It is also a process surrounded by a number of popular misconceptions, such as the following:

Common Myths of Culture

Myth #1   To collect their data in the field, anthropologists tend to "go native."

Myth #2   The goal of anthropological fieldwork is to produce a complete description of a group's way of life.

Myth #3   Anthropological fieldwork is impressionistic.

Myth #4   In anthropology, questionnaire-based surveys provide the most accurate, objective data.

ANTHROPOLOGICAL FIELDWORK: A HISTORY

In 1871 Sir Edward B. Tylor, whose definition of anthropology we reviewed in the previous chapter, published *Primitive* Society: *Researches into the Development of Myth, Philosophy, Religion, Art, and Custom.* It is a massive, two-volume work based on Tylor's assimilation of information collected by assorted travelers, missionaries, and civil servants. By 1915, Sir James George Frazer, a Scottish anthropologist, had published an even more massive work, in twelve volumes, *The Golden Bough: A Study in Mythology and Religion.* Both *Ancient Society* and *The Golden Bough* were influential, widely read not only by scholars, but also by a general audience. Though separated by more than thirty years, these anthropological works share an important trait: they were written by scholars using data collected by other people. Neither Tylor nor Frazier did active fieldwork. This was not illegitimate; it was simply an early stage in the development of anthropology, later referred to, with a certain amount of scorn, as "armchair anthropology."

The next generation of anthropologists, many of them civil servants in the employ of the British Colonial Office or the United States Government, actually left their armchairs, went to the field, and relied on data that they had collected themselves. Still, these data were often generated in artificial circumstances, where the anthropologists questioned informants exclusively in formal settings, and often through interpreters, actually or metaphorically "on the veranda" of an official European or American colonial building. There were no university courses in field methods, and most anthropologists felt it important not to "go native," that is, not to live too intimately or identify too closely with their informants, the people whose communities they were studying. In the words of the eccentric linguist and cultural anthropologist, Jaime de Angulo, who worked with the native people of northern California in the 1920s, "Decent anthropologists don't associate with drunkards who go rolling in ditches with shamans" (Leeds-Hurwitz 2004:10). In this observation de Angulo was referring to himself, because in collecting linguistic and other data, he actually *did* drink and otherwise socialize with his informants, some of whom were shamans. He may even have rolled in a ditch or two. In the early years of the twentieth century this kind of fieldwork, now quite common, was considered unacceptable and undignified by most anthropologists.

The idea of what "decent anthropologists" do started to change forever when **Bronislaw Malinowski** began his fieldwork in Melanesia, most notably in the Trobriand Islands. Malinowski was a Polish graduate student in mathematics and chemistry recovering from a serious illness when he encountered Fraser's *Golden Bough* and decided to become an anthropologist. A few years later he conducted fieldwork in the Trobriand Islands north of New Guinea, where he became trapped by the outbreak of World War I. This was a British-controlled region; and because Malinowski was a native of the Austro-Hungarian Empire with which Britain was at war, he was not permitted to return to Europe. As a result, Malinowski had plenty of time to conduct fieldwork and to develop his philosophy of how anthropological fieldwork should be carried out. He summed up his approach well in his book, *Argonauts of the Western Pacific*: "The final goal of which an anthropologist should never lose sight is to grasp the native's point of view, his relation to life, to realize *his* vision of *his* world" (Malinowski 1961 [1922]: 25). If the antique use of a term like "native," and the exclusive reliance on masculine pronouns are a little hard to take in the twenty-first century, we need to remember (as mentioned in the previous chapter in the case of Tylor) that we are all (including Malinowski) to some extent hostages to the culture of our own time and place. Despite this, Malinowski was breaking new ground. As he repeatedly reminded anthropologists, the only way to understand the perspective of the group under study was to get "off the veranda" and into the community. That is, the anthropologist must, so far as she or he is able, share the experiences of the people whose lives he or she is studying, and do so through the medium of the local language. To describe this approach, Malinowski coined the term, still widely used by anthropologists today, **participant observation**.

The goal of grasping "the native's point of view" was first proposed by Malinowski, and it was revolutionary. Of course, as the reader will no doubt recognize, the "native's point of view" is what anthropologists later came to call the *emic*, (as opposed to the *etic*) view, as discussed at length in the previous chapter. Malinowski was merely ahead of his time; the emic/ etic distinction in anthropology was not made for another thirty years.

To be sure, Malinowski was not the first anthropologist who ever lived and worked in the community he studied. In the last quarter of the nineteenth century the American Frank Hamilton Cushing lived and worked with the Zuni and Hopi people of the American Southwest. And Franz Boas, the German-born founder of American anthropology, worked closely with several Native American groups in the United States and Canada. Even more important, Boas emphasized to his many students, who soon populated anthropology departments in universities throughout the United States, the importance of fieldwork conducted through participant observation and informed by the principle of cultural relativism, as we saw earlier.

Figure 2.1   Bronislaw Malinowski (1884–1942), during fieldwork in the Trobriand Islands (1918).
Source: Wikipedia.

Since the time of Boas and his students we have seen another shift in the nature of fieldwork in anthropology. In recent decades, there has been increasing use of so-called "participatory" modes of fieldwork, where local individuals and community groups collaborate with the anthropologist in research. Here the boundary between the observer and the observed begins to fade. Local persons become active in the research process and research results are shared immediately and directly with community members (Lamphere 2004). Such participatory fieldwork is especially used in the area of applied anthropology (see Chapter 10). And finally, anthropological fieldwork is being affected by globalization, a topic covered in the next chapter. Human populations are more mobile then they were fifty or even twenty years ago, so that anthropologists studying them have to be on the move, too. Thus, an anthropologist studying transnational migrants or, say, Kurdish refugees, may have several field sites to cover and not just one demographically stable community.

TRANSFORMING THE OBSERVER: THE MAKING OF AN ANTHROPOLOGIST

Participant observation was devised as a method for collecting ethnographic information. There is, however, another, quite different, consequence of participant observation: it transforms the anthropologist. No one who engages in long-term participant observation can remain unchanged; he or she will never be the same person after the experience as before. To some extent, participant observation is like basic training in the military: to turn new recruits into soldiers, they must first be stripped of everything that ties them to their previous lives as civilians. Their hair is cut in a non-civilian style; their clothing is taken away and replaced with new, uniform, non-civilian clothing. They are no longer called by their civilian names, but by their rank or job description. They have little comfort or support from friends or family, but only rigid demands made of them by unsympathetic superiors. Having broken down the new recruits, the military then builds them up again, now with military information, expectations, assumptions, values, and most of all with a military identity.

In fieldwork the anthropologist is similarly stripped of his or her original identity, assumptions, and support network. Often the anthropologist is unable to speak the language of the new community with adult-like competence, so that every utterance is painful and uncertain, and every conversation reduces the anthropologist to the position of a child or an idiot. Elizabeth Warnock Fernea, who accompanied her anthropologist husband to rural Iraq in the 1950s, spoke very halting Arabic when she first arrived. When she was preparing to leave two years later, the local women, now her friends, recalled her early attempts at speaking to them, saying that they had thought she was not quite mentally competent (Fernea 1965).

Other aspects of the culture are also difficult to understand and manipulate for the newly arrived anthropologist. How should one greet old people? Young people? Children? How should one respond to common questions, like "How are you?" or "What's happening?" What kind of clothing is appropriate? What kind of clothing is not appropriate? When someone urges you to have more to eat, should you really eat more, or is what you leave uneaten the food that will be fed to the children after you have finished? To what extent can you be a part of the group with whom you are living, and to what extent must you remain different?

When anthropologists are first in the field they often experience what is referred to as **culture shock**. That is, they feel lost in an alien culture, with no guideposts by which to navigate, and unable to rely on their own familiar cultural assumptions. The food is different; the smells are different; the sights and sounds are different; even taking care of the most insignificant personal need may become an enormous difficulty. It is hard to ask a simple question, and there may be no privacy at all. Most North Americans find periodic privacy essential to their sense of well-being, but not all people do. Not only do people in many societies dislike being alone (and thus assume that everyone must feel the same way), but newly arrived anthropologists are very likely to be a curiosity, so they have constant attention paid to them. Many anthropologists have experienced almost perpetual questioning and observation from community members: "How much did that watch cost?" "Why don't you have any children?" "Why are you here by yourself?" "Are you going to stay here forever?" "Why not?"

Just as the first wave of culture shock is wearing off, the anthropologist may find that he or she is now beginning to question some basic beliefs, principles, or assumptions that had formerly seemed unassailable. With no one around to shore up these convictions, it can be hard to maintain them. And as the anthropologist considers the problem, it seems clearer and clearer that a great part of what individuals believe is very much dependent upon the continual reinforcement of people with similar beliefs.

Culture shock operates in two phases. The first one occurs with the difficulties of coping in a new cultural system and maintaining one's bearings without the support of participants in one's own culture. But after long residence in a fieldwork community, anthropologists often report that reentry into their own culture induces a second phase of culture shock. Part of this reverse culture shock is the unfamiliarity of the formerly familiar: crowds of people look different; they are all speaking English; there are flush toilets and electricity everywhere. Dogs are friendly, and you can drink water right out of the tap. Although they have not forgotten their own culture in the year or two they have lived within another one, anthropologists are now transformed by their field experience. While not a genuine part of the culture they have researched, this culture has forever altered the eyes with which they assess both their own and any other culture. No longer can they simply accept the practices of their own society as "normal" or "ideal." From now on their native culture practices will always be seen as only one set among many in the world. In addition, as a result of participating in another culture, anthropologists often gain a new perspective that allows them to see flaws in the operation of their own cultural system when they return. One common difficulty anthropologists returning to the United States often have is coming to terms with the relative wealth and consequent waste in North American society. They may have become accustomed to greater outward shows of emotion in other societies, and find that North Americans seem cold. And frequently these returnees find that, however American they may feel, they now have a bond to another place and culture that they can never give up. Many anthropologists retain ties to a field site throughout the rest of their lives. Fieldwork, particularly when it takes the form of participant observation, transforms the anthropologist forever.

THE FIELDWORK PROCESS

Fieldwork is a process, one that often takes considerable time. For their doctoral degrees most cultural anthropologists spend one to two years in the field. Many anthropologists see this fieldwork as an initiation into the profession. One reason fieldwork takes so long is that time may be needed to become adept in a new language and to build rapport with local people. Here we discuss some preparatory and preliminary phases of fieldwork.

Getting Ready for Fieldwork: A Theory and a Question

In the early days of anthropology, the beginning anthropologist would pick a place to do fieldwork (or have a place chosen by his or her professor), read whatever information was available, and head off to explore the area and the people. Sometimes the anthropologist had a topic of investigation in mind, but often the purpose of the research was simply to provide a general account of the culture of a group; that is, an ethnography. The beginning anthropologist seldom consciously selected a theoretical focus for fieldwork. S/he simply operated according to the prevailing theoretical focus at the university in which he or she was a student.

Today, things are different. In the first place, there is much more published information available, so a general ethnography of a community is less in demand today than it was a hundred years ago. Chances are that several such ethnographies have already been produced for almost any society. Today, an anthropologist decides on a much more specific issue, question, or problem to explore. Instead of asking, "What is life like for impoverished residents of the Texas-Mexico border region," an anthropologist today might ask, "What strategies do impoverished residents of the border region employ to survive in an unstable, economically depressed area?" Or "What is the domestic structure of impoverished households headed by never-married mothers? What strategies do these women employ to survive? And what consequences are likely to result?" A new researcher headed to an indigenous community in lowland Ecuador might ask, "What are the consequences in this community of the shift from subsistence horticulture to wage labor?" And an anthropologist working in Haiti might ask, "How do the experiences of persons living with HIV/AIDS vary according to gender, and what circumstances correlate with more successful medical outcomes?" Clearly, the questions explored by contemporary anthropologists are both very specific and almost infinitely varied. And the societies explored now vary, as we have seen, from the extremely unfamiliar to the community next door.

In addition to reading published information available on an issue the anthropologist plans to explore, he or she also needs to decide on a **theory,** a scaffolding of ideas that will serve to organize his or her research and analysis. A theory is not a baseless set of guesses, though that is the way the term is sometimes used outside the academic world. Rather, a theory is a set of assumptions or guiding principles used to analyze or explain phenomena, especially cause and effect. In the note at the end of the previous chapter we briefly considered post-modernist theory. A somewhat less extreme theoretical perspective in anthropology is **cultural materialism**, an approach advocated by anthropologist Marvin Harris. This theory takes as its guiding principle the idea that cultural beliefs and practices are primarily shaped by the material circumstances of a people's existence, in particular their technology in interaction with a particular natural environment. The different ways that peoples satisfy basic needs (as for food and shelter) and basic proclivities (as for reproduction) are seen as the root causes of human variation in social structure, worldview, values, religion, art and other cultural expressions. Thus, when cultural materialists seek to explain a cultural belief or practice, they look first to its role in a people's material circumstances. Later in the book (Chapter 8, Religion) we will see an example of how the approach of cultural materialism has been used to account for some particular religious beliefs in India.

Very different from cultural materialism is the theoretical approach known as **interpretative anthropology**, advocated by anthropologist Clifford Geertz and very popular in the second half of the twentieth century. Here a guiding principle is that any understanding of cultural phenomena is inescapably subjective. The aim is not to explain cultural beliefs and practices, but while admitting our subjective biases, to *interpret* those beliefs and practices, to decipher the meaning they have for those who hold them. One then "reads" a culture as one might read a play or a poem, and one offers an, admittedly subjective, interpretation of it, much as a literary critic might offer an interpretation of Shakespeare's *Hamlet*.

There are several other theoretical perspectives in anthropology, some of which we will encounter in subsequent chapters. But as we can see from these two brief examples, not all of the theoretical approaches in anthropology follow the model of science. Those that do, such as cultural materialism, can generate **hypotheses,** or provisional cause and effect statements, which are subjected to constant testing and revision. When adopting such a theoretical perspective, one of the most important issues to consider is how to **operationalize** a research question. That is, the research question will contain concepts that need to be turned into identifiable (possibly measurable) entities. For example, let us suppose a researcher formulates the following question: In community X does poverty negatively impact health and, if so, how? Here, the concepts of "poverty" and "health" need to be operationalized. What will constitute poverty? What criteria will be used to detect it—income, living standard? And what about "health"? Will people simply be asked about their health status, or will other criteria be used? These are the kinds of operationalization questions researchers need to answer before the research goes further.

Different researchers are likely to find different theoretical perspectives congenial, depending upon their interests, and useful, depending upon the kinds of questions they want to explore. Different theoretical perspectives are not necessarily mutually exclusive, nor do they remain static through time. But even given this fluidity, a specific theory serves to construct one's research question, to organize one's research, and to direct one's analysis and conclusions. The theoretical basis of an anthropologist orients every aspect of his or her scholarly work. It may change over time, but it prevents the work from being chaotic and difficult for others to assess. Theoretical choice is also relevant to how a researcher is going to formulate the research question to be explored, and what research methods (to be explored later in this chapter) will be employed.

Working in the Field: First Contacts

As an anthropologist begins fieldwork, the first problem is often how to connect with people who can serve as guides to the society. This is a critical issue, because it can have a powerful effect on the rest of the field experience. The anthropologist has arrived in the field, and is doing his or her best to follow Malinowski's century-old advice that it is essential to live in the community one is studying and to speak the local language. The next step for the newly arrived anthropologist is to establish contact with congenial and well-connected residents who can help introduce the anthropologist to other community members. Since the early days of anthropology, such a person has been referred to as an "informant."

Recently, this term has been questioned by some anthropologists and by some community members, as well. Part of the reason for this is that the word sounds like "informer," or betrayer of one's group. Another part of the reason is that some people feel that the term is insufficiently respectful of the value of the community member's contribution to anthropological research. We continue to use the term "informant," however, because we feel it is the clearest option and shows no intrinsic lack of respect for the role of the people without whose cooperation and insight we would be entirely unable to complete our part of the anthropological effort.

For a newcomer to any community it is difficult to figure out who is a helpful, knowledgeable resident, offering assistance because he or she is simply thoughtful or interested in the anthropologist, and who is offering assistance largely because he or she is alienated from the group and seeks friendship with another kind of outsider. It usually becomes apparent during fieldwork that well-integrated, successful community members are rarely eager to establish friendships with outsiders, while more marginal residents may seek out an anthropologist's company. Making a friend of a marginal person may hamper the anthropologist's ability to form future alliances with more representative community residents. On the other hand, it is also true that marginal people have interesting insights about their culture and society.

It can also happen that early offers of friendship and assistance may come from persons who are motivated primarily by their own material gain. Anthropologists from the United States, however modest they may perceive their circumstances at home, are likely to have economic resources far beyond those of the people whose communities they are studying. Seeing this, it may be tempting for some community members to offer information that is false and services they cannot provide, as well as to ask for or demand gifts or payments from the anthropologist. While the anthropologist must be wary of such situations, she or he must also understand that the disparity between a middle class North American and most local persons in the field is so great that extractive attempts are both comprehensible and nearly inevitable.

Early friends often serve as long-term guides to a culture for anthropologists, These guides often serve as **culture brokers**, or individuals who mediate between two cultures, introducing participants in each culture to one another, and helping to explain cultural differences and peculiarities. Often these culture brokers prevent disastrous cultural gaffes, and help to foster cross-cultural understanding. With luck and persistence, some culture brokers become more than helpful guides to the anthropologist; they become lifelong friends.

Working in the Field: Some Preliminary Steps

Having found a place to live and made a few initial contacts, many anthropologists begin fieldwork with some traditional strategies that have been used since the end of the nineteenth century. Any strategy that allows the anthropologist to get out into the community and meet and speak to people is usually a good idea. One classic early activity is mapping the research area, the neighborhood, or the village. This activity permits the anthropologist to explore the area, to develop an accurate idea of its resources and organization, and to be seen by the community residents. Later on, as the anthropologist becomes more familiar with the area and its residents, and as the residents become more familiar with the anthropologist, this map can serve as the basis for a later census. It can also serve as the basis for selecting residents for interviews, or for calculating networks of family members, friends, and political or other alliances. Maps are also useful as a framework for noting the condition of houses, outbuildings, and other structures, as well as their number, elaborateness, and size. Finally, the map is a handy basis for calculating such phenomena as land tenure and access to other resources, such as water, garden plots, pasturage, and transportation, as well as stores, schools, medical facilities, and the like.

Often anthropologists do a census of the community early in their fieldwork. Like mapping, this activity increases their general familiarity with the area and its residents, and also further exposes the residents to the anthropologist. One common census strategy is to use a standard system of kinship notation (see chapter 6), so that important relationships within a household and among households can be understood. The anthropologist will generally ask about age, gender, marital status, occupation, and educational attainment of household residents, but there are other kinds of questions one can ask to elucidate particular aspects of life. Where do family members who are not part of the household live? What church, doctor, healer, school, and market do family members use? Family history can also be part of this kind of census, so the anthropologist may want to know where family members were born, when they were married, and when parents, grandparents, or other kin died.

Once a map and a census are complete, the fieldworker may be ready to apply particular anthropological methods for gathering data, as discussed next.

FIELD METHODS

Early cultural anthropologists were primarily geared to what is today referred to as "qualitative" methods of research, such as participant observation and informal conversations and interviewing. Today more anthropologists have added quantitative methods to their research arsenal, while by no means abandoning qualitative approaches. **Qualitative** research methods are usually less formal and not rigidly structured. They tend to be flexible; the group studied is fairly small; and both the researcher and the social context of the activity are recognized to affect the research results. Because of these factors, qualitative investigations, whether they make use of organized interviews, focused observations, or of more diffuse participant observation (or of all three) are likely to be variable, intensive, and somewhat intuitively organized. By contrast, **quantitative** research methods are more formal and rigidly structured. The groups studied can be quite large, and pains are usually taken to ensure that the researcher and the social context have as little impact as possible on the data obtained. Because the data collected are by nature quantitative, they can be analyzed statistically.

While many researchers are primarily geared to either quantitative or qualitative research, the two approaches are not inimical to each other, nor are their goals necessarily opposed (Bernard 2011:24). It is simply that for answering some kinds of questions and collecting some kinds of data, in some kinds of circumstances, one approach may be more appropriate than another. Often it is helpful to combine these approaches. It would be interesting, for example, to analyze poverty through a quantitative survey of such information as income, nutrition, age at which children leave school, number of rooms per residential unit, and the like. One might then combine this information with data derived from a qualitative approach, like that of the anthropologist Oscar Lewis. Lewis began by doing traditional participant observation, and then developed a distinctive method of extensive audio recordings of conversations with impoverished informants. These hundreds of hours of taped recordings were then assembled into coherent, seamless narratives, in which informants discussed their experiences, thoughts, dreams, expectations, and regrets. The results of this technique include the books *The Children of Sanchez* (1961), an account of an impoverished family in Mexico City, and *La Vida* (1966), the story of a Puerto Rican family in New York and Puerto Rico. The books are powerful and detailed ethnographic accounts of the effects of poverty on human lives and the culture in which they participate. They are very different from a quantitative account, but both approaches are valuable and useful. Lewis, himself, enriched his work with some quantitative information.

By far the most used method of fieldwork in cultural anthropology is the one-on-one interview, a qualitative method. Interviews may take a variety of forms; the most flexible follows what is called an "open-ended interview schedule." This is a list of questions or topics for questions that do not have preset responses from which the interviewee is to choose. Some of these interview schedules are more structured, with only the listed questions asked. Others are "semi-structured"—they can be enlarged or modified at will and on the spot, if the interviewer decides to ask for elaboration of a particular response. Because it is time consuming and distracting to take notes as a respondent talks, a more practical approach is to record the responses. Although transcribing recorded interviews and survey responses is extremely time consuming (especially when they are not in the anthropologist's native language), the detail and complexity reflected in such responses makes the procedure well worthwhile.

Another instrument for social science research is the closed questionnaire survey, a quantitative method. These contain questions with a predetermined ("closed") set of possible responses ("How helpful did you find your student counselor? () very helpful () somewhat helpful () not helpful"). Questionnaire surveys are administered (either in person, by phone or through the mail) to a random sample of a target population, generating information that is, statistically speaking, representative of the whole population. Questionnaire surveys can yield masses of quantitative data relevant to large populations.

Many people (and some in social science fields other than anthropology) consider questionnaire surveys to be more accurate and objective than other methods such as participant observation and informal interviewing. This is not necessarily the case. Questionnaire surveys can generate data that are strictly quantitative—full of impressive numbers, percentages and statistical correlations—but that may be completely inaccurate. This is because respondents may misunderstand a question, or, from any number of motives, give false information. This potential flaw of the questionnaire surveys is magnified whenever it is applied cross-culturally, where those who design the research instrument do not share or adequately understand the cultural background of the respondents.

In one interesting case, three anthropologists conducted an experiment to test the accuracy of questionnaire surveys in rural Nepal (Stone and Campbell 1984; Campbell, Shrestha and Stone 2011). For this they devised a survey instrument that consisted of questions taken from actual national surveys previously conducted in the country. These covered several census items along with questions about landholdings, livestock, crop yields, health behavior, and knowledge of family planning methods. Following the national surveys, this survey was designed to be administered to male household heads, except for the family planning section, which was designed for any household woman aged 15 to 45. The anthropologists then hired Nepalese researchers to administer this survey to a sample of households in three rural villages where the anthropologists themselves had lived for a considerable period of time, in one case for over two years. When the survey data came in and were computed, the anthropologists then visited the three villages to conduct a cross-check of the survey information by discussing the survey at length with the respondents, all of whom they had known for many years. This experiment found that the survey data were quite accurate on the census items—number of people per household, their ages, their fertility history and so on. But the survey produced decidedly inaccurate data in the other categories. Respondents had systematically under-reported land and livestock holdings and over-reported annual expenses. Over and over, these respondents told the anthropologists that they under-reported economic assets because they feared that if the government got access to this information (and it *was* written down on official-looking forms) they would have to pay more taxes. They similarly over-reported expenses because, they said, they wanted to appear poor, thinking that this would result in some special assistance from outside agencies. But the most inaccurate data of all concerned the family planning section of the questionnaire. Family planning is a sensitive subject in rural Nepal because of its associations with sexual behavior. In much of rural Nepal, sexual activity is surrounded by notions of ritual impurity, strict privacy and reserve. During the questionnaire, women respondents systematically denied any knowledge of contraceptive methods because, as they later explained to the anthropologists, they felt *laj* (embarrassment, shyness), especially since the questionnaire interviewers were male and the questionnaire was administered in a public setting (a setting hard to avoid anywhere in rural Nepal) with neighbors and relatives present. Also, they had interpreted questions asking for their knowledge ("Have you heard of condoms? Have you heard of the pill?") as questions asking if they personally had used a particular method, so they fended all these questions off with "no" responses.

Along with ideas about their accuracy, it is commonly thought that closed questionnaire surveys provide objective data, whereas the standard anthropological methods of participant observation and interviewing can provide only data that are "impressionistic" and lack objectivity. The truth is, however, that *all* methods of social research are subjective and introduce biases. This problem can be mitigated only by becoming aware of the biases.

Certainly questionnaire surveys strive for objectivity. The sample population is selected randomly to avoid biases in selection. Variables are operationalized so that they can be objectively measured. Questionnaire administrators try to be "neutral" in demeanor and tone so as not to influence respondents. And the resulting data are processed according to standard mathematical procedures. But even with all this effort, subjective biases inevitably creep into the design and data collection of a questionnaire survey. First, the decision of what topic to study in the first place, what questions to ask respondents, and how to operationalize variables are subjective mental processes that a researcher undertakes before the survey begins. The researcher cannot invoke rules or a formula or a standard external to his or her own reasoning and judgments to justify why certain variables are selected and how they are operationalized. Second, the predetermined "closed" response choices of questionnaires introduce a bias: potential responses outside, beyond or between these closed categories are automatically excluded. Responses are forced into these subjectively delineated categories. Third, no matter how "neutral" the questionnaire administrator, "interviewer bias" can never be eliminated (except in mailed-out questionnaires and even here the language of the written questions may bias responses). And in some cultures neutral interviewers might be offensive, or at least seen as very peculiar.

At the same time, anthropological qualitative methods are not as impressionistic as some would suppose. Anthropologists do not simply live in a community and record their off-hand impressions. They carefully record what they observe, what people say, and what people do. Like any scientists, they must give convincing evidence for any statements they make or conclusions they draw from their fieldwork. And finally, anthropologists are trained to recognize, admit and then *suspend* their own biases—even their most deeply felt and ingrained convictions—while immersing themselves in the field. They realize that they must suspend their own views in order to understand beliefs and practices in another culture. For example if one is studying witchcraft in another culture, he or she should suspend the bias that witchcraft beliefs are "superstitions" or "misguided ideas about cause and effect." In the end, survey questionnaires pursue objectivity by seeking detachment between researchers and subjects; qualitative methods pursue objectivity through controlled attachment, through admission and suspension of value judgments. Neither attempt is perfect.

There are some additional methods used by anthropologists. One is focused group discussions. Here a certain category of people is brought together and the anthropologist leads a group discussion on some topic. For example, mothers of young children may be brought into a group to discuss child-rearing practices or issues of child health. Many anthropologists ask informants to perform certain tasks to gain insight into how they think about a variety of phenomena. One Amazonian anthropologist asked women to make colored pencil maps and drawings of what were important to them. Not surprisingly, most women drew maps of their gardens and produced drawings of particularly important plants (Allison 2010). Another anthropologist, who works in sub-Saharan Africa, asked her informants to sort a stack of photographs into those things that were local and those that were "foreign." Interestingly, many imported (or "foreign") items had gained such acceptance that they were included in the local pile (Abdul-Karim 2012).

Two psychological tests often used by psychologists and sometimes by anthropologists are the Rorschach test and the Thematic Apperception Test (TAT). Rorschach tests are the classic "ink blots," which are depicted on cards and are then presented to informants who tell the researcher what the blots represent to them. TATs involve cards depicting ambiguous scenes in silhouette, which are interpreted by informants. Rorschach tests and TATs are most often employed by psychologists, to elucidate the unconscious convictions and motivations of their clients. But they are also used by some anthropologists to gain insight into cultural values and beliefs. For example, in one soci-

Figure 2.2   A Rorschach ink blot.

ety informants may frequently interpret a TAT image of a person in bed while another person stands over him as a representation of death and mourning. In another society, by contrast, the same image may usually be seen as a depiction of a mother checking on a sleeping child. These differing interpretations, along with other cultural information gathered by anthropologists, may indicate a generally pessimistic or fearful attitude toward life in one society, while in the other, people's outlooks appear to be more sanguine and confident.

FIELDWORK RESPONSIBILITIES

In exploring the communities in which they pursue their research, anthropologists would do well to follow the maxim inculcated in all medical students since the middle of the nineteenth century: *Primum, non nocere* (First, do no harm). Anthropologists just starting out seldom think of themselves as having the power to do much harm, but given their (often) comparative wealth, cultural ignorance, and lack of fieldwork experience, they may inadvertently create damage. For example, one anthropologist, just beginning doctoral fieldwork, made the mistake of telling a longtime key informant about her conversations with another local woman, a neighbor of the first woman, whom she had observed collecting special tree branches for use in a traditional curing procedure. The anthropologist had discussed the branch collection with this neighbor, and then asked her longtime key informant for additional information. This latter woman responded with anger and hurt feelings, first because she saw herself as "progressive," and was embarrassed that the anthropologist had observed the branch collection right across the street. But more important, the older informant's feelings were hurt that the anthropologist had not gone to her first for an explanation of the branch collecting. "You should have come to me first," the informant told the anthropologist. "I could have explained it the right way, and besides, my neighbor consults a particular healer sometimes. She believes that healer, but it's just witchcraft" (*pura brujeria*). These two neighbors maintained a frosty relationship for several months as a result of the anthropologist's lack of awareness of her role in her older informant's life. At that point the anthropologist remembered what another informant had told her: "You will leave when you get what you want, but we have to stay here forever."

Even after having established good working relationships with informants within a community, there are still issues to be dealt with. One issue is how to compensate local people appropriately for the valuable information they provide the anthropologist, for example by participating in surveys or interviews. But what form should compensation take? In many societies, including the United States, payment in money is simple and acceptable, while in other societies some other kind of exchange may be more appropriate. Whatever the medium of compensation, the anthropologist must make sure that it is adequate to convey respect for the assistance rendered, but not so great as to render the informant an object of envy or resentment within the community. The anthropologist must also be careful not to insult an informant who has become a genuine friend by diminishing the significance of that friendship by paying in money for assistance that the friend now sees as help given by one friend to another. In such a case, some other acknowledgement of gratitude must be found.

Responsibilities to residents of a fieldwork community also persist beyond the fieldwork, itself. What if an anthropologist writes a book based on his or her experiences in the field? True, the anthropologist is the author. True, the anthropologist has collected the data, organized them for the publication, and written the account. But without the community, without the informants, there would have been nothing to write. Many academic books make little or no money for their authors, but some do. Should the anthropologist/author retain all the royalties from a book? And if not, with whom should the anthropologist share the income? With key informants? But who is key? With the whole community? But how can a few thousand dollars be distributed to a whole community? Some anthropologists have established funds that provide educational and other benefits to people with whom they have worked, and to which they make contributions from their book royalties. One of the best known of these is the Kalahari Peoples Fund, established in 1973 by members of the Harvard Kalahari Research Group. Other anthropologists, whose collaboration has been restricted to a small number of informants, share the profits of publication directly with these individuals.

Some anthropologists have facilitated the delivery of medical supplies to their field sites, contributed to educational projects, or have become involved in the marketing of locally produced commodities. Such assistance can be among the most rewarding aspects of a long-term relationship between an anthropologist and the community of individuals who have provided the information on which that anthropologist's career is based.

As more and more populations in the world gain access to modern means of communication, like cell phones and computers, the relationship between anthropologists and their informants in other cultural communities endures over time, well beyond the fieldwork. Malinowski could leave his informants in the Trobriand Islands when he returned to Europe, and there would be no further communication between them. But today anthropologists find that their informants, though they may have little interest in reading the anthropologist's books or articles, can easily access their departmental websites. There they can find statements that the anthropologist may have written about them, accompanied by photographs. Through social media and other means of modern communication, they may comment upon this information, with approval or disapproval. Today residents of areas studied by anthropologists are gaining and exercising more control over the information they provide about their culture. This is generally seen by professional anthropologists as a welcome development.

SUMMARY

In this chapter we have briefly explored the history of anthropological research and have noted some ways in which anthropological methods of acquiring information have changed. We have also looked at specific approaches now employed by cultural anthropologists and noted the increased importance of selecting a theoretical perspective that will organize and inform the anthropologist's research, as well as the specific field methods and techniques that will work most productively with a particular research question or problem. At this point we are able to consider the myths we identified at the beginning of the chapter.

Myth #1   To collect their data in the field, anthropologists tend to "go native."

Although contemporary anthropologists no longer sit in their book-lined studies and make observations about information collected exclusively by others, the image of the anthropologist who disappears into the bush and "goes native," becoming a "member of the tribe," is a fantasy—a myth. True, today's anthropologists do spend extended periods of time in the field, and may return again and again to the same community. They may develop important, lifelong friendships with community residents who began as informants. While anthropologists are in the field they will speak the local language, eat the local food, and observe local customs as well as they are able. They will drink beer or chicha or tea or fermented mare's milk, and they may even go rolling in ditches with shamans, as Jaime de Angulo claimed to do.

They will never be unmarked by the experiences they have had in the field; they will never see the world again in the way they saw it before they began their fieldwork. But they remain anthropologists, and they almost always go home, even if they return to the field, often for the rest of their lives. Their informants may like them or despise them or forget about them altogether when they leave the field. But they never forget that, however much they may come to like and value a particular anthropologist as a friend, the anthropologist is an outsider. And however much anthropologists may come to feel at home in the field, they are under no illusion that they are "part of the tribe." Despite real and important friendships, they remain anthropological outsiders, forever looking for meaning and analyzing cultural patterns.

Myth #2   The goal of anthropological fieldwork is to produce a complete description of a group's way of life.

At one time a complete description of a group is exactly what anthropologists aimed to do when they went into the field. They were aiming to fill a huge gap in the western world's understanding of peoples different from themselves and cultures different from their own. There was little information about many tribal groups, and even large, state-based societies were known primarily through unsystematic and often ethnocentric accounts of travelers, colonial administrators, and missionaries. But today there is a wealth of general ethnographic material available on which to build. Contemporary fieldwork in cultural anthropology, therefore, can be more specific and better organized. Today anthropologists select specific questions, issues, or problems they wish to explore, informed by particular theoretical perspectives, and pursued through methods and technique appropriate to their research interests. These contemporary studies, when taken together, can provide a far more complete and fine-grained description and analysis of a society and culture than was possible a century ago. In pursuing modern field research, however, we need to remember that we are standing on the shoulders of giants, without whose work our own would not be possible.

Myth #3   Anthropological fieldwork is impressionistic.

Anthropological fieldwork is very different from watching steel balls dropping in a vacuum or mold growing in a petri dish. In general, it does not involve replicable experimentation. And in general, it *does* require that the researcher have a personal relationship with the people of his or her study.

But these facts do not yield the inevitable conclusion that anthropological fieldwork is impressionistic. Like all social sciences (and more than some), anthropology is a hybrid, involving many of the approaches, techniques, and conventions of science in conjunction with some of the values and interpretive skills of the humanities. This does not mean that anthropology is impressionistic. With the exception of some approaches like interpretative anthropology (discussed earlier in this chapter), anthropology generally aims to be objective, systematic, and explicit in its goals, its research methods, and its analyses. Most important, anthropology is *empirical*. Anthropological conclusions and general statements are based, not on intuitive notions, however thoughtful, or on impressionistic responses to disorganized experiences, however interesting. They are based on the concrete findings of their systematically planned, carefully executed, and transparently described fieldwork.

Myth #4   In anthropology, questionnaire-based surveys provide the most accurate, objective data.

Questionnaire-based surveys can be very helpful in collecting a large quantity of certain kinds of information from certain kinds of informants in a short amount of time. Both of the authors of this text have used questionnaire-based research. But this kind of research carries with it several built-in difficulties that can make it neither accurate nor objective. Questionnaires are usually administered by non-specialists hired specifically for the purpose. They may have no experience with the population under investigation, and the population may fear, mistrust, or dislike them, and thus provide inaccurate responses. The items on the questionnaire may include controversial or tabooed subject matter that local people never discuss with strangers. Even a seemingly bland question like "Where were you born?" or "How long have you lived here?" may evoke fear from a respondent who is an undocumented immigrant. In a forced-choice questionnaire, the possible responses may not include a response the informant considers applicable. And finally, questionnaires can never permit the detail and nuanced responses that allow for accurate interpretation of a person's responses. If an informant says "Some things happen because of fate," does this mean that the informant believes she has no control over her own life, or does she mean that powerful socioeconomically-based structural forces beyond her control shape many aspects of her life? Only through extensive fieldwork, including one-on-one interaction with members of the community will allow a researcher to extract an accurate interpretation of this kind of response. Questionnaire-based research can be productive, but its utility is to a great extent dependent upon the informed interpretation of the researcher, whose experience is usually based on traditional anthropological field methods, like participant observation and one-to-one interaction.

QUESTIONS FOR THOUGHT AND REFLECTION

1. Before you read this chapter, did you have any idea of how anthropologists collected their information? What was it? Where did your idea come from?

2. What do you think would be the most difficult part of doing anthropological fieldwork? What do you think would be the most rewarding part? Is fieldwork something you would like to try? Why or why not?

3. Sometimes people ask if paying respondents in a study interferes with the honesty or accuracy of their answers. What are your views on paying informants, both pro and con? Have you even been a subject in a social science investigation or experiment? Were you paid in some way?

4. Anthropologists routinely try to make connections with people they have never met before and who come from very different cultural systems. Yet most people living in North America have never had a stranger from another culture move into town, start hanging out, and ask local people detailed questions about their lives. How do you think you and your family would react to this kind of experience?

5. You are an anthropologist who wants to explore the effects of the desire for high priced, imported consumer goods (like fancy athletic shoes and cell phones) on the part of teenagers in an impoverished rural community in Madagascar (an island off the southeast coast of Africa). What kind of quantitative approach would you take? What kind of qualitative approach? Be specific, but do not worry about not knowing anything about Madagascar. Knowing that the country is very poor and that the community you are interested in is a rural area is enough to start thinking about this question.

6. If you were an anthropologist, what kind of a question would you like to research? Where would you like to go to do this research? What kinds of questions would you ask to investigate your problem?

REFERENCES CITED

Abdul-Karim, Christa
    2012 *There Is No Development Here: Social Power and the Shaping of a Southern Zambian Community.* Unpublished PhD dissertation, Washington State University.

Allison, Kerensa Louise
    2010 *Manioc Mothers: Stability and the Influence of Tourism among the Napa Kichwas in the Ecuadorian Amazon.* Unpublished PhD dissertation, Washington State University.

Bernard, H. Russell
    2011 *Research Methods in Anthropology: Qualitative and Quantitative Approaches.* Second Edition. Walnut Creek, California: Alta Mira Press.

Campbell, J. Gabriel, Ramesh Shrestha and Linda Stone
    2011 *The Use and Misuse of Social Science Research in Nepal.* 2nd ed. Kathmandu, Nepal: Mandala Book Point.

Fernea, Elizabeth Warnock
    1961 *Guests of the Sheik: An Ethnography of an Iraqui Village.* Garden City: Doubleday and Company.

Frazier, Sir James George
    The Golden Bough: A Study in Magic and Religion. London: Macmillan and Company.

Lamphere, Louise
    2004 The Convergence of Applied, Practicing and Public Anthropology in the 21st century. *Human Organization* 63(4):431–443.

Leeds-Hurwitz, Wendy
    2004 *Rolling in Ditches with Shamans: Jaime de Angulo and the Professionalization of American Anthropology.* Lincoln: Unoversity of Nebraska Press.

Lewis, Oscar
    1961 *The Children of Sanchez:Autobiography of a Mexican Family.* New York: Random House.
    1966 *La Vida: A Puerto Rican Family ion the Culture of Poverty—San Juan and New York.*

Malinowski, Bronislaw
    1961 [1922].   *Argonauts of the Western Pacific: An Account of Native Enterprise and Adventure in the Archipelagoes of Melanesian New Guinea.* New York: E.P. Dutton.

Pike, Kenneth L.
    1954 (rev 1967). *Language in Relation to a Unified Theory of the Structure of Human Behavior* (2nd. ed.). The Hague: Mouton.

Stone, Linda and J. Gabriel Campbell
    1984 The Use and Misuse of Surveys in International Development: An Experiment from Nepal. *Human Organization* 43(1):27–37.

Tylor, Sir Edward Burnet
    2010 (1871) *Primitive Culture: Researches into the Development of Myth, Philosophy, Religion, Art, and Custom* (2 volumes). Cambridge: Cambridge University Press.

CHAPTER 3

CULTURE CHANGE AND TRANSFORMATION

The origin, evolution, and dynamics of culture

This chapter explores the origins and transformations of culture. Where does human culture come from? Why and how does culture change? And what form is human culture taking in our current shrinking world? Here we cover the topics of the evolutionary beginnings of culture, and the processes of culture change and globalization, focusing on the following myths:

Common Myths of Culture
Myth #1   Culture is unique to our species.
Myth #2   Human cultural evolution is progressive; over time, cultural developments and transformations have generally improved the well-being of humanity.
Myth #3   Globalization is breaking down cultural barriers and homogenizing culture around the world.

CULTURE AS EVOLUTIONARY ADAPTATION

Over thirty years ago a primatologist observed an interesting chimpanzee behavior at Arnhem Zoo in Holland. A subordinate male was approaching a female for sexual activity; but just as another, dominant male entered the scene, the first chimpanzee used his hands to cover his erect penis (de Waal 1982). This fascinating incident, taking only seconds to occur, suggests a number of capabilities of chimpanzees, such as an awareness of the self, an awareness of the social status of others, and a capacity for deception.

In the early 1950s on the Japanese island of Koshima, a woman farmer observed a young female Japanese **macaque** (named Imo by researchers) take a sweet potato to a fresh water stream and wash the soil off the potato before eating it. Later, Japanese researchers reported how Imo continued her behavior and how it spread, first to Imo's playmates, then to her mother and then widely throughout the community. Over time, the behavior persisted and persists to this day. Hence, a new, innovative behavior was transmitted over the generations in this macaque community.[1]

By now, there have been many long-term studies of wild and captive nonhuman primates and several laboratory experiments. These have confirmed that many species of primates show social, communicative, and cognitive capacities far more complex than what was assumed to exist even a few decades ago. This is especially true for common chimpanzees (*Pan troglodytes*) and the closely related **bonobo** chimpanzee (*Pan paniscus)*. This growing body of knowledge has raised new questions about how and in what ways humans are unique from other living primates, or about the extent to which what we call *human* culture is unique to our species.

It is easy enough to look at "culture" in such a way that it *is* unique to *Homo sapiens.* If, for example, we say that "culture" entails human language, or that it refers to the making and manipulating of symbols in particular ways, then, yes, only humans have it. Another, and in our view, more productive, position is to consider culture as the social (non-genetic) transmission of patterns of behavior over the generations. Of course, to say that cultural adaptations are non-genetic is not to imply that these adaptations occur apart from biological/ genetic evolution. Indeed, all cultural capacities (for example, human language, technology, symbolic expression and so on) depend on and are inseparable from evolved biological dispositions. Further, biological and cultural adaptations are intertwined in that they impact and shape one another. For example, in human evolution the increase in brain size and changes in brain structure were undoubtedly interlinked with the cultural development of increasingly complex tools (Stone & Lurquin 2007:30).

"Culture," understood as learned and socially transmitted behavior patterns, is an evolutionary adaptation used to some extent by many primates and even other animals[2] but most especially by human beings. We are the only species to rely primarily on culture as opposed to genetic mutation and biologically-produced change in our efforts to survive and reproduce. This view of culture ties us in with all other life forms, rather than opposes us as special, unique, superior, and somehow apart from mere "nature" (de Waal 2002). This view of culture also emphasizes its evolutionary origins; it helps us to see where culture came from.

In this section of the book we discuss "culture" among the living nonhuman primates. We then look at human ancestors such as ***Homo erectus***, and at other extinct species like the **Neanderthals**. An interesting question about the way human culture evolved is this: just when and why did the human line come to depend more on culture than on genetic change as an adaptation?

Living Primates

One of the more impressive cultural adaptations among nonhuman primates is the making and using of tools; and here, the most impressive nonhuman primate of all is the chimpanzee. Common chimpanzees in Gombe National Park in Tanzania (the site of the work of **Jane Goodall** [1986] and her colleagues over many decades) remove leaves from twigs and then use the twigs to "fish" for termites by inserting them into termite nests, pulling them out and then eating the termites that cling to the twig. Twigs are also modified and used to "fish" for ants, and sticks are used to extract honey from beehives. Chimpanzees also use "sponges" (made of leaves that they have chewed) to extract water from tree hollows. They drink the water off the sponges and also use sponges to dry themselves and clean babies.

Perhaps the most striking tool-use among chimps is their use of hammer stones and anvils to crack open fruits, seeds, and nuts, as observed among chimps of the Taï forest (Ivory Coast) in Africa. Here the chimps find and carry hammer stones to the tree roots or flat rocks that serve as anvils, and then pound the stones on the anvils to crack open hard shells. Observers now agree that this use of stones and anvils is taught by older chimps to younger ones; that is, real instruction occurs. The young chimps do not simply learn the technique through observation of older chimps but are slowly and deliberately instructed by them (Boesch 1991, van Hooff 1994).

As with human culture, chimpanzee tool-use traditions show variation among different local groups (McGrew 1998). For example, the Gombe chimps do not use twigs to fish for tree-dwelling ants available in their area, whereas chimps that live south of them do so. This kind of variation in the

Figure 3.1.   A bonobo fishing for termites. San Diego Zoo.
Photo: Mike Richey. Wikimedia. CC BY-SA 3.0

tool use of groups within the same species and living in similar environments strengthens the assertion that primate tool use is cultural.

In addition, there are reports of social differences among nonhuman primate groups of the same species, for example differences in grooming styles. One very interesting study traced social interactions of a troop of olive baboons in Kenya over many decades, beginning in 1978 (Sapolosky & Share 2004). Among these baboons, females stay put in the troop and young males migrate out to join other troops. The baboon troop under study lived near a garbage pit next to a tourist lodge, where the more aggressive adult males of this troop scavenged for food (only aggressive males could compete with each other at this pit). In 1983, many of these males died of tuberculosis from infected meat in the garbage. Indeed, nearly half of the troop's adult males perished in this way, leaving a troop consisting of the less aggressive males and doubling the ratio of females to males. By 1986 this troop exhibited a strikingly different social pattern than before—there was a far more relaxed dominance hierarchy among males, higher ranking males showed less aggression toward lower ranking males, and males showed less aggression toward females and engaged in more grooming with them. What is significant is that this new social pattern was maintained over time as new males from other (less peaceful) troops migrated into the troop at puberty. Ten years later (by which time no adult males of the original 1983 troop remained in it) this more peaceful baboon culture was still intact. It seems that the new social style was transmitted to and adopted by the incoming males.

Most primates live in groups, are highly social, and construct fairly complex social structures. This is especially true of higher primates such as apes and monkeys. Often these primate societies are marked by interpersonal dominance relationships or **dominance hierarchies**. In about 60 percent of primate species, males are clearly dominant over females,[3] and in many species males and females have dominant-subordinate relationships among themselves. From the point of view of the development and use of culture, it is notable that the organization and social life of many nonhuman primate societies, as with many human societies, rests on the primate recognition of **kinship** bonds (family ties) among themselves. Research has consistently shown that among primate societies, behaviors such as grooming, forming alliances, and peacefully feeding together, are strongly biased in favor of kin (Chapais & Berman 2004). Among Gombe chimps, maternally related males form close cooperative groups, often engage in cooperative hunting and may help one another rise in rank or fend off aggression from other unrelated males (Goodall 1986).

With regard to kinship, a look at the larger social order of many primate species is even more impressive. For example, monkeys such as rhesus monkeys, vervet monkeys, common baboons and Japanese macaques live in groups that consist of subunits of females with their young and subunits of adult males. Young males disperse out to join and mate within other groups when they mature. The adult males have a dominance hierarchy among themselves. The female units are more complex: here, there are distinct units of mothers with their young that may extend over a few generations. For example, a unit may consist of an old mother, her daughters (her sons will have dispersed out) and her daughters' infants. Interestingly, these "**matrilineal**" (traced through the mother, see Chapter 6) units are themselves ranked. Thus all of the females in Matriline A are dominant over those of Matriline B, who are dominant over Matriline C, and so on. Within each unit, a mother is dominant over her daughters and the daughters are in turn ranked, with the younger ones ranking higher than the older ones.[4]

Among these species, then, we see two extraordinary and very human-like features of social organization. First, this structure shows recognition of kinship, not just between mothers and their children or among siblings but recognition of kinship over the generations. As we will see in Chapter 6, this recognition of kinship over the generations is crucial to the development of fully human-style society. This kinship structure in addition provides a social basis for the transmission of knowledge over the generations.

Secondly, this structure shows that an individual's placement and rank within the society is, at least in part, established by his/ her birth, or ancestry, another important feature of human societies. In these primate species, females' ranks are determined by the position of their matriline and their birth order. For males, those born of high ranking matrilines are also high-ranking and treated deferentially by all individuals inside their natal societies; but later they will migrate out, join new groups and establish their own rank among the males of these new units.

Humans are distinct from all other primates in their elaborate use of symbols. Indeed, human culture is saturated with symbols as seen vividly in ceremonial behavior, religious rituals and artistic expressions. Symbolic capacity is also at the heart of language development. And yet, many nonhuman primates do show an impressive capacity to learn and engage in symbolic communication. For example vervet monkeys make different learned vocal sounds as warnings of the approach of different kinds of predators—snakes, eagles, and leopards (Cheney and Seyfarth 1990). In experimental settings, chimpanzees have been taught to communicate through use of different symbols on a computer keyboard, and chimpanzees and gorillas have been taught some sign language (see Chapter 7).

Aside from using it more, human use of culture is distinct from that of other primates in a few ways. Regarding tool technology, only humans use tools to make other tools, although chimpanzees can be taught to do so. For example, the bonobo named Kanzi has been taught to make simple stone tools in this way. Also, as far as is known, only human culture is cumulative; that is, innovations made by one individual are then built upon or modified by others. Thus many aspects of human culture, such as technology, have histories of development.

Human Ancestors

Alongside seeing the use of cultural adaptations among living primates, we can also look at culture among our own **Hominin** ancestors, as revealed in the fossil record. The term "hominin" is a category that covers humans and their extinct ancestors after the divergence of the human line from its common ancestor with chimpanzees, our closest evolutionary cousins. This split occurred five to seven million years ago in Africa. Hominins are characterized by bipedal (two-footed) locomotion and upright posture along with the associated anatomical changes brought about by this new mode of locomotion, especially changes in the foot, arms, legs, hands, pelvis, spine, and braincase. Bipedalism may have been favored in human evolution by a number of different factors; but clearly this new mode of locomotion, itself, enhanced tool development and more efficient foraging (searching for food), as it freed the hands to manipulate the environment. It also allowed the carrying of food and other items over longer distances.

After the human line diverged from the last common ancestor with chimpanzees, a number of different genera and species of hominins lived for considerable periods, often overlapping in time with one another. Members of the lineage that eventually led to us, *Homo sapiens*, were rarely, if ever, the only hominins on the planet.

Among the earliest hominins were the **australopithecines**, covering 6 or more different species, in eastern and southern Africa, who lived 4.2 to 2 million years ago. Although australopithecines were able to walk upright, they undoubtedly still spent considerable time in trees. They had a similar brain size to that of chimpanzees (about 415 cubic centimeters). Since living chimpanzees make and use tools, it is assumed that australopithecines did so as well, although clear archaeological evidence for these tools has not been found.

The first evidence of tools in association with hominin fossils comes with Homo *habilis*, a member of the genus *Homo,* now believed to have evolved from the australopithecine species know as *afarensis* (the famous "Lucy" was part of this group). These **habilines** lived in Africa from 2.5 to 1.7 million years ago. *H. habilis* had an enlarged brain size (averaging 650 cubic centimeters), and is associated with stone tools such as flakes, choppers, scrapers and stone hammers. *H. habilis* was followed by *Homo erectus,* whose span on earth lasted over a million years (roughly 1.8 to 0.8 million years ago). *Homo erectus* had an even larger brain size (from 727–1067 cubic centimeters), more elaborate and efficient stone tools (including hand axes), and covered a wider territorial range that included not only Africa but also parts of Asia and, most likely, Europe. New fossil finds of *Homo erectus* indicate that this species was quite diverse in size and shape (Lieberman 2007). Archaeological evidence is controversial, but some finds do suggest that *H. erectus* cooperatively hunted game with weapons. Of particular interest is the likelihood that *H. erectus* had mastered fire and used it to cook food. However, archaeological discoveries of charred animal bones and what may be hearth sites remain controversial.

Figure 3.2. A reconstruction of a Homo erectus (adult female). Reconstruction by John Gurche.

Photo: Tim Evanston. Smithsonian Museum of Natural History, Wikimedia. CC BY-SA 2.0.

Recently a newly discovered fossil hominin has added complexity to our view of human evolution. In 2013 a cache of fascinating and puzzling hominin fossils was discovered in a cave near Johannesburg, South Africa by two amateur spelunkers, or cave explorers. These hominins, provisionally named *Homo naledi,* have some characteristics (like modern feet and legs) of *Homo erectus,* or even *Homo sapiens.* Other characteristics (like shoulders, curved fingers, and small brains between 450 and 550 cubic centimeters), however, are much more characteristic of *Australopithecus.* Even more surprising than this unexpected mix of traits is that multiple individuals (but no other animals) were found together in a nearly inaccessible cave chamber. This has suggested to some researchers that *Homo naledi,* despite their small brains, may have intentionally disposed of their dead in some culturally meaningful way. Analysis of the implications of *Homo naledi* is still ongoing, and will receive a significant boost when the fossil remains are dated.

In Africa, Asia and Europe, *H. erectus* was replaced by *Homo heidelbergensis* who lived from 2 to 0.1 million years ago. Exactly where and how often this transition took place is in dispute. In Europe the successors to the *heidelbergensis* are known as the Neanderthals. Compared to modern humans, Neanderthals were short and stocky with heavy, massive bodies. They had pronounced brow ridges, no chin, faces that protruded from the braincase and large worn front teeth. Many of these distinctive features suggest adaptations to the cold climate in which they lived.

Figure 3.3 Fossil skulls. From right to left are Australopithecus afarensis, Homo erectus and Homo sapiens.
Source: Museum of Anthropology, Washington State University. Authors' collection.

For a long time the status of these Neanderthals was hotly contested. Some considered them a direct ancestor to and a subspecies of modern *Homo sapiens*. Others saw them as a late form of *heidelbergensis* and a separate species. More recent DNA analysis has concluded that the Neanderthals were not a direct human ancestor but a side branch that went extinct, although some interbreeding between Neanderthals and fully modern humans did occur (Green et al. 2010), very likely in the Middle East.

Neanderthals are of special interest because they are quite recent in the fossil record (they lived in Europe from 350,000 to 39,000 years ago); they overlapped with modern humans (and may have been killed off after modern humans appeared); they showed a brain size slightly larger than that of modern humans (averaging 1400 cubic centimeters compared to the human average of 1350) and they had made important cultural adaptations. These included an advanced and varied tool tradition known as Mousterian and consisting of refined flakes, flakes hafted onto handles, scrapers, borers and stone points. In addition, it is now agreed that Neanderthals controlled fire, cooked their food and buried their dead. But most important are speculations about Neanderthal symbolic abilities and even religious beliefs. Although they often buried their

Figure 3.4 A reconstruction of a Neanderthal (adult male).

Source: Zagros Paleolithic Museum, Kermanshah, Iran. Wikimedia CC BY-SA 3.0.

dead and placed the bodies in a fetal-like position, it is not really known if these burials were accompanied by religious ritual or provision of grave goods, which would indicate the use of shared cultural symbols and possibly beliefs in an afterlife. For Neanderthals there is some evidence for ornamentation or art. For example, a Neanderthal site in Hungary yielded a mammoth tooth covered with red ochre. It is not known what this object may have meant, but apparently it had no utilitarian function. Other evidence, some from sites in Spain and Italy, suggests that some Neanderthals wore jewelry and decorated their bodies with pigment (Wong 2015).

It is not known why the Neanderthals went extinct, but it may have been that bio-cultural processes allowed modern humans to out-compete Neanderthals and other archaic groups. Anthropologist Rachael Caspari (2011) notes that the dramatically more complex tool technology of modern humans that appeared around 30,000 years ago in Europe occurred at the same time that human longevity increased and grandparents became common. This evolution of grandparents, she suggests, was interlinked with and a driving force behind the development of this new technology and the new elaborate forms of art that also appeared at this time. This new class of elder grandparents could have played important roles (as they continue to do in all societies), namely, the passing on of vital knowledge and the providing of economic support to their children's descendants. Thus grandparents fostered intergenerational accumulation and transfer of technological, environmental, and social knowledge. In addition, an increase in human longevity would have increased population density which would in turn have promoted greater complexity of social organization.

To what extent any of our hominin ancestors possessed language is unknown. Although still debated, it is now more widely supposed that Neanderthals did have some form of language communication. Genetic and other evidence suggesting that they were physically and mentally capable of language adds weight to this idea, as does any evidence of symbolic expressions in body ornamentation. In addition, anthropologist Stanley Ambrose (2001) argues that the distinctive Neanderthal tools with flakes shafted onto handles relied on three separate processes: making a handle, inserting a stone flake into it, and binding the product together with some other material. Ambrose draws a parallel between these composite tools and the assemblies of sound to produce meaningful utterances. Thus language ability may have evolved in tandem with the mental abilities Neanderthals needed to make their composite tools.

Our acknowledging of the symbolizing capabilities of Neanderthal is fairly recent; for a long time the very word "Neanderthal" was synonymous with "brutish" or "dim-witted." We are beyond this view now, but granting the Neanderthals these capabilities raises the question: How far back in human evolution does symbolic capacity and artistic expression go? Possibly the earliest forms of artistic expression were body decoration, as by using ochre for coloring the skin (Morriss-Kay 2010). The earliest evidence of this comes from South Africa, dating to over 150,000 years ago. Later are zig-zag engraving patterns made in ochre blocks or flint, also from South Africa and once thought to be the earliest expressions of art outside the human body. However, a recent find of zig-zag engraving on a mussel shell in Indonesia dating back some 500,000 years ago and made by *Homo erectus* (Joordens 2015) challenges this view and opens the possibility that Homo *erectus* had capacities for symbolizing.

There are also examples of early recognition of animal-like forms in rock that were then modified with incised lines to draw out the similarity. This resulted in rough, figurine-like artifacts, found in the Middle East and North Africa as far back as 250,000 years ago. By around 35,000 to 40,000 years ago we find the famous Upper Paleolithic cave paintings in France and Spain and similar cave drawings in Indonesia and elsewhere in the same time period. Also from Europe during this period are the intriguing "Venus" figurines, three-dimensional representational objects that go beyond enhancement of pre-existing, suggestive forms in the material. Since these Venus figurines show such exaggeration of women's hips, breasts and abdomens, there has been considerable speculation that they were associated with female fertility, possibly used in some way to enhance human fertility or ease childbirth, but we simply do not know what they meant or how they were used by their makers.

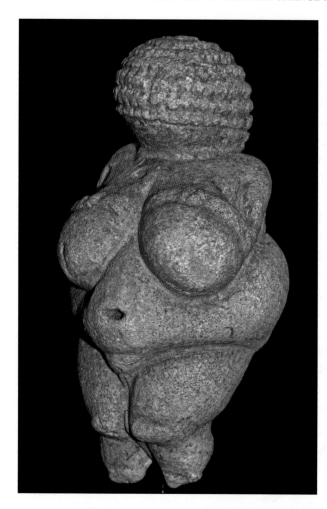

Figure 3.5 Venus figurine. The Venus of Willendorf.

Source: Museum of Natural History, Vienna, Austria. Author: Oke. Wikimedia CC BY-SA 3.0.

As far as we know, fully developed sculpture and cave paintings are restricted to our species, *H. sapiens*, but it is clear that this art has a long history in our evolution. It is probable that there were connections between this evolution of artistic expression and the development of tool-making that provided us a survival advantage in hunting (Morriss-Kay 2010). Cognitive processes needed for the making of specific tools were similar to those needed for certain artistic expressions. At some point we became able not only to recognize the potential for, say, animal shapes in stone, but also to imagine a compete tool or a piece of art that could be made as an entirely new creation.

Our understanding of human evolution continually changes as researchers make new fossil discoveries or analyze fossil evidence with new methods. So many new kinds of hominins have been discovered in recent decades that the human family tree is now thick with branches. For example, in 2004 researchers found on the island of Flores (Indonesia) skeletal remains of a new, never-before-seen hominin which was named *Homo floresiensis*, representing creatures popularly known as the Hobbits on account of their small size. These hominins, once interpreted as descendants of *Homo erectus* who underwent island dwarfism, are now thought by many to pre-date *Homo erectus* and to have been the first hominins to migrate out of Africa (Wong 2009).

The Hobbits lived as recently as 17,000 years ago, co-existing with modern humans. In 2008, an archaeologist found a chip of finger bone that, through DNA analysis, was determined to represent a new species of human that came to be known as the Denisovans, closely related to the Neanderthals. In 2009, news of a new, upright-walking fossil hominin "Ardi" (*Ardipithecus ramidus*) dating to 4.4 million years ago in Ethiopia was revealed. In 2010 a new type of Australopithecine (*Australopithecus sediba*) was reported from South Africa. And in 2013, a fossil jaw unearthed in Ethiopia is now considered to be the earliest evidence of *Homo*. This fossil, dated at 2.8 million years ago, pushes back the origin of our genus of *Homo* by 500,000 years. It was found some 40 miles from where Lucy was found in 1974. The fossil may be an evolutionary link between *Australopithecus afarensis* and *Homo habilis*.

But while new fossils, DNA, and other modes of analysis help fill in the picture of human evolution, the exact evolutionary line from Australopithecines to humans has been and remains controversial. Different scenarios, all fairly complex, have been proposed (see one possibility below) and the status

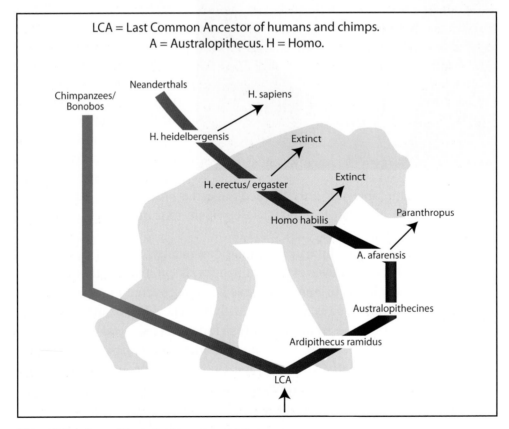

Figure 3.6   A possible path of human evolution.

of many fossils is in dispute. For example, a fossil hominid from Kenya, know as *Homo ergaster* and dated at about 1.8 million years ago, is seen by some as a link between *H. habilis* and the first *H. erectus*, whereas others see *ergaster* as itself an early erectus.

Theories of the Transition to Modern Humans

Adaptations through cultural mechanisms, relied on so extensively by humans, carry one clear advantage over those based on genetic change alone: they are much more rapid and flexible. Genetic mutations occur by chance and it may take generations for favorable ones to emerge. With cultural mechanisms, by contrast, humans can respond quickly to environmental changes and can quickly communicate these responses to others. Thus for their adaptations, humans do not need to wait around for chance genetic mutation or even wait for biological reproduction (Stone & Lurquin, 2007).

As we have already discussed, humans are unique among all species on the planet in that they rely primarily on culture as a mechanism of adaptation to their environment. Other species may use cultural mechanisms, but their adaptation and evolution have rested almost completely on the process of natural selection operating on genetic mutation. We will return here to a question raised earlier: When and why did the transition to a primary reliance on culture occur in the human line? It is easy to see what the advantages were, but what was the take-off point for human culture and what propelled it?

We do not yet have the answers to these questions, but scholars have proposed a number of interesting ideas on this issue. Anthropologist Robin Fox (1980) proposed that a major leap in human cultural adaptations occurred with the development of big game hunting. He places this hunting transition at around the time that Australopithecus was evolving into *H. habilis* and suggests that the transition was well under way by the time of early *H. erectus*. Fox suggests that big game hunting entailed a new division of labor by sex: males engaged in the hunting of large game while females specialized in the gathering of plant food. Before this time males and females foraged for themselves, with some hunting of small mammals and some food sharing, as among contemporary chimpanzees. But the new hunting and gathering order brought about a trade between men and women—meat for vegetables. This changed the relationship between men and women. Before, they interacted sexually and there was male protection of females, but now the sexes were interdependent on one another for food. Fox wrote that this meat and vegetable trade between the sexes "is probably at the root of a truly human society" (1980:143). For Fox, as for other anthropologists before him, the first truly human society was one in which local groups exchanged mates (spouses) among themselves to form peaceful alliances with one another. In Fox's view, the male/female/meat/vegetable trade brought males into closer association with females and their young in domestic units. Ultimately, with their control over the nutritionally-valuable meat protein, males came to have official power over the allocation of females as mates (in humans, brides) for other groups of men.

Primatologist Richard Wrangham (2009) hypothesized that it was not hunting as such but the cooking of food that led our hominin ancestors on the path to distinctively human adaptations. Wrangham places the human transition at a slightly later point than did Fox, namely at the *H. habilis/H. erectus* interface. For him, the cooking of food brought about the evolution of a branch of habilines into *H. erectus*. He wrote:

> I believe the transformative moment that gave rise to the genus *Homo*, one of the great transitions in the history of life, stemmed from the control of fire and the advent of cooked meals. Cooking increased the value of our food. It changed our bodies, our brains, our use of time, and our social lives. It made us into consumers of external energy and thereby created an organism with a new relationship to nature, dependent on fuel. (2009:2)

Wrangham demonstrates that compared to raw food, cooked food is energy-rich and carries further advantages such as providing food that is safer and more diverse. He shows how the adaptation to a cooked diet that yields softer, more easily digestible food may have allowed for the development of the smaller teeth, smaller mouths and weaker jaws of *H. erectus* and *H. sapiens* compared to other hominins and to nonhuman primates. These are good examples of how cultural adaptations can change us physically and affect our biological evolution. Wrangham also shows how energy from cooked food may have been instrumental in the impressive growth of brain size, and accompanying mental capacity, in *erectus* and, later, *sapiens*.

In addition, Wrangham speculates that as men specialized in hunting, women came to do the cooking and that this convenient division of labor brought a new relationship of mutual dependence between the sexes in a way somewhat similar to what Fox had proposed. However, Wrangham's emphasis on female cooking (rather than just gathering of plant food) gives a different slant to his scenario. Men, he wrote, protected their mates from being robbed of their food while cooking, and in turn women prepared their mates' meals. In this way, cooking led to human-style pair-bonded mating within domestic units.

These ideas of Fox, Wrangham and many others on the human transition are not necessarily in conflict with one another, although they emphasize different factors primarily responsible for the cultural "take off" in the human line. At present, all these ideas remain speculative; only future findings in fields such as archaeology, genetics, and primatology will clarify human evolutionary transitions whereby culture becomes our primary means of adaptation. Meanwhile, it appears that although anthropologists differ in their ideas on how the transition to fully human culture came about, they generally agree on when or among what species it did occur. It is now widely considered that *Homo erectus*, who lived between 1.8 million and 400,000 years ago, was the first creature to develop recognizable human culture. *Homo erectus* started out with a brain roughly half the size of ours, today, but later members of the species ended up with brains that were only about eight percent smaller than ours. During the time they existed, *Homo erectus*, as we saw, developed more useful and more efficiently made tools than had existed before, and began to use fire. We cannot know whether *Homo erectus* had language, though it seems reasonable to many anthropologists that this species had developed at least a rudimentary form of linguistic communication.

To conclude, we have seen that many primate and hominin species have made use of culture in their adaptations to the environment. Humans are distinctive for their far greater use of cultural mechanisms and the cumulative nature of their cultural developments. Also, nonhuman animals do not develop complex webs of learned behaviors on their own; they develop no symbolic systems of their own: no art, no religion, and no language, though they do communicate with each other (see Chapter 7). Why are nonhuman animals, especially the very intelligent nonhuman primates, so relatively limited in their use of culture? The answer is that they lack the biological basis for it. And more than any other biological characteristic, the basis for culture is a complex brain.

As noted, cultural innovations, unlike genetic change through mutation and natural selection, can help a species to adapt rapidly and flexibly to environmental challenges. This was undoubtedly a tremendous advantage to the evolving human line which came to spread over and dominate the entire planet. But, as with many evolutionary adaptations, this one has entailed costs as well as benefits. Helpful as it is, culture is also destructive, as seen, for example, in the development of warfare. Human culture has brought global warming, deforestation, environmental pollution, and new infectious diseases.

It has driven many of our fellow primates to the brink of extinction. Now the human species appears to be locked into global economies and life-ways that are seriously destructive to our own habitat. A question for our species' future is this: will human culture be able to change quickly enough to avert our own demise through the environmental destruction we have wrought?

CULTURAL DYNAMICS

All cultures change over time. Here we discuss more fully some reasons for culture change and mechanisms for transformations. We begin by dispelling the common notion that cultural change and transformations are progressive.

Cultural Transformations and the Concept of Progress

The view of human culture as inherently progressive through time has a long history. In the nineteenth century, anthropologists saw human culture as progressing through distinct stages, each more advanced than the last. The endpoint of their schemes was their own "advanced" Western culture. In many cases the names they gave to the stages they posited for cultural evolution revealed their biases. Thus, for example, **Lewis Henry Morgan** in the United States posited that cultures passed through three basic stages of, first, "Savagery," then "Barbarism" and finally "Civilization." This kind of thinking was ethnocentric and later discredited, largely through the impact of the notion of cultural relativism (discussed Chapter 1) in anthropology.

Later anthropologists, and especially archaeologists, did continue to study transformations in culture over time, although they gave less pejorative names to different cultural stages or forms, such as "band societies" "chiefdoms" "states" and so on (see Chapter 5). Still, these schemes seemed to imply a kind of "progress" in at least technology and complexity of political organization. Even in the present time, popular conceptions of cultural evolution are progressive in nature, focusing, for example, on steady advancements in medical science. Most people reading this book will probably consider that their lives and life chances are better than were those of their grandparents.

In the longer, global view, however, there is one disturbing pattern discernible in the transformations of human culture, and that is increasing socioeconomic inequality. This point has been forcefully drawn out in the work of anthropologist John Bodley (1997, 2003). Bodley sees cultures in terms of how they organize social power, which he refers to as their "cultural scale."

In Bodley's analysis there are three broad categories of cultural scale—small, large, and global. Small-scale cultures (bands, tribes) are characterized by autonomous (or independent) households and local communities of about 500 to 1000 people; they exhibit socioeconomic equality, at least within gender and age groups, and an ethic of sharing; in these societies there is no central authority above the household level; and economic production is for subsistence rather than the accumulation of wealth. Large-scale cultures (chiefdoms, states and empires) consist of institutionalized political hierarchies; households and villages are no longer autonomous but under the authority of these political institutions. These cultures have denser populations and are divided into social classes with the ruling elite supported by the taxes, tribute and labor of the lower social orders. Economic activities serve and support the political organization. Global-scale cultures are dominated by multinational profit-seeking corporations within a commercial market economy. Here, in a reversal of the situation among large-scale cultures, political organization is in the service of these corporate economic interests.

All three types of cultures can still be found in the world today, but over time many humans have passed from small-scale to large-scale to global-scale culture. As they have done so, world population has increased dramatically, economic production has intensified and power has become increasingly concentrated. Small-scale society has been the longest lived; the whole world was small-scale and tribal from 50,000 to 8,000 years ago. Large-scale cultures had taken over about half the globe by C.E. 1200, but within a few centuries global-scale culture began its rise and by the year 2000 had engulfed the world, with only a few thousand people living in small-scale societies as "indigenous persons."

What Bodley sees as the prime movers in the passage from small-scale through large-scale to global-scale culture is neither organizational necessity nor technological inventions, but deliberate, human action carried out by a relatively few ambitious individuals, the would-be "power elites." The growth of cultural scale is an elite-directed process. These elites are not necessarily evil people, but merely opportunists who simply seek to expand their power in an effort to enhance their own material comfort and life chances along with those of their descendants. "Elites can use their more powerful imperia [command over others] to transform culture for their own benefit. Elites gain their added power from increases in the size or scale of societies, polities, and economic enterprises (2004:5)."

The growth of cultural scale has clearly not benefited humankind in Bodley's view. On the contrary, the passage from small-scale through large-scale to global-scale culture has meant increasing social inequality. Indeed, the only cultures in which what we would now call human rights were enjoyed by all (or at least all adult men) were small-scale tribal cultures. "In the tribal world every member of the tribe was born with a 'natural' entitlement guaranteeing the opportunity to enjoy a full life" (2003:15). The quality of life was high and poverty unknown. In large-scale societies inequality increased markedly. To maintain these societies many people were reduced to servitude and slavery— "for the first time vast numbers of people were treated like domestic animals" (2003:21)—wars became devastating with high casualties, and in ancient civilizations large numbers of human beings were ritually sacrificed for various purposes. Warfare and other inhumane atrocities continue in global-scale culture, and here we see some new problems such as mass poverty and environmental pollution. One may disagree with Bodley's rather grim overview of world history; one may debate the relative merits of different types and scales of societies; but Bodley has a point: human cultural evolution has been grossly inequitable in its costs and benefits, and this inequality increases with the growth in culture scale.

Mechanisms of Cultural Change

Bodley focuses on the actions of opportunistic powermongers as primary agents of cultural evolution. There are, of course, other processes of cultural change. One is **acculturation,** which occurs when a dominant group overtakes the territory of indigenous peoples whose cultural traditions are then rather rapidly lost and new cultural forms are adopted from the dominant culture. This has been the fate of innumerable tribal societies under colonization, as among native peoples in the Americas.

Other changes can come about through the processes of **innovation** (especially techno-economic innovation) and then **diffusion** (spread), first through the population of the initial culture of invention and then gradually to other cultures that come into contact with the first one, and so on from culture to culture. Agriculture, having been independently invented in different parts of the world, and earliest in the Middle East, may have spread in this way, triggering all sorts of other changes in residence patterns, human disease, division of labor by sex, and so on. Thus it ushered in substantial subsequent cultural change wherever it was adopted. Another perspective now contends that it was not the *idea* of agriculture that spread by diffusion from the Middle East into Europe; rather, agriculture may have moved into Europe as human agricultural populations themselves expanded and migrated out from the Middle East.

Cultural groups also contain within themselves a source of change: *internal variation*. Within any culture, even within small-scale, relatively slow-changing ones, members of the group will have different perspectives on their shared world. As mentioned in Chapter 1, men may have different views from women; young people will see things differently from older people. Also, some cultural ideas are expressed as variations on a theme. There are slightly different ways to hunt a giraffe or build a house; there are different conceptions of a god or different levels of belief in the god's power, and so on. Culture change can occur whenever there is a shift in the dominance of one cultural idea or variation over other competing ones.

Another source of cultural change is migration; change can occur whenever a subgroup migrates out or splinters off. There may be subtle shifts in the migrating culture if most or all of the migrants are male or most are younger people. Or, a splinter group may break away from a parent population precisely because its members hold a particular cultural trait in common (say a religious or political belief) or have a conviction not widely shared in the parent population, for which they may be discriminated against. This belief or conviction then has free rein in their new location and with time becomes a widespread, stable trait in the new location. An obvious example of this kind of cultural drift is the Pilgrims who migrated to the **New World**. Persecuted in England for their religious beliefs, they migrated to New England where they founded religious communities. Their core values—prosperity as the outward sign of virtue and universal conformity to their religious beliefs—not only became entrenched in the new land, but have remained prominent features of American life to the present time (McKee & Stone, 2007).

Internal variation and migration, then, are sources for change in any culture. Often we think of cultural change in connection with major technological innovations—fire, agriculture, electricity, etc., and indeed changes are brought about through these innovations. Or we consider major transformations such as the changes brought about by the fall of empires, wars, revolutions, or conquests of indigenous peoples by colonizing powers. But a lot of what we see in terms of human culture change is in fact a subtle and gradual process rooted in the internal variation in cultural ideas.

GLOBALIZATION

A very particular kind of cultural change is taking place in the world today. We now see, for example, that people from one country (such as Grenada in the

Caribbean) are more numerous in cities like New York than in their homeland. We all know that with the click of a computer button we can send our written thoughts and photographs anywhere in the world to a virtually unlimited number of other people. And we are all aware that certain powerful symbols of our times—such as the MacDonald's Golden Arches—are now recognizable worldwide. This new set of changes is often referred to as "**globalization**." Globalization is the accelerating movement of people, goods, ideas, and money over the world. It is facilitated by technologies of transportation, e-mail, the Internet and changing economic forces (or what Bodley called global-scale culture). We see the effects of globalization everywhere today in, for example, the processes of urbanization, transnational migration, and increasing travel for business or tourism. One of the inevitable results of this large-scale movement of humans is an increase in the spread of infectious diseases.

In many ways, globalization is nothing new. Our species has always been on the move, as seen as far back as the initial out-of-Africa migrations of *H. erectus* 1.7 million years ago and later *H. sapiens*, some 130,000 years ago. Wherever they went, our ancestors took their worldly goods and cultural practices with them; and where these groups bumped into one another, in peace or conflict, their goods and cultural ideas began to flow over boundaries of languages and life-ways. What is new with globalization is the accelerated pace of this movement and its connection with an increasingly global economic system. Economically, globalization is rooted in the expansion of capitalism, especially notable after the end of the Cold War in the early 1990s. As such, globalization is an important part of the sustaining and deepening of poverty and economic inequality in the world today. Global capitalism involves an increasing incorporation of local, small-scale economies into a broader international economy dominated by multinational corporations. These corporations relentlessly pursue profits, depend on economic growth, and foster the commoditization of more and more goods and services in more and more countries. Together with international financial institutions, these corporations have favored a global economy based on so-called *neoliberalism*. Neoliberalism promotes unrestricted world trade, privatization, and less interference of governments generally in the economy. These policies benefit the rich but often devastate the world's poor. For example, beginning in the 1990s, the World Bank made loans to developing countries that were contingent on those countries agreeing to undergo economic "structural adjustment." To meet these requirements, poor developing countries were required to adopt neoliberal economic policies and, to implement these, they needed to cut back social services such as education, public health, and anti-poverty measures.

Today's accelerating migration of people around the globe is largely for the purpose of finding jobs. Wage-labor migration may be temporary or "circular;" that is, persons move back and forth from rural to urban areas in their home country or move between two or more different countries, sending remittances to family members back home. This circular movement between countries is referred to as *transnational migration*. Today transnational migration is largely a flow of persons from poorer developing countries to wealthier ones for work. In recent decades this movement has been feminized; women now outpace men as transnational migrants, as, for example, in Sri Lanka, where many very poor women work for months or years as housemaids in Middle Eastern countries such as Saudi Arabia (Gamburd 2008). This migration (involving up to 13 percent of working-age women) has a significant impact on gender roles among migrant families in Sri Lanka, where males are expected to be primary breadwinners, with wives subordinate to husbands. Husbands of migrants now take over childcare and other household work, while their wives work outside the home and outside the country.

Another type of global flow of persons that reflects world inequalities is transnational adoption. Today many children and infants move from poorer "donor" countries to become members of families in wealthier nations. This movement of children is fairly recent, having become significant only in the latter half of the twentieth century. Earlier, transnational adoptions were sporadic responses to natural disasters, economic crises and wars (Kapstein 2003:2). In these cases, the motives for adoption were often humanitarian, with many adoptive parents already having children of their own. Today the transnational flow of children is spurred by couples or individuals who desperately seek to have children and are for a variety of reasons unable to produce their own. In North America and Europe a rise in the age of marriage and increasing postponement of attempts to conceive after marriage has meant that couples have fewer children of their own. Because fertility decreases with age, couples are more likely to be infertile by the time they decide they want children. At the same time, few children in these countries are available for domestic adoption due to the availability of contraception and abortion and also to the reduction of social stigmas attached to out-of-wedlock births and single motherhood. At present, about 40,000 children are transnationally adopted each year. Although the United States remains the largest receiver of transnational adoptees, dramatically rising numbers of adoptions are now noticeable in European countries. The highest donor of children is China, followed by Russia, and the majority of transnationally adopted children are female.

Globalization is affecting all of us in many ways and is now intensely studied by a wide variety of different disciplines. But the question for us here is this: how is globalization affecting human culture? The dominant opinion is that globalization blurs cultural boundaries, that it is promoting a homogenization of culture, or, ultimately, a world monoculture and the loss of cultural diversity (Nederveen Pieterse, 2004). After all, many people worldwide, especially young people in urban areas, now eat and shop in the same transnational food and clothing chains, listen to the same popular music, and watch the same movies. Some have further suggested that wealthy nations are becoming culturally dominant, or culturally imperialistic, as they are economically in the lead and at the receiving end of labor migrations. As a result, a global cultural transformation is, in this view, actually Westernization or possibly even an Americanization of the world. Is any of this happening? Most anthropologists think not.

Take McDonald's for example. These fast-food restaurants now exist in 119 countries, serving basically hamburgers, French fries, chicken, and salads. McDonald's is a powerful multinational corporation, itself a symbol of globalization and a prime target of anti-globalization movements. But is the experience and meaning of eating at McDonald's everywhere the same? Not at all. For one thing, McDonald's itself has morphed to fit local customs and ideas, for example serving mutton instead of beef for its "Maharaja Burger" in India, where Hindus avoid beef. At the same time, local consumers further transform McDonald's on their own. David Wu (2006:129) describes the atmosphere of some Taiwanese McDonald's as like "an old-fashioned temple bazaar" in terms of the bustle, noise, and lively human interaction among diners. In some places in Taiwan, McDonald's restaurants have become a hang-out for primary and junior-high school students, who spend hours there together talking and studying in the afternoons. From Korea, Sangmee Bak (2006:148) reports that "Young people (especially women college students and dating couples) often convert McDonald's restaurants into cafés where they chat over coffee or soft drinks." In some locations in Seoul, McDonald's have become convenient places for meetings, with bulletin boards for messages provided in the lobbies. And in Korea, where many foods are normally shared from the same pot, "even when friends purchase separate packets of fries, they often pour the contents onto a tray and together eat from the resulting pile" (Bak 2006:157).

In these and many other cases, McDonald's restaurants become localized as much as they are globalized. James Watson concludes from these several

Figure 3.7   McDonald's in Ashkelon, Israel.
Source: Wikimedia. Uploaded by Ingsoc. CC BY-SA 3.0.

studies of McDonald's in East Asia that some untrained observers fail to distinguish cultural form from content. They see outward forms of what looks like "Americana"—like McDonald's, but also Nike shops, Starbucks and so on—and "jump to the conclusion that globalization has changed the essential core of non-Western cultures." (2006:196). What they fail to see is the *content* of a new form in its transplanted cultural context, that is, the use and meaning it has to local people. Thus "[t]he perceived 'sameness' of world cultures is an illusion, a mirage that masks a vast panoply of local responses to globalization" (2006:197).

We see similar processes at work in terms of other aspects of culture such as marriage and the family. Some have assumed that globalization, especially the processes of urbanization, exposure to Western media, and labor migration, would result in the decline of arranged marriages, the rise of marriages based on romantic love, and the breakdown of large, extended families worldwide. It is true that globalization has had an impact on marriage and the family in many areas of the world, but the reality of this impact is more complex than these assumptions would lead us to think. In India, for example, new ideas about romantic love *have* entered marriage, and yet most marriages are still arranged by kin groups, not the individuals, themselves. At the same time more and more single people in the United States now pay impersonal on-line services to arrange their "matches."

Daniel Smith (2011) has discussed the mixing of the old and the new in marriage among the **Igbo** of Nigeria, as this country enters an increasingly globalized world. The Igbo over the past several decades have seen increasing economic diversification, urbanization and labor migration. Education, for women and men, is now highly sought and seen as crucial to securing good jobs. Igbo youth in urban areas are daily exposed to new life styles and values through music, films, television, and the Internet. All of these and other forces of globalization are impacting marriage and family formation. But this transformation does not merely reflect an adoption of Western forms of family; rather the transformation is taking its own new path.

On the one hand, most contemporary Igbo marriages are based on individual choice and romantic love, rather than on arrangement by parents and among kin groups. On the other hand, a couple's ties to kin remain strong, and final marriage choices still depend on the preferences and consent of the parents and extended families of the couple. In a similar way, modern marriages show husbands and wives operating as a team with greater gender equality than in the past. However, Smith noted that this gender equality fades after the courtship phase of a union and that after marriage, a patriarchal situation prevails in terms of sexual freedom. Previously premarital chastity was expected of women although not of men. Today a rising age of marriage for women, along with the availability of contraception, has led to an acceptance of premarital female sexuality. But after marriage there is a clear double standard: Women are "supposed to be faithful in marriage *and* tolerate men's extramarital affairs" (Smith 2008:228, emphasis his). Male peer groups encourage male infidelity and these extramarital affairs are for a man a display of masculinity toward other men.

A retention of old patterns is also seen in that Igbo stress on the continuing importance of kin networks in securing access to resources in the new, global economy. Finally, attitudes toward fertility show both change and continuity with older models. Many Igbo today want to limit their fertility due to challenging economic times and the cost of educating children. At the same time, most persons whom Smith interviewed wanted to have at least four children. Igbos still feel that "having people" (that is, coming from and having large families for support) is essential to life in Nigeria (Smith 2011:59).

Clearly, with the now great and ever accelerating movement of people across the globe, "culture" has become geographically untethered. Gone are the days when anthropologists could draw bounded circles within continents and label them as distinct cultural groups. And this flow of persons amid the spread of global capitalism is bringing about a great deal of cultural change. But so far it does not appear that we are headed toward any kind of global monoculture. Rather, we are seeing new cultural mixtures or what Jan Nederveen Pieterse (2004) has called the "hybridization" of culture within globalization.

SUMMARY

This chapter has explored the evolutionary origins of human culture, covering culture among nonhuman primates and our hominin ancestors. We then moved to the topics of culture change and a recent kind of change known as globalization. In the process we have discounted the following myths:

Myth #1 Culture is unique to our species.

This is a myth that is nearly as old as the discipline of anthropology, primarily for two reasons. First, humans seem to need to establish rigid and unquestioned boundaries that distinguish themselves from nonhuman animals. And second, until the middle of the twentieth century, there was very little empirical evidence for the ways nonhuman primates lived in the wild. Now that most anthropologists and biologists are less concerned with distinguishing themselves from apes, and we know much more about how monkeys and apes live in their natural habitat, we are more willing to accept the idea that culture is not an exclusively human adaptation. We have seen in this chapter that various nonhuman primates make and use tools, recognize kinship over the generations, establish dominance rank through ancestry, and engage in rudimentary symbolic communication. A community of chimpanzees is not likely to develop religious beliefs or write *Hamlet*, but it does develop and socially transmit behavioral conventions. Human culture is unique, however, in its elaborate creation and use of symbols and its cumulative capacity.

Myth # 2 Human cultural evolution is progressive; over time, cultural developments and transformations have generally improved the well being of humanity.

This has been a common assumption pervasive both within academia and in the popular imagination. However, modern or more recent cultural practices are not necessarily "better" in any sense than earlier ones; indeed, human cultural transformations have consistently brought at least one unsettling feature—increasing socioeconomic inequality—in their wake.

In biological evolution more complex organisms have developed over time, but it does not follow that the later, more complex forms are in any sense "better" than earlier ones. Humans, for example, though far more complex than bacteria, are not better adapted to their environments and may, in fact, be less suited to long-term survival. Similarly cultures may transform with time, becoming more complex, but this does not suggest progress or betterment in any sense. Though technology and medicine, for example, have become more powerful, the benefits these changes have produced for some of the world's peoples have proven disastrous or unavailable for others.

Myth #3   Globalization is breaking down cultural barriers and homogenizing culture around the world.

Some see a loss of cultural diversity as a threat of globalization, and this is one of the reasons for anti-globalization sentiments and movements. Often implied in this objection is the cultural imperialism of the West or even the United States (sometimes cultural globalization is referred to as McDonaldization, a term introduced by sociologist Geore Ritzer [2008]). In many ways, globalization is bringing about a "shrinking world" and a new global consumer culture of sorts. However, the process of globalization is so far showing a localization of new cultural expressions or a reworking of new cultural traits into older local patterns. Globalization is bringing culture change everywhere, but the world is not headed toward a global monoculture.

QUESTIONS FOR THOUGHT AND REFLECTION

1. Depending upon how one defines "culture," it is possible to argue either that some nonhuman primates have culture or that they do not. Explain this statement, providing specific definitions and examples.

2. Using the example of Old World monkeys, explain some of the elements of kinship that are evident in their social organization. What similarities do you see with some varieties of human kinship and family life?

3. What does it mean to say that humans are unique among the animal species on the planet in that their adaptations to circumstances are primarily cultural rather than biological? Are there nonhuman animals that use cultural adaptations? Explain. Do humans also rely on biological adaptations? Explain.

4. What are some of the cultural effects of the transition from small-scale to large-scale to global-scale organization? What has driven this transition? In general, who has benefitted from these transitions, and how? Who has suffered from them? Is it possible to make a single, overall evaluation of the good or bad effects of the transition?

5. What is globalization? How has it resulted in a certain degree of imposition of external cultural phenomena throughout the world? On the other hand, explain how local cultural values and practices have modified the imported cultural phenomena so as to retain important indigenous identity and institutions. Provide specific examples.

ENDNOTES

[1]Some have questioned whether this is a case of true imitative learning, where an organism models its behavior on that of another, or it is just a case of "resource enhancement," where one organism is directed to a new or improved resource by another (see van Hooff 1994).

[2]Other animals for which cases of cultural transmission have been suggested include some species of birds (where songs are learned by infants from mothers), whales, and dolphins. In some whales, for example, hunting techniques appear to be learned (de Waal 2001).

[3]Among squirrel monkeys and some lemurs, females are dominant over males. Other species such as muriqui monkeys exhibit sexual equality (Strier 1992).

[4]It is not known why among these species younger sisters rank over elder ones. It is known that mothers assist the younger females to rise in rank.

REFERENCS CITED

Ambrose, Stanley H.
  2001 Paleolithic Technology and Human Evolution. *Science* 291:1748–1753.

Bak, Sangmee
  2006 McDonald's in Soeul: Food Choices, Identity, and Nationaism. In Watson, James, L. editor, *Golden Arches East: McDonald's in East Asia. 2nd edition*. Pp. 136–160. Stanford, CA: Stanford University Press.

Boesch, C.
    Teaching among Wild Chimpanzees. *Animal Behavior* 4:530–532.

Bodley, John H.
    Cultural Anthropology: Tribes, States and the Global System. Mountain View, CA: Mayfield
        Publishing Company.
    2003 *The Power of Scale: A Global Approach*. Armonk, NY: M.E. Sharp.

Caspari, Rachael
    The Evolution of Grandparents. *Scientific American* 305(2):44–49.

Chapais, Bernard and Carol M. Berman, eds.
    2004 *Kinship and Behavior in Primates*. Oxford: Oxford University Press.

Cheney, Dorothy L. and R,M, Sayfarth
    How Monkeys See the World. Chicago: Chicago University Press.

de Waal, Frans
    Chimpanzee Politics. London: Jonathan Cape.
    2001 *The Ape and the Sushi Master: Cultural Reflections of a Primatologist*. New York: Basic Books.

Fox, Robin
    1980 *The Red Lamp of Incest*. New York: E. P. Dutton.

Gibbons, Ann
    2009 A New Kind of Ancestor: Ardipithecus Unveiled. *Science* 326:36–43.

Goodall, Jane
    The Chimpanzees of Gombe: Patterns of Behavior. Canbridge, MA: Harvard University Press.

Green, Richard E. et al.
    2010 The Neanderthal Genome. *Science* 328(5976):710–722.

Joordens, Josephine C. A. et al.
    2015 Homo Erectus at Trinil on Java Used Shells for Tool Production and Engraving. *Nature*
        518:228–231.

Kapstein, Ethan B.
    2003. The Baby Trade. *Foreign Affairs* 82(6):115–125.

Lieberman, Daniel E.
    2007 Honing in on Homo. *Nature* 499(20):291–292.

Morriss-Kay, Gillian M.
    2010 The Evolution of Human Artistic Creativity. *Journal of Anatomy* 216:158–176.

McGrew, W. C.
    Culture in Nonhuman Primates? *Annual Review of Anthropology* 27:301–328.

McKee, Nancy P. and Stone, Linda
    2007 *Gender and Culture in America*, 3rd ed. Cornwall-on-Hudson, NY: Sloan Publishing.

Nederveen Pieterse, Jan
    2004 *Globalization and Culture*. Lanham, MD: Roman and Littlefield.

Ritzer, George
    2008 *The McDonaldization of Society*, 2nd ed. Thousand Oaks, CA Pine Forge Press.

Sapolsky, Robert M. and Lisa J. Share
  2004 A Pacific Culture among Wild Baboons: Its Emergence and Transmission. *PLoS Biology* 2(4):0534–0541.

Stone, Linda and Paul F. Lurquin
  2007 *Genes, Culture and Human Evolution: A Synthesis*. Malden, MA: Blackwell Publishing.

Strier, Karen B.
  Faces of the Forest: The Endangered Muriqui Monkeys of Brazil. Cambridge, MA: Harvard University Press.

Van Hooff, Jan A.R.A.M.
  Understanding Chimpanzee Understanding. In Wrangham, Richard W., W.C. McGrew, Frans B.M. de Waal and Paul G. Heltne, eds., *Chimpanzee Cultures*. Pp.267–284. Cambridge, MA: Harvard University Press.

Watson, James L.
  2006 Update: McDonald's as Political Target: Globalization and Anti-Globalization in the Twenty-First Century. In Watson, James, L. editor, *Golden Arches East: McDonald's in East Asia. 2nd edition*. Pp. 183–197. Stanford, CA: Stanford University Press.

Wu, David Y.H.
  McDonald's in Taipai: Hamburgers, Betel Nuts and National Identity. In Watson, James, L. editor, *Golden Arches East: McDonald's in East Asia.2nd edition*. Pp. 110–135. Stanford, CA: Stanford University Press.

Wong, Kate
  2004 Rethinking the Hobbits of Indonesia. *Scientific American* 301(5):66–73.
  2015 Neanderthal Minds. *Scientific American* 312(2):36–43.

Wrangham, Richard
  Catching Fire: How Cooking Made Us Human. New York: Basic Books.

CHAPTER 4

MAKING A LIVING

Patterns of subsistence and their cultural and environmental interactions

In the nineteenth century, when anthropology was just developing, travelers and colonial officials from Europe and North America began to undertake systematic observations of ways of life different from their own. It was inevitable that nearly all of these early observations were suffused with ethnocentrism, the notion, as discussed in earlier chapters, that one's own way of life is not only the best, but also the only normal, sensible one. Though all kinds of cultural practices attracted the notice of these observers, one activity that struck many as central was the ways in which people obtained food, or in a more general sense, made a living, which anthropologists generally refer to as "**subsistence**." In the eighteenth and nineteenth centuries, the subsistence system that Europeans and Euro-Americans considered normal and natural was agriculture, and echoes of this perspective remain in the myths that color many common views today. Here are a few influential myths we will examine in this chapter:

Common Myths of Culture

Myth #1 The normal and natural subsistence method for humans is agriculture.

Myth #2 People who do not practice agriculture live precarious lives that are "nasty, brutish, and short," in the words of seventeenth-century English philosopher, Thomas Hobbes (mentioned in Chapter 1 of this book).

Myth #3 The standard human pattern is for men to dominate subsistence and for women to be involved in other, domestic activities.

Myth #4 The production of food, from simple horticulture to modern, mechanized agriculture, has produced a generally more prosperous and leisured life for the world's population.

EARLY VIEWS OF CROSS CULTURAL SUBSISTENCE

It is true that agriculture is the backbone of modern, industrial society. By the middle of the eighteenth century, industrial occupations were becoming increasingly common, but they were all dependent upon agriculture for their existence. Without agriculture, the technology that made industrialization possible would not have developed. The huge food surpluses that released large numbers of people from food production and allowed (or forced) them to find employment in other occupations would not have been possible, either. Despite the fact that a decreasing proportion of their population engaged in agriculture, many Europeans and Euro-Americans considered agriculture a sign of "civilization," and agricultural occupations a sign of virtue and hard work. People who hunted wild animals and collected wild plant foods, as well as those who relied on herding domesticated animals, were thought of as indolent and primitive, while those who practiced food production on a small scale and moved their garden plots every few years were seen as poor and wasteful precursors of agricultural farmers. All non-agriculturalists were, ironically as it turns out, seen as poor stewards of the land over which God had granted humans dominion. In fact, in sharp contrast to large, urban-based societies, hunter-gatherers leave most of their territory unoccupied and unexploited at any given time. They live "lightly on the land," leaving little evidence that they have been there. But when metropolitan, agriculturally-based societies first encountered foraging peoples, they considered their way of life, generally, and their subsistence system, specifically, wasteful and unproductive.

As anthropology matured as an academic discipline, anthropologists ceased to pass such unfounded and inaccurate judgments on societies and cultural systems different from their own, and began to concentrate on describing these cultures in detail and to consider *why* they varied. These descriptions contributed valuable information and allowed anthropologists to make comparisons and establish hypotheses about the reasons for cultural variation.

Early hypotheses about why cultures varied tended to focus on environmental phenomena as determining how societies were organized, but much of this thinking was crude and over-generalized. For example, some scholars proposed that hot, humid climates discouraged certain cultural innovations. But let us look at some real cases. Today in the hot and humid Amazon Basin, much of the indigenous population practices simple, small-scale farming, shifting their gardens from place to place every year or two. It is not hard to see why early European invaders might have decided the environment determined subsistence practices so different from their own. But consider hot and humid Southeast Asia, where people have been practicing labor intensive wet rice agriculture in elaborately constructed terraced fields for thousands of years. Clearly, climate alone does not determine people's general ways of life or even their subsistence systems. The environment *does* impose limits on how people live, but human technology has always allowed people to transcend many environmental limitations. It used to be said, by way of illustrating the restrictions imposed by the environment, that "you can't grow corn in the Arctic." Now, however, we know that technology *does* allow us to grow corn even in the Antarctic (though it is hardly an economically viable option). In the same way, much earlier technology produced elaborate irrigation systems that extended the Nile's flood waters, so that the ancient Egyptians were able to grow wheat in the marginal land bordering desert, proving that "you *can* grow wheat in the desert."

After coming to terms with their cultural biases and abandoning their strict environmental determinism, anthropologists came to study and understand cross cultural variation in new ways, considering a wide variety of phenomena. But they have tended to retain one view of nineteenth-century observers, namely that subsistence systems are of central significance. Today most anthropologists consider a society's dominant subsistence system as a primary factor in influencing the contours of its culture. We will examine four broad varieties of subsistence below.

HUNTING AND GATHERING/FORAGING

For most of the time humans have existed on the planet, they have made a living through hunting wild animals (including fish) and gathering wild plant foods. This system of subsistence is referred to as **hunting and gathering** or as **foraging**. Our information about this way of life comes from a variety of sources. Some of them are derived from archaeology, some from historical information, and some from those contemporary peoples, like the **!Kung** people (who call themselves the **Ju/'hoansi**) of Botswana and Namibia (see Lee 2012), or the **Aka** of the Central African Republic and the Republic of the Congo (see Hewlett 1991), who have retained a foraging way of life into the present.

Division of Labor

In general, hunting and gathering is based on a gendered division of labor that maximizes the capabilities of men and of women for the good of the whole group. Men, as a rule, are responsible for hunting large animals, while women take charge of acquiring and procuring plant foods. Virtually everyone in foraging communities prefers meat to vegetable foods. Because of this preference, along with the risks involved in hunting, substantially higher status, praise, and attention accrue to men as hunters than to women as gatherers. But for virtually all hunting and gathering peoples, the vegetable foods provided by women form the essential basis of the diet and amount to well over half of all food consumed by the group.[1] In Arctic regions, where plant foods play little role in the diet, women's status is correspondingly low, though it is acknowledged by all that their labor in producing the tailored skin clothing necessary in the bitter cold is essential to group survival. Still, such essential contributions to group well-being do not necessarily translate into power or status.

The gendered division of labor in hunting and gathering societies is not an arbitrary one, nor is it a cynical sexist plot to subordinate women to men (as has crossed the minds of some students). Hunting large animals with spears and bows and arrows requires substantial upper body strength and the ability to put forth considerable bursts of energy. These are capabilities more common in men than in women. In addition, women young enough to be of any use in hunting are very likely to be pregnant or involved in the nursing and frequent carrying of small children. Hunting and gathering peoples breastfeed small children for several years, and routinely carry children on their backs or in slings across their chests, both of which techniques make it difficult to stalk, chase, and kill large animals.

Figure 4.1   Inuit family 1929.
Photo: Edward S. Curtis.

RESIDENCE AND MOBILITY

From the perspective of outsiders, a notable characteristic of hunting and gathering peoples is that with very few exceptions they do not live in one place throughout the year, but instead move in what anthropologists refer to as a "seasonal round." This means that as foraging communities use up the resources in one place, they move on to exploit resources in another area within a territory. Foraging peoples do not move around randomly. They are very familiar with the environmental niches of their territory, and they make travel plans carefully, based on many generations of experience.

In general, hunting and gathering peoples spend most of the year living in very small groups. Keeping the size of the group small makes it easier to find adequate food, water, and other resources, especially in seasons or locations of scarcity. Perhaps a pair of siblings with their spouses and children will travel together, or a nuclear family plus a grandparent or a widowed aunt. A family or small group may travel toward a specific geographic goal, say a known source

Figure 4.2   Hazda men hunting.
Photo: Idobi. Wikimedia CC BY-SA 3.0

of reliable food, where they may just camp for a night or two, building a simple brush shelter to protect themselves from the wind. In seasons in which resources are abundant, as when fish are running, or prey animals have put on weight, several small groups may congregate together for an extended period of time. Coming together in larger groups is generally enjoyable for hunter-gatherers. People can see old friends, catch up on family news, and the young people can flirt while their elders plan marriages and remember old times. But eventually the local resources begin to wear thin, the continued presence of a large number of people in one encampment without sanitation becomes oppressive, and quarrels may break out. At that point it is time to break camp and separate into smaller groups once again. This flexibility and spontaneity of living arrangements is one of the hallmarks of hunting and gathering societies, and it serves two purposes. One is the ease of exploiting resources, and the other is social harmony, providing an escape valve for personal conflict in societies that lack coercive authority (chiefs, laws, police, etc.) for regulating social interaction.

There have been some groups of hunting and gathering peoples who have not been nomadic. Such peoples occupy territory that is so rich in resources that moving is not necessary. In historic times many of the Native American peoples of the northwest coast of what is now the United States and the southwest coast of Canada lived in such permanent settlements. These Indian peoples subsisted primarily on the abundant marine resources of the area, including fish, shellfish, and sea mammals. It is quite likely that in the remote past, before settled peoples with large populations and powerful technology had come to occupy most of the desirable ecological zones, more foraging groups were relatively sedentary.

Because most hunting and gathering peoples *do* move in a seasonal round, they need access to sizeable tracts of land. These territories are far too large to be patrolled by the people who use them, so there is no way of preventing other groups from using the land or other resources. From time to time a family that does not customarily use a particular area may ask the group using it if they may share resources. The request is usually granted, because the survival value of sharing and reciprocity is ever present in the minds of hunter-gatherers. Unless sustained, widespread ecological disaster takes place, or population pressure from modernized groups pushes foragers into a space too restricted for survival, armed conflict over territory rarely occurs.

Ownership and Sharing

The necessary mobility of most hunting and gathering peoples imposes limitations on their lives. To members of settled societies, one of the most striking limitations is the small number of possessions owned by foragers. Consider how many pounds of possessions we haul along with us every time we go on a brief vacation or move into a dormitory for a semester, not to mention how many tons of possessions must be transferred by moving van every time a family moves. By contrast, contemporary hunter-gatherers, as Lee (2012) tells us, are likely to have no more than 20 pounds of possessions per adult. These possessions include primarily the tools and containers used for subsistence and the clothing and ornaments people wear daily. They may also include coverings and blankets used for shelter and warmth. Hunter-gatherers usually have no domesticated animals other than dogs, so they must carry their possessions, themselves, as well as all babies and small children who cannot walk long distances. The practical impossibility of moving large quantities of possessions precludes the possibility of hoarding, and effectively discourages any individual from amassing more wealth than any other.

Because of the unpredictability of hunting (the likelihood of a successful hunt is only about 25 percent [Lee, 2012]), as well as the communal effort often required to achieve hunting success, meat in foraging communities is commonly shared among all members of the group, whether they have assisted in the hunt or not. In some groups the meat is distributed according to the whim of the person deemed most responsible for a successful hunt, as with the

!Kung. In other groups, like many precontact Inuit (Eskimo) peoples, a man's hunting partners have a right to a particular part of the prey animal (shoulder, haunch, etc.). Indeed, Inuit hunting partners called each other by the name of the body part they would receive ("My Shoulder," "My Haunch").

It is tempting to think of the foraging practice of food sharing as demonstrating a level of morality superior to what prevails in stratified, metropolitan societies like our own, where there are huge differences in wealth, and where the rich do not willingly share with the poor. But for hunter-gatherers, food sharing is not merely ethical; it is also a sound survival strategy. A hunter-gatherer who has meat and shares it with someone who has none can reasonably expect that when he has no meat someone will supply him. Hunters and gatherers are not saints. They quarrel, gossip, and lie like everyone else on the planet. But their groups are small, and their members depend heavily upon each other. Thus, they do not allow anyone in their group to starve if there is food available, and huge discrepancies in wealth do not develop among them.

However it is accomplished, the distribution of meat from male hunting is typically a very public, celebrated and rule-governed affair. Because the gathering of plants is less risky and more predictable, there are fewer rules and less ceremony attached to their distribution. As a rule, each woman does her own gathering, and sharing is private and informal. Along with the division of labor, itself, this difference likely affects gender relationships. According to anthropologist Ernestine Friedl (1978), the status of women is relatively high in societies where they contribute substantially to primary subsistence, as among most hunter-gatherers, but it is somewhat diminished because their plant foods are both less desired and only privately distributed to others. We will return to Friedl's ideas on gender and subsistence later in this chapter.

Among foragers, land and other environmental resources, like trees or water, are not privately owned. Instead, land is conceived as a resource to which local family groups (perhaps even the entire ethnic group) have a right of use. Needless to say, this is a dramatically different approach from that of the inhabitants of large, urban-based societies, as we will see.

The Shape of Foraging Groups

Along with their equality and mobility, as discussed above, foraging societies are shaped by their small size. With small size, foraging communities are face-to-face groups, made up of people related by blood or marriage, or both. For most of the time foragers have existed, this small size has been easy to maintain for a number of reasons. First, until the last century or so no one on earth has had access to modern medicine, so that life expectancy has not been much more than half what it is now. This has not been the result of people dying in droves at the age of forty. Rather, it is largely the result of what occurs when nearly half of all children die before they attain reproductive age. Babies in their first year of life are particularly susceptible to lethal infections that today are easily and routinely cured by antibiotics.

The second factor contributing to the maintenance of small forager population size is the fact that hunter-gatherers tend to be very lean. This is because their lives require strenuous activity and their diets involve little fat and limited intake of carbohydrates. In women, extremely lean, muscular bodies can result in irregular ovulation, which means that such women are less likely to become pregnant than women with more body fat.

In addition to having lean bodies, women in foraging societies are also likely to breastfeed their children for far longer than is common in modern, metropolitan societies. Because many wild foods require substantial processing before they are suitable for babies and small children, foraging mothers typically nurse their children for three to five years, often supplementing breast milk with solid food that they have partially chewed, themselves, so as to begin the process of digestion. Breast feeding, in addition to providing infants with high quality nutrition and some protection against disease, also has the effect of somewhat suppressing the mother's ovulation. This is not a reliable method of birth control for those whose diets are rich in fats and carbohydrates (so do not try this at home!), but in combination with an extremely lean body, it does reduce a woman's chances of becoming pregnant.

Finally, some foragers resort to infanticide when a woman with a small child gives birth to another infant before the first one is weaned. The thinking is that nursing two infants may threaten the mother's health (breastfeeding requires a huge number of calories), as well as the health of both children, neither of whom may get adequate nutrition. If there is no woman in the group who has recently lost a nursing infant to death, and who may be able to breastfeed the new baby, an older female relative, often the mother's own mother, may reluctantly decide that to save the life of the child the family already has, it is essential to kill the new infant. To those living in a world of modern medicine, jarred baby food, and infant formula, this may seem heartless. But for foragers, such difficult choices must sometimes be made. For the reasons cited above, as well as others less well understood, annual population growth among foragers is less than one-hundredth of a percent, while the rate jumps to one tenth of one percent once a population turns to food production and becomes sedentary (Bently, Goldberg, & Jasienska, 1993).

HERDING AND PASTORALISM

Pastoralists are groups of people whose subsistence primarily revolves around the care of domesticated herd animals. With domesticated animals, we are talking about animals that are in some biological way different from their wild ancestors, as is also the case with domesticated plants. Archaeologists in some parts of the world such as **Mesopotamia**, have charted the changes in the bones of sheep and goats, as the animals went from wild to domesticated. Recently, DNA comparison of remains of ancient with that of modern horses has shown how human domestication of horses may have altered characteristics dealing with horse locomotion, physiology, and cognition (Shubert et al. 2014).

Though the term "pastoralist" is derived from *pastor,* the Latin word for "shepherd," not all pastoralists depend upon sheep. The ancient Hebrews,

Figure 4.3   Sami with reindeer (1890–1900).
Photo: Anne-Sophie Ofrim. Wikimedia CC BY-SA 2.0

whose sacred books included the Old Testament of the Christian Bible, *were* primarily herders of sheep and goats, as are some residents of the same territory today. By contrast, in East Africa, such pastoral peoples as the **Dinka**, the **Nuer**, and the **Maasai** rely for their food and many of their other needs on their large herds of cattle. In Central Asia (in such countries as **Kazakstan**, **Uzbekistan**, **Turkmenistan**, and **Kyrgyzstan**), many people continue to make their living by herding sheep, goats, and the small Central Asian horses that have been raised in the area for thousands of years. And in northern Scandinavia some of the nearly 100,000 **Lapps**, or **Sami** people, continue to herd reindeer.

Residential and Territorial Patterns

Pastoralists are less mobile than foragers and do not spend each year in a nomadic seasonal round. Most of them are described as "semi-nomadic" or "**transhumant**." This means that the people orient their subsistence around a fixed residence but move away from it on a temporary basis at certain times of the year. The fixed residence will often consist of a dwelling that is a permanent structure, and sometimes gardens. But livestock cannot usually remain in one place throughout the year, because they will deplete all the vegetation available in that place. Sometimes the entire family or tribal group moves with the animals from a permanent, winter home to a temporary, summer home or series of summer camps, often at a higher elevation. At other times the animals may be moved to locations nearer the family's permanent home and tended by a few family members while other family members remain at home taking care of garden plots. Not all pastoralists raise plant foods, but some do, and these gardens may require continual cultivation or need to be protected from garden thieves.

The permanent houses, gardens, and animal stockades of pastoralists all represent a substantial investment in time, energy, and resources. Thus pastoralists have both greater incentive to protect and defend their territory and, with their larger populations, greater ability to do so. Skirmishes between herders and their neighbors are not uncommon, and though national governments have now generally curtailed raids on the part of herders, they were a frequent part of herding life in the past.

Division of Labor and Ownership

Herding populations are known to anthropologists as characteristically **patriarchal**. That is, these societies are generally dominated by men, while women have a clearly lower and dependent status. The reason for this is probably that the primary source of subsistence, herd animals, is generally under the control of men. Ernestine Friedl (1978), whose ideas on gender among foragers we encountered earlier, posited that women's status is highest in societies where they are owners or controllers (not just laborers) of productive resources. To Friedl, ownership or control of the primary source of subsistence is the greatest determining factor in power and status between the sexes. And in general, in herding societies it is men who own or control the herds.

There is, of course, no biological necessity for men to take charge of herd animals, most of which are fairly placid and relatively easy to control. But among pastoralists men often also serve as semi-military defenders of the flocks and herds from raiders, and have been known to raid other groups' livestock themselves. On the other hand, there is the case of the Navajo people of Arizona and New Mexico, who for more than 300 years have based their subsistence on the herding of sheep, originally acquired from Spanish settlers. Unlike the division of labor in most herding societies, it is Navajo women who are thought of as the owners of the flocks, and who often handle the actual herding of the sheep, either on foot or on horseback. The Navajo people are **matrilineal** and **matrilocal** (see Chapter 6 for a discussion of these cat-

Figure 4.4   Navajo woman and child with sheep.
Photo: Ken Hammond. Agricultural Research Service.

egories), which means that membership in a family group is traced through the female line, and that men marry into their wives' families and live with them. Though political leadership positions are usually filled by men, Navajo women have very high status. Whether this is the *cause* of their ownership of sheep, or whether it is the *consequence* of sheep ownership, or whether the two phenomena reinforce each other is difficult to say. But the Navajo case is both an exception to the usual pattern of stock ownership among pastoralists, as well as a good illustration of Friedl's idea about gender status and the ownership of the means of subsistence.

With most herding peoples, ownership of herd animals and the territory they require is frequently held collectively by male members of a family group, rather than exclusively by individuals. Among many of the cattle-herding peoples of East Africa, individual cows are recognized and ornamented by their young male caretakers, who have an elaborate system of naming cattle according to their markings, and who compose romantic poetry using cattle imagery. Women in these societies may milk the cattle, process the milk into butter and cheese, and perform other caretaking chores for cattle, but they do not own them. Cattle belong to men. Also, in earlier times in some East African cattle-based societies like the Maasai, no crops were grown, and cattle provided virtually the only source of food. With this, it is not surprising that men, the owners and primary herders of the cattle, came to have substantially higher status and much greater power than women.

The Shape of Pastoral Groups

As we have seen, foraging peoples usually live in small groups based on the nuclear family, and their populations show little growth. Herders, by contrast, because they are less mobile and have higher fertility rates, tend to live in larger, extended family groups and to be parts of substantially larger ethnic groups overall. The larger, denser populations of pastoralists are often organized into **lineages** and **clans** (described in Chapter 6) and people feel a primary allegiance to these units, rather than to the whole group.

Also, unlike hunters and gatherers, pastoralists own property beyond their clothing and tools. Along with permanent houses, this property may include furniture, storage vessels, elaborate enclosures for animals, sheds, and outdoor shelters or *ramadas*. And most important of all, there are the animals. Given this property, it is not surprising that among pastoralists there is considerably less sharing and more individual and family ownership of property than what we see among foragers. Also, with this kind of property ownership, some dif-

Figure 4.5   Maasai man with cattle.
Photo by Professor Mark E. Richie, courtesy of *Syracuse University Magazine*.

ferential wealth and power develop in pastoral societies. Herding peoples do not usually have social classes or castes, but some families acquire more property than others, and they can pass this property on to their children, a practice that can maintain and intensify the wealth and influence of particular families.

Like most foraging groups, pastoral societies permit **polygyny**, or marriage to more than one wife at a time. But whereas only a few hunter-gatherer households in any single society are polygynous, in some herding groups many senior men have multiple wives, most of whom have several children. The numerous wives and children are useful in caring for the animals on which herding peoples rely, and can greatly contribute to a senior man's wealth, prestige, and power within the group.

HORTICULTURE AND SMALL-SCALE FARMING

Though at one time the universal subsistence pattern was hunting and gathering, some people eventually turned to herding domesticated animals, a pattern that continues today in some parts of the world. Another subsistence strategy, which proved more widespread and which is also still in use by some people today, developed as well. This is the practice of **horticulture**, or the cultivation of domesticated plants on a small scale, without the use of plows or irrigation. It seems like a greater leap of imagination to decide to raise domesticated plants than to herd domesticated animals. And, as we will see, horticulturalists experienced greater changes in their ways of life than did foragers who adopted herding.

At various times, and at various places throughout the world, groups of people independently took up horticulture, and the practice spread further as humans migrated outward from those regions. Archaeological evidence indicates that the very earliest beginnings of horticulture occurred independently in Mesopotamia around 12,000 B.C.E., in Southeast Asia around 7,000 B.C.E., and in the New World (Mexico, the Andes, and the Amazon basin) beginning around 5,000 B.C.E.

The food crops raised in these areas were different, and the ways of life that ultimately developed in each place also varied. But all these locations shared one important similarity, namely a range of environmental niches within easy reach of the groups who lived there. Without moving far, these groups could take advantage of a variety of resources from the hills and valleys, from the rivers and plains, or from swampy areas and from groves of trees. As the inhabitants of these areas loosened the soil around wild food plants to encourage growth, or constructed fencing around wild food plants to protect them from animals, they began to invest in the modification of the environment and the plants that grew there. Over time this resulted in horticulture. Gradually these people became more and more compromised by the investments they had made in labor and resources, and less and less able to move away from the scene of their efforts to pursue a hunting and gathering way of life.

Of course, this did not happen overnight, and many early horticulturalists continued to send at least some of their family members to hunt and to collect wild plant foods. But horticulture did make a dramatic difference in the way people lived, such a difference, in fact, that it is often referred to as "the **Neolithic** Revolution." The "Neolithic" (which means "new stone") in this term has to do with a new style of stone tool manufacture that developed around the same time as the beginnings of horticulture in Mesopotamia, from 10,000 to 8000 B.C.E. and in the New World (Mexico and the Andes) between 10,000 to 8000 B.C.E. This new style is the practice of grinding the edges of roughly flaked stone tools, which provided a sturdier edge that was less brittle than the sharper edges of chipped stone tools that earlier had been manufactured

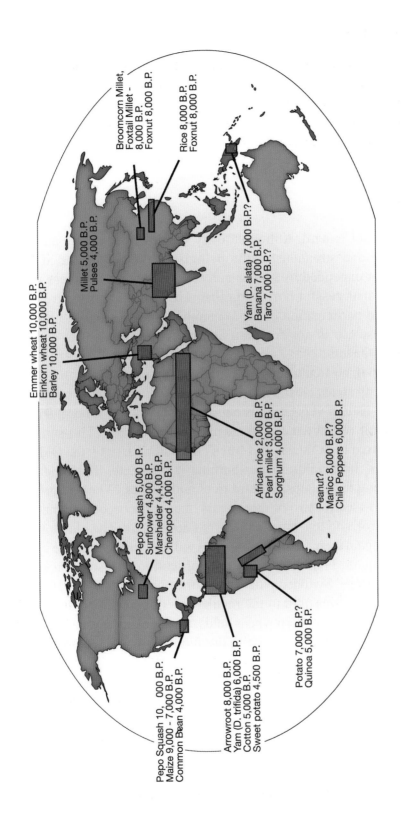

Figure 4.6   Agricultural origins

97

for hundreds of thousands of years. But what is important about the Neo-lithic Revolution is the revolution part, and that has to do with the effects of domestication. People settled down in permanent villages and began to rely more and more heavily on domesticated plant foods. Most of these people also added some domesticated animals, which further restricted them to a fixed location.

Division of Labor

Horticultural labor is hard. Although today we think of hunting and gathering as insecure and strenuous, anthropologists have demonstrated that the amount of labor expended by hunter-gatherers is substantially less than that required to be a successful horticulturalist. This work is also more constant and requires the participation of more members of the group. Child participation in subsistence is not common among foragers, but it is widespread among food producers.

The first step in horticulture is the initial clearing of the land to be used for planting. In many areas, clearing the land requires the removal of weeds and brush. First the natural vegetation is cut down, and then it is burnt so that the ashes of the burnt vegetation contribute nutrients to the soil. This style of horticulture is referred to as "**slash and burn**" horticulture, or by the Old English term, "**swidden**" horticulture. After burning is complete, the garden area is planted, in among the stumps of burnt trees and bushes. When a horticultural garden has been used for two or three years, the weeds become numerous and difficult to control, and it is time to move to another plot. The old plots will be abandoned to regain their fertility; new plots will be cleared; and the cycle will begin all over again. Thus slash and burn horticulture is also often known as "shifting cultivation." Swidden plots are not the organized fields of more elaborate agriculture; to eyes used to the regular rows of contemporary cornfields or the huge expanses of modern wheat fields, they look messy and skimpy. But they represent a substantial increase in productivity over the nomadic gathering of wild plant foods.

In horticulture, the initial clearing of the land, which is the hardest labor, requiring the greatest muscular strength, is generally done by men. Men also usually burn the fields, while women generally plant, weed, and help harvest the garden plots. Women are also the processors of the harvest, converting the crop into food, often a laborious endeavor. They are also responsible for the processing of foods derived from animals, such as meat, eggs and milk. While these activities are much more laborious than the processing of foraged food,

Figure 4.7   Yanomami women in Venezuela carrying manioc.
Wikimedia. CC BY-SA 3.0

they do yield a larger result. This food can also be stored for the future and is more suitable for feeding to small children than are the minimally-processed bush foods of foragers.

Ownership, Distribution, and Residential Patterns

Horticulturists have substantial investment in their land. Because of this and the fact that their land base is much less extensive than is the territory of foragers, horticultural groups are much more protective of their land than are foragers. They may engage in land disputes with their neighbors, and these skirmishes may involve violence, including raiding for land, stock, and women, and the killing of enemies.

On the other hand, horticultural peoples often do not own land as individual private property. Land may be thought of as the collective property of the group; it is not considered a commodity—as something that can be bought or sold. Members of the group who need land have a natural right to use it to grow their crops, and from time to time outsiders who have married into the group or who have been absorbed into it in other ways also obtain the right to use the land. But the notion of selling the land, of exchanging it or losing it, does not exist.

With this in mind, it is easier to understand the famous transaction of 1626, in which the Canarsie (Lenape) Indians "sold" a piece of their territory, the island of Manhattan, to Dutch settlers for 60 guilders' worth of trade goods (roughly $23 by nineteenth-century calculations). The Canarsie were an Algonkian group who lived primarily on Long Island, where they were horticulturalists, though they also fished, gathered, and hunted. The Canarsie certainly figured that the metal utensils they obtained from the Dutch and the beads of a variety they had never seen before were worth far more than a peripheral piece of hunting territory that neither they nor the Dutch imagined would one day be the most valuable real estate on the planet. Such ideas had no place in the universe of a horticultural people.

Horticulturalists who practice shifting cultivation need less territory than hunter-gatherers, but they need substantially more territory than is under cultivation at any given time. Becausee slash-and-burn horticulture requires that garden plots remain fallow for several years, substantially more land is *not* cultivated at any given time than *is*. In general, the longer the fallow period, the better for the land and the harvest. Thus, horticulturalists attempt to control as much land as possible, so that they will not have to reuse garden plots after only a short fallow period. Some horticultural groups, including many of the manioc cultivators of the Amazon region, move the location of their villages when they have worn out the garden space, when the village site has been overused, or when illness has afflicted a village for some time. Such groups thus require space not only for shifting cultivation, but for shifting habitation sites, as well.

Gender

The status of men and women in horticultural villages is variable, but in general it appears to be unequal, with male status superior to that of females. Applying Friedl's principle that gender status is to a great extent determined by control of the means of subsistence, the higher status of men should not surprise us. Though women's labor is essential in caring for gardens and in processing the crops and animal products into food, clothing, and other necessities, the land and large animals are generally thought of as being controlled or collectively owned by men. Thus women's labor, however necessary, is conceived of as of secondary importance, while men's labor and administrative control, as well as their heavy exertion in the initial clearing of garden plots, result in their higher status and greater authority.

It is sometimes suggested that because many horticultural peoples personify the earth as a woman, and revere supernatural females as embodying the much revered principle of fertility, this indicates that everyday women in horticultural societies must have (or have had) very high status. At first, this argument sounds plausible, but upon closer examination its weakness becomes apparent. We can look at the status of the Virgin Mary and female saints in Christian, especially Catholic, countries for the last two thousand years. It is undeniable that the status of these figures is very high, and that they are of great importance in the lives of many individuals, both women and men. But it is equally clear that the high status of female spiritual figures has not carried over into the lives of human females in the Christian world. This is not to deny the cultural power of such spiritual figures, whether in the Western world or elsewhere. It is merely a warning not to engage in too simplistic an analysis of the connection between the symbolic world and the world of everyday life.

The Shape of Horticultural Societies

Universally, as hunting and gathering peoples settled down in relatively permanent villages and began to domesticate plants and animals, populations began to increase. This may seem surprising for a couple of reasons. First, in settled villages, people and animals exchange pathogens constantly, and human and animal waste is never far from human living spaces. The close quarters and constant exposure to human and nonhuman pathogens transmitted through air, water, and bodily effluvia ensure that diseases are exchanged more easily in horticultural villages than they are among foragers. Second, horticultural people also rely on a smaller variety of foods than their foraging ancestors because they no longer do much hunting or gathering, but consume primarily the relatively small number of foods they cultivate. This can result in less adequate nutrition, especially if one or more of the staple food crops fail.

Nevertheless, two other features of horticultural villages counteract these factors that would otherwise restrict population growth. One is that because women are now less likely to eat a low-fat, low-carbohydrate diet, their body weight increases, and as it does, so does their fertility. In addition, because cultivated foods and a settled life lend themselves to more appropriate foods for infants, the dangerous period of weaning is more easily bridged, and fewer children die at that stage. Thus, while there are negative factors affecting survival in a settled village, these are usually outweighed by increased fertility and increased availability of infant food, with the result that populations increase.

Increase is, in fact, the name of the horticultural game. Population, labor, and the amount of food people acquire all increase. The combination of food *production* (rather than food *collection*) and a stable location for food *storage* means that horticulturalists can amass food surpluses, and this surplus has further consequences. Among early horticulturalists there were few specialists who were not primarily engaged in the raising or processing of food. With the creation of surpluses, however, it became possible for some people to devote much of their time to the pursuit of specialized activities. In this context, a man who is unusually proficient at woodworking, for example, may spend his time after the harvest in making tools for his neighbors, or helping them with construction. And the neighbors, who have more food than their families can consume, can exchange food for labor, or food for specialty manufactured items. Though most people continue to be farmers and housewives, some people with special capabilities may turn into full-time specialists, supported by the surpluses that can now be generated from gardens and pastures.

As a few full-time specialists develop, they are able to concentrate on their crafts and increase their skill. That is, as occupational specialization increases, so does technological development. If every man makes his own farm implements in addition to providing food for his family, no one has much time or energy for innovation and experimentation. But as a few men become specialty toolmakers, they can devote their entire energy to such endeavors, and as a result they are inclined to produce better and better products. The same principle applies to other occupations, from pottery to weaving to midwifery, and it is true for both men and for women. Occupational specialization increases technological innovation.

The combination of occupational specialization, the amassing of surpluses, and the inheritance of property promotes stratification within the horticultural community. Though small horticultural villages are often made up of groups of related families, the foraging principle of sharing as a high ethical principle no longer prevails. Families are now interested in fostering their own well-being rather than that of the group as a whole, and they look primarily to members of their family to help them out in difficult times.

With this focus on the family (rather than the whole group) combined with interests in the ownership of property, horticulturalists and some herders become concerned with the legitimacy of their children. Husbands in foraging societies may be angry if their wives have sexual affairs with other men. But they are not concerned that their property will descend to the children of another man, because there is no property to speak of. With horticulturalists and some pastoralists, however, one of the ramifications of the piling up of wealth and its primary control by men is that men begin to feel a need to protect their wealth from inheritance by other men's children. Thus the concept of illegitimacy develops substantially greater power, and with it often an exertion of stronger control over women. To ensure that one's wife's child is also one's own, many horticultural and pastoral societies develop cultural practices that intensify the inequities between male and female autonomy and status, and impose severe limits on female self expression, self determination, and sexuality.

AGRICULTURE AND LARGE-SCALE FARMING

The shift by some foragers to herding or to horticulture left many other foraging peoples perfectly content to continue their hunting and gathering way of life for thousands of years. As long as they retained political independence and enough productive territory for their needs, there was no universal rush to food production. In the same way, many herding and horticultural groups maintained their subsistence system and the political and other cultural traits that accompanied it for millennia. As new styles of subsistence developed, older ones remained, until in relatively recent times many foraging peoples have been forced into more modern subsistence styles as they have lost control of their former territories.

The tendency of food producing groups to expand their populations, the ability of such groups to advance technology and administrative capabilities, and the ability of these groups to develop differential access to wealth, resulted in some significant changes in certain horticultural groups. These changes produced a shift to a more elaborate and more productive style of food production, which we refer to as **agriculture**. The word "horticulture" is derived from the Latin word *hortus*, or "garden," whereas the word "agriculture" is derived from the Latin word *ager,* or "field." Real changes occurred in this transition from garden to field, from small-scale to large-scale farming.

The characteristics of agriculture involve the use of intensive methods of cultivation, which vary from region to region and from crop to crop. Traction, first provided by animals such as horses, oxen, or mules, and later by fossil fuels, is one common trait of agriculture. So is the use of fertilizer—first natural fertilizers, such as manure (both animal and human), and later chemical. And finally, agriculture involves permanent alterations of the landscape, including irrigation structures such as ditches, dams, dikes, and canals; limiting structures like walls, fences, and other barriers; and the construction of additional croplands. These additional lands include terraced fields like those in Southeast Asia; raised crop beds, like those constructed in the Mayan lowlands of Central America; and the ***chinampas*** of the Aztecs, artificial islands and peninsulas constructed of turf in marshy areas along lake shores to provide additional growing space.

Division of Labor, Ownership, and Distribution of Wealth

The gendered division of labor in agriculture is not dramatically different from that of horticulture. Men are generally responsible for the work that requires considerable physical strength, which now often involves the management of draft animals, while women are primarily in charge of the processing of raw materials into food and clothing, as well as the management of kitchen gardens and such small domesticated animals as fowl or (in the Andes) guinea pigs, and the milking of cattle and goats. Once the harvest is brought in, sometimes with the help of women, women process crops like corn, wheat, barley, or manioc (in lowland South America) into high-carbohydrate staples like bread and porridge, as well as into fermented drinks like beer.

The distinctive feature of the agricultural—as opposed to the horticultural—division of labor is not the way tasks are divided by gender. That process is a continuation of what occurred in horticulture. Instead, it is the division of labor by status and wealth, which comes to fruition in agriculture. Consider the construction of terraced rice fields in South or Southeast Asia, or the creation of the elaborate network of irrigation ditches, canals, sluice gates, and dams in Mesopotamia. In the first place, such an elaborate system is unlikely to be necessary unless there is a large population requiring extensive areas for cultivation. In the second place, the group would need substantial sociopolitical organization to undertake such an elaborate building project. In the third place, this organization would probably require some kind of differential power to exist; otherwise, it would be difficult to convince people to put in long days of tedious labor for a project from which they might not derive much personal benefit. And this is generally what happens in agricultural societies. The division of labor is vertical, or hierarchical, with a small group of people who own or control large quantities of wealth, especially land, determining the activities of the majority of the population, who own or control little wealth.

There has been considerable variation in the way agricultural workers articulate with the land they work. Four varieties of worker-to-land relationships predominate in agriculture. The first is what can be called "the family farm," where a farm is privately owned by the family who live on it and work it, often with the assistance of a few hired laborers. In many parts of the United States (or what became the United States) from the seventeenth through the nineteenth centuries, such family farms predominated, and formed the icon in the American imagination of hard work and virtue. Because good farmland was scarce and expensive in Europe, many European immigrants flooded to the United States for a chance to own farmland and thus to achieve prosperity and independence.

In a second type of worker-to-land relationship, agricultural landowners own the labor of others, and sometimes also their persons. The cotton, tobacco, and sugar plantations of the southeastern United States depended entirely on enslaved labor, a tradition that has existed at various times in many other agricultural societies throughout the world. In some agricultural societies, including many in Europe, labor was performed by workers whose persons were not (usually) the property of their employers, to be bought or sold, but who had no right to leave their employers' land. They owed their labor to their employers, and they could not offer it to anyone else. This institution, known as "serfdom," ensured that landowners could rely on a steady supply of labor for their often huge holdings. Serfdom (which existed in Russia until 1861) has existed in many societies and at many times. [2]

Even in many societies without explicitly coerced labor, only a small number of the people who work in agriculture own the land they work. Many of the rest are merely tenants of the landowners, often paid through a system of sharecropping—a third variety of worker-to-land relationship. This system allows the tenant farmer to keep a share of the crop he harvests as payment for his labor, while the rest of the crop is returned to the landowner, in payment for the use of the land on which the tenant lives and farms. Tenant farmers usually have the use of a house and a personal plot of land for raising a few animals and crops for their own personal use, but they own neither the house nor the land. In an agricultural system, farmland is very expensive. It *can* be bought and sold for a profit, but tenant farmers are often too poor to amass enough money to buy any land. In addition, they may find that they are always in debt to the landowner for whom they work, and who may have advanced them money or seed against their share of the upcoming harvest.

Still, sharecroppers may be in a more economically advantageous position than those farm laborers who have no arrangement with a landowner for a place to live and a plot of land from which they share the profits. In this fourth variation of worker-to-land relationship, freelance agricultural workers have only their labor to offer in exchange for pay. They have neither the buffer of a house and a kitchen garden, nor do they have the (admittedly not always reliable) patronage of a landlord who can sometimes be prevailed upon to offer loans and other assistance. But the labor of these independent agricultural workers is usually preferred by large landowners. A large-scale landowner can simply pay for agricultural work when he needs it, and can ignore workers when he has no need for their labor. With traditional sharecroppers, by contrast, the landowner must set aside a house and garden plot for each family, and must also cope with the continuing human needs of the sharecropper and his family. In the off season, when there is little or no need for the sharecropper's labor, he is still a presence on the land.

As time has worn on, and as agriculture has become increasingly mechanized, two things have happened. First, fewer and fewer people are required to produce agricultural commodities, as technology has replaced intensive use of human labor with devices powered by fossil fuels. Second, the people who are today involved in agriculture have increasingly become wage-earning employees, rather than farm owners or sharecroppers. In the United States in the middle of the nineteenth century, half of all Americans were engaged in agriculture. Today, the figure is under one percent. And of this one percent, more than three-quarters are employees (who earn an average of $7.70 per hour [U.S. Department of Labor: Bureau of Labor Statistics. http://www.bls.gov/oco/ocos285.htm]). Today most of the population in all First World agricultural societies, and increasing proportions of Second and Third World societies, devote their labor to non-agricultural activities such as manufacturing and service industries. In this sense, we can think of ourselves as living in a *post-agricultural* subsistence system.

The Shape of Agricultural Societies

Agricultural subsistence allows for the development of extreme variation in wealth and status. It is the only subsistence system in which some members of a community may have access to plenty of food and other resources while other members of the group may literally starve. Even in herding and horticultural societies, where disparities in wealth may develop, the basic necessities of life are seldom withheld from any group members.

We tend to think of agricultural societies as providing a higher standard of living for their residents, mostly because many of us come from such a society, but this is not the case. As mentioned earlier, members of agricultural societies, like those of all food-producing societies, work longer hours than foragers, and usually with less control over their labor than foragers. Resources are much less evenly distributed in agricultural societies than in those groups with other subsistence patterns. And because agricultural societies usually rely upon only a small number of crops, if a drought strikes the region or a pest attacks the staple crop, thousands or even millions of people may die or be dislocated.

The United States received a huge influx of immigrants in the middle of the nineteenth century as the result of a blight that struck the Irish potato crop

Figure 4.7   Starving Irish peasants. Great Famine (1847) by James Mahony (1810–1879).

from 1845 to 1849, and then again in the 1870s. Many of those who are now reading this text, like one of its authors (McKee), are North Americans thanks to what came to be known in Ireland as "The Hunger." At the time of the potato famine the Irish peasantry were living under atrocious conditions, on plots too small to sustain them. They were almost wholly dependent for their survival upon potatoes, a crop originally imported from the New World to Ireland in the sixteenth century by Sir Walter Raleigh. When that crop failed several years in a row, roughly a million people died of starvation and disease, and another two million emigrated, mostly to English speaking countries like England, Australia, Canada, and the United States. Such famines are characteristic of agricultural societies, but are uncommon in foraging societies, and even in pastoral and horticultural societies, where populations are less dense, and where people rely on a wider range of resources.

The increase in population that has ineluctably accompanied food production is today accelerated by technological advances in medicine, which have allowed more infants to survive, and more adults to live longer lives. Traditionally, food producers have valued large families, partly to provide insurance against the inevitable death of some children, and partly because numerous children were helpful in subsistence activities and could care for parents in their old age. These conditions are changing but meanwhile, the successes of the agricultural subsistence system have contributed to an increase in population that has become a serious world problem.

Another problem that has resulted both directly and indirectly from the successes of agriculture is environmental degradation. This phenomenon has numerous interlocking causes, including increased population and intensive agricultural practices. It has also been fostered by the creation of manufacturing and extractive industries, made possible by increased technological power, that provides more and more manufactured products demanded by the ever increasing population. Societies whose subsistence is based on agriculture have found it difficult to rein in their productive successes, and to take a look at the implications for their future. In this they are no different from people who have used other subsistence systems. Foragers live lightly on the land and do not develop large populations or destructive subsistence practices. Even herders and horticulturalists tend to shift their herds and flocks and the locations of their gardens, and so restrict the impact they have on the environment. But these practices should not be romanticized. They are the result not so much of thoughtful and considered restraint, as of limitations to exploitation imposed by smaller population and simpler technology. Today we do not have the luxury of doing whatever seems convenient and assuming that the generations who come after us will take care of the mess we leave behind. The successes of agriculture have put us in a position in which we must learn the restraint that was never necessary for practitioners of other subsistence systems.

SUMMARY

It is clear from our discussion of subsistence systems that increasing technological complexity and control over the environment were not brought about because people were pressured into extracting ever more food from the planet as a result of population pressure. Population pressure came *after* the introduction of food production, not before it. In general, once people settled down and began to produce food, they were trapped into a way of life from which they could not escape, even though it required more effort, yielded a more uncertain outcome, resulted in environmental degradation, and ultimately produced greater inequality.

Looking at the splendid monuments of agriculturally-based civilizations, like the glittering Babylonian Gate of Ishtar, the moving Gothic cathedrals of medieval Europe, or the transcendently beautiful Taj Mahal, it is tempting to think that the glories of the societies that produced these monuments—all made possible by an agricultural subsistence system—leave the accomplishments of smaller scale foraging, herding, and horticultural societies in the dust. But it is essential to remember that the cost of great monuments and other impressive accomplishments is paid for by the majority of the populations of agricultural societies who do not participate in their benefits. Those who live in foraging, herding, and horticultural societies, by contrast, are all likely to share in whatever benefits accrue to those societies.

We cannot go backward in time or complexity. We cannot will ourselves to live in the world of hunter-gatherers, of whom very few remain. Nor can we take up herding or simple horticulture. There are too many people on the planet in the early twenty-first century for the majority of human groups to give up agriculture. It is the only subsistence system that will provide enough food for the six and a half billion people who today inhabit the earth. But we must develop a strategy that will allow us to distribute the food we now produce to all of those who need it, and to allocate the resources of the world in an equitable way. Ironically, this was something our ancestors did in the past and our foraging, herding, and horticultural cousins still do today. We must find a way to combine their balance with out technological skill.

At this point, let us consider specifically how this chapter has addressed the myths about subsistence that we considered at its beginning.

Myth #1   The normal and natural subsistence method for humans is agriculture.

Any way you slice it, this is simply not the case, though early European and Euro-American colonial adventurers certainly believed it was. For one thing, as we have seen, there are three subsistence systems other than agriculture employed in the world today: foraging, pastoralism, and horticulture, though agriculture dominates the contemporary world. Secondly, the archaeological record clearly shows that from the time humans evolved until roughly 12,000 years ago, *all* societies survived by hunting wild animals and gathering wild plant foods. After that time *some* groups began to domesticate plants and animals, and the subsistence strategies of herding (or pastoralism) and simple farming (horticulture) developed. It was not until much later, around 6,000 years ago, that large-scale agriculture developed, and even as agriculture developed, most human groups still lived by foraging, herding, and small-scale farming.

Myth #2   People who do not practice agriculture live precarious lives that are "nasty, brutish, and short," in the words of seventeenth-century English philosopher, Thomas Hobbes.

From our examination of the lives of contemporary hunting and gathering peoples, anthropologists know that although the lives of foragers—as of all other peoples in the world—were certainly shorter on average than they are today, they were not nasty or brutish. They were, in general, more leisured than those of farmers and herders, and people enjoyed the full complement of human activities like arts and religion that make human life rewarding and meaningful.

Myth #3   The normal human pattern is for men to dominate subsistence activities, and for women to be involved in other, domestic activities.

Cultural anthropologists have roamed around the world, examining the myriad ways in which people live today. Historians and archaeologists have looked at the lives of people in times past throughout the world. From the evidence these scholars have gathered, it is clear that women have played a major role in subsistence, both today and in the past. In hunting and gathering societies, women have contributed well over half of the food consumed by the group. Residents of these societies prefer meat, which is largely procured by men, but it is women's plant foods that are absolutely necessary for survival. Even in food-producing societies, where men are generally considered the owners of the means of subsistence, women's contributions to the maintenance of gardens and domestic animals, as well as their dominance in converting crops and herds onto food, are essential for the survival of the family. Today, of course, in state-based societies like our own, women's contribution to subsistence through wage labor is often essential to a family's well-being. Indeed, in the increasing numbers of female-headed households in state-based societies, women's wage labor may be the only contribution to a family's livelihood.

Myth #4 The production of food, from simple horticulture to modern, mechanized agriculture, has produced a generally more prosperous, leisured, and enjoyable life for the world's population.

The production of food definitely produces more food than foraging. And modern, mechanized agriculture definitely produces more food than herding or simple farming. But this increase in production comes at a high human and environmental cost. Fewer and fewer people are needed to produce food, as large-scale, mechanized agriculture relies more and more heavily on machinery, which throws increasing numbers of former small farmers and farm workers out of work, and in many places raises the cost of food for people who once grew much of their own. The environmental costs of agriculture, resulting from plowing, monocropping, heavy use of chemical fertilizers and pesticides, and reliance on irrigation, are enormous. The formerly fertile lands around the ancient city of Ur in present-day Iraq once supported one of the earliest and most powerful city-states of the ancient Near East. Thousands of years of intensive agriculture were a powerful agent helping to reduce this area to the desert it is today. The destructive power of agriculture is not a recent phenomenon, but it continues into the present.

QUESTIONS FOR THOUGHT AND REFLECTION

1. Sometimes people talk about hunting and gathering as a "natural" way of life. There are at least two senses in which "natural" may be understood in this context: as reflecting the biological aspects of humans, and as reflecting humans as an integral part of the natural world. Considering these two aspects of the term "natural," discuss how the foraging way of life may be seen as natural. Is equality natural?

2. Use Friedl's argument about the influence of subsistence practices as a powerful influence on gender status to account for the patriarchal nature of most pastoral societies. What about the Navajo? Why do you think they are an exception to the general tendency of pastoral societies to be patriarchal?

3. What characteristics do pastoral and horticultural societies seem to share as a result of being food producers that set them apart from foragers? Why do pastoral and horticultural peoples tend to be more interested in the legitimacy of their children than foragers are?

4. What kinds of cultural changes occur as a horticultural society becomes an agricultural society? They are both farming groups, so why should they be so different?

5. What does it mean to say that the division of labor in agriculture is vertical? What are some of the results and implications of this vertical division of labor?

6. Agriculture is certainly here to stay, unless we manage to bomb ourselves back to the Stone Age or fry ourselves through global warming. What do you see as the strengths of agriculture? The weaknesses? How do you think we might solve some of the problems that agriculture brings?

ENDNOTES

[1]There are some exceptions. In the most recent ice age, which ended about 10,000 years ago, ice and snow covered Europe and North America, and the environment was similar to what the Arctic is today. In such circumstances, vegetation is severely limited, and the majority of all food consumed is derived from animals, and thus obtained by men.

[2]Another variant of the concept of coerced labor is "peonage," a system prevalent in parts of Latin America. In this system agricultural and other workers could be forced to work through either the imposition of a minimal payment for which peons then had to work in recompense, or more commonly through more or less perpetual indebtedness that could be passed on to heirs.

REFERENCES CITED

Bentey, Gilian R, Tonu Goldberg, Grazyna Jasienska
    1993 "The Fertility of Agricultural and Non-Agricultural Traditional Societies." *Population Studies*
        *49:*269–281.

Friedl, Ernestine
    1978 "Society and Sex Roles." *Human Nature:*1:8–75.

Hewlett, Barry S.
    1991 *Intimate Fathers: The Nature and Context of Aka Pygmy Paternal Infant Care.* Ann Arbor:
        University of Michigan Press.

Hobbes, Thomas
    2012 [1651] *Leviathan,* Noel Malcolm, ed. Oxford: Clarendon Press.

Lee, Richard B.
    2012 *The Dobe Ju/'hoansi.* 4th edition. Belmont, California: Wadsworth.

U.S. Department of Labor: Bureau of Labor Statistichttp://www.bls.gov/oco/ocos285.htm.

Shubert, Mikkel, Hákon Jónsson, Dan Chang et al.
    2014 Prehistoric Genomes Reveal the Genetic Foundation and Cost of Horse Domestication.
        Proceedings of the National Academy of Science 111(52):E5661-E5669.

CHAPTER 5

LIVING TOGETHER

The organization of societies and the ways they address universal human needs

WHY "TAKE ME TO YOUR LEADER" DOES NOT ALWAYS MAKE SENSE, AND OTHER MYTHS ABOUT SOCIAL ORGANIZATION

We have all seen cartoons in which the alien, whose flying saucer is parked in the background, says to the startled earthlings he meets, "Take me to your leader." And we all learned in elementary school that when the Pilgrims climbed off the Mayflower and onto Plymouth Rock, they essentially said the same thing to the Wampanoag people, the Native American ethnic group who lived in the area. The Wampanoag did have a "sachem," or senior elder who coordinated group activity, but, though influential, he could not act on his own and relied heavily on consultation with other senior group members. And since the Wampanoag were matrilineal, women played a role in important decisions, too. The Pilgrims only gradually came to understand these cultural factors, and then dimly. Indeed, most colonial invaders from Europe and Asia had severe difficulty understanding how other societies were organized. Their general assumption was that all communities would be organized according to the same underlying structures and principles as their own. In discussing the variety of ways in which human societies are organized, this chapter will explore and refute some of the most common myths that have prevailed for a long time.

Common Myths of Culture
Myth #1 All societies require a few people who rule (a central, coercive governing authority) and a majority of people who are ruled.
Myth #2 All societies should have some central coercive authority; otherwise the society would be chaotic and unworkable.
Myth #3 It is in the nature of human societies to divide into social classes that vary according to people's occupations, relative wealth, and prestige.
Myth #4 A person born into a low position in society can generally rise above that position through hard work.

SAVAGES AND BARBARIANS

By the nineteenth century in Europe, the idea of social evolution had been a subject of human thought at least since the Greeks. In England this idea intensified with the increasing population and social change that resulted from the dramatic progress in technology that began in the eighteenth century. Two of the most influential thinkers in this area were political economists, **Thomas Malthus** (1766–1834) and **Herbert Spencer** (1820–1903) the latter of whom was a friend of Charles Darwin. Malthus, an Anglican clergyman by occupation, was famous for his notion that the population was rising faster than the ability of the world's resources to sustain it. He recommended that the lower classes should practice sexual abstinence to limit the number of children they had and that the price of wheat should be kept high enough that cheap food would not encourage excessive reproduction on the part of the poor. Spencer, who coined the term "the survival of the fittest," believed that intervention in this process through social welfare legislation, such as the British Poor Laws, should be curtailed, so as to prevent the survival of the unfit. Not surprisingly, Spencer, a chronic hypochondriac but a member of the privileged classes, did not consider himself among the "unfit."

In the United States these ideas of social evolution and their consequences were also under discussion. In 1877 the American anthropologist and student of Native American cultures, **Lewis Henry Morgan** (1818–1881) published *Ancient Society*, in which, as mentioned earlier in this text, he laid out his notion of the inevitable stages through which human groups must pass: savagery, barbarism, and civilization. "It can now be assumed upon convinc-

Figure 5.1 Lewis Henry Morgan

ing evidence," he wrote in the Preface to *Ancient Society*, "that savagery preceded barbarism in all the tribes of mankind, as barbarism is known to have preceded civilization" (1877: vi–vii). Morgan concluded that the interconnection of these three "conditions" formed a "necessary and natural sequence of progress."

Morgan acknowledged that at one time all humans on the planet had lived in a state of "savagery," and that the more recent ancestors of those who in 1877 lived in "civilization" had previously lived in "barbarism." But all these terms used to discuss social evolution were so loaded with either positive or negative value that it was impossible to escape their ethnocentric impact. Though Morgan, himself, was sympathetic to Native American peoples with whom he worked, the terms he used strongly suggest that participants in small scale societies are brutal, barely human "savages," or crude, unthinking "barbarians."[1] Savagery and barbarism were not presented so much as legitimate and coherent ways of life as temporary stops along the route to "civilization," the natural goal of all humans and pinnacle of human achievement.

In 1962 Elman Service, then a professor of anthropology at the University of Michigan, published *Primitive Social Organization*, and the terms "savagery" and "barbarism," which had by then made anthropologists uncomfortable, dropped forever from anthropological usage. Instead, Service used terms that were more value-neutral and simply classified the social organization of human groups according to their degree of social complexity. In ascending order of complexity, Service used the terms "band," "tribe," "chiefdom," and "state." In the fifty-some years since this sequence of terms was introduced, there has been considerable debate over its value. Despite debate, however, the utility of Service's system of classification remains, and we will use it as a framework for this chapter. As with all classification systems, it is important to remember that this one is not concrete reality, or a thing in itself. Rather, it is a heuristic device developed to help us think about and understand the world around us, in this case, to understand variation in social order. It is emphatically not a system of ascending moral or intellectual value.

BANDS

As we learned in the last chapter, at one time all people on earth were hunters and gatherers. That is, they raised no crops and herded no animals, but relied on wild plants and animals for their food. At this time, all humans were also organized into small, acephalous groups anthropologists refer to as bands. "Acephalous" is a term derived from the Greek word for "headless." The reason for this designation is that one of the most striking features of band based societies to European explorers and colonizers was the fact that many of the small-scale societies they encountered had no central coercive authority (or "head"), which to these Europeans was simply inconceivable.

Figure 5.2. Space alien encounters a member of a small-scale society.
Cartoon by Gilberto Guerrero Garza.

As a result, the Europeans often imposed their own notions of leadership and hierarchy (organized levels of power and prestige) onto the peoples they met, imagining "chiefs" and "princesses" where they did not actually exist. Of course, there were definitely some hierarchical societies in Africa and in the **New World** (North, Central, and South America) to be discussed later in this chapter. But many indigenous, or native, inhabitants of North America lived in acephalous societies, many of them organized into bands.

If band based societies have no central, coercive authority, the first question that comes to modern, metropolitan minds is how are they governed? The answer is that they are not governed at all in the sense that large-scale societies like our own are governed. There is no person or group of persons in a band who makes rules that are then imposed upon the group as a whole. For one thing, a band consists of a very small number of people, usually no more than fifty, and often as few as a single family, slightly extended by a grandparent, adult sibling, and perhaps the sibling's spouse and children. In such a small group the bonds of kinship, or systems of relatives (discussed in the next chapter), bind it together, making more formal authority unnecessary.

Of course, as classic narratives in our own cultural system relate, even close relatives like brothers can fall out with each other. The Old Testament tells us that Cain slew Abel, and Joseph's brothers sold him into slavery. What happens in band-based societies when people disagree seriously with each other is usually far less dramatic. Part of the group is likely to split off, either permanently or for an unspecified time, and each subgroup goes its own way. This splitting, or "fissioning," characteristic of bands, offers a handy safety valve in situations of conflict, as noted in the previous chapter.

What mechanisms do bands rely on to organize the routine activities of life? As we will see, the most important elements organizing band life are the interlocking principles of kinship, equality, seniority, and consensus.

Kinship

The most important single institution organizing band level societies is kinship, the system of relationships established by birth, marriage and sometimes adoption. A full exploration of kinship and marriage will be taken up in the following chapter, but it is useful to provide a brief discussion here of the role of kinship in band-based societies. In some sense, kinship is a "natural" organizational system, in that humans, like all animals, reproduce biologically, providing such "natural" relationships as mother, father, son, daughter, brother, sister. But the significance human groups attach to these biological relationships, and the uses to which they put them vary remarkably from society to society.

People who live in band-based societies often establish relationships with other bands through marriage, and they use these relationships to negotiate other alliances and the use of vital resources. For this reason, it is useful for band-based peoples, who live throughout most of the year in very small groups, to establish relationships with a large number of people. In this way they have the widest possible choice of allies as well as marriage partners, a relationship that is typically negotiated by parents for their children. Generally, band-based peoples marry someone who is only distantly related to them. Relationships with these distant relatives can be strengthened through marriage and can then provide a safety net for the people involved, who can reasonably call upon each other for such assistance, such as the sharing of resources in times of scarcity.

Most band-based peoples consider themselves equally related to their fathers' and their mothers' relatives, and to those family members connected to them by both male and female links. Such groupings of kin traced out from one individual are referred to as **kindreds**, Kindreds are characteristic groupings of both band-based societies and large, state-based societies like the contemporary United States. But the way kindreds work differs between these types of societies. People in the United States have numerous institutions to help them solve their problems; they do not need to call upon their extended families for assistance. Considering themselves part of kindreds, these people can activate only those relationships they care about and ignore those relatives they do not know or like. People in bands, on the other hand, have virtually no institutions to rely on except their kin networks. Large kindreds allow them to draw upon the widest possible range of connections.

Another advantage to kindreds in band-based societies is that they provide cohesion across separate bands. As we have seen in the previous chapter, hunting and gathering peoples, most of whom are organized into bands, usually spend some parts of the year in larger groupings, especially when and where resources are abundant. At these times members of bands, who share a language and a cultural system, but who may spend little time together, reestablish group solidarity and ethnic identity through kinship links with people whom they see infrequently.

Consensus

Though fissioning, or splitting apart, is always possible when members of a band have serious disagreements, most bands go to some trouble to avoid confrontations that threaten group stability. With no specific mechanism or institution for resolving disputes, band members generally engage in lengthy discussion and argument, in an attempt to come to a conclusion with which everyone can be comfortable. A process such as voting is seldom used in kin-based band societies. With voting, there are always clear winners and losers, and this may prove alienating to members of the group whose views do not prevail.

One aspect of consensus that is particularly significant in band society is the power of social pressure to produce behavioral conformity to the group's cultural norms. Though mild personal peculiarities are tolerated, bands are not communities that harbor many eccentrics or hermits—people who make little contribution to the group while they work on personal goals and interests. Lazy or generally obnoxious people are usually shamed into relative conformity through ridicule and negative gossip. Those who are destructively aggressive or chronically violent may be shunned and driven from the group. The latter is a serious fate, because it may be difficult or impossible to find another band willing to accept such a person. In extreme cases a violent or otherwise intolerable individual may be killed. Where there are no prisons, no mental hospitals, and no coercive means for removing a destructive person who will not leave on his or her own, homicide can be the only alternative.

To prevent disputes from reaching a crisis, and to keep them from developing into feuds that continue from one generation to another, members of bands often strive to end bad feelings through making one person or group donate reparations (some items of value) to another, injured, person or group. The idea behind such a strategy has less to do with "justice" in the modern, Western sense, or even "equity," than it does with social healing and unity. The goal is to heal the group and make it function well again, rather than to punish someone. This approach is well described by Richard B. Lee (2012) in his definitive ethnography of the !Kung, during their existence as an independent group and beyond. It is easy to understand why healing of social ruptures through reparation is the prevailing principle in an acephalous society, which does not have institutional mechanisms for dealing with serious strife.

Seniority

Though band-based societies lack institutions that put specific individuals in official roles of authority (chief, governor, or king, for example) the principle of seniority usually serves as a method for loosely establishing relative authority within the group. In general, older people are considered to be wiser and more experienced than younger ones, and thus their suggestions and advice are usually heeded by other group members. In the absence of writing, elders are the living libraries.

Inequality

Bands generally achieve a level of equality unknown to contemporary urban-based societies. In bands there are no differences in wealth (as seen in Chapter 4). In general, any desirable possession that one person acquires can equally easily be acquired by any other member of the group of the same gender and age. And as noted earlier, there are no individuals who possess coercive authority over any other adults (except, in some groups, wives). In any group of people, however, it is inevitable that some individuals will manifests talents and capabilities that others do not have to the same extent. Thus some people will be intelligent, good at hunting, or adept at healing, while others will be contentious, clumsy, lazy, or foolish. Those individuals whose personal characteristics lead others to respect them often develop positions of informal authority and leadership within the community, roles that result in increased prestige. Such prestige is referred to by anthropologists as **achieved** status, because it is the result of an individual's own efforts. Achieved status is contrasted with **ascribed** status, which accrues to an individual as the result of factors beyond the individual's control, such as gender, age, or parentage. Status in bands must be earned individually; unlike wealth or patents of nobility in large-scale, stratified societies, it cannot be inherited from one generation to the next.

Some band-based societies go to considerable effort to maintain equality within their group, so that no individual will develop an arrogant sense of importance. Lee (2012) reports that the !Kung of Botswana go so far as to engage in a practice they refer to as "insulting the meat." According to this tradition, the !Kung never compliment a member of the group on his hunting success, but instead tell him that the animal he has killed is small, scrawny, and so insufficient that people will complain about the meager portions of meat they receive. In this way the !Kung aim to prevent the successful hunter from becoming too pleased with himself and likely to cause trouble, fueled by vanity, within the group.

Division of Labor

In general, labor is organized in bands according to two principles: age and gender. Small children do very little, and old people make less of a contribution to subsistence as they age. Older adolescents and adults in the prime of life are responsible for the majority of subsistence activity: men for hunting, and women for collecting wild plant foods.

But there are other activities that bands must attend to besides subsistence, for, like the residents of metropolitan societies, the participants in band-based societies do not live by bread (or antelope meat or camas roots) alone. They are also involved in a wide range of other essential activities, like the making of clothing, ornaments, tools, containers, and housing, as well as healing the sick, performing religious duties, caring for children, and producing art. Naturally, some individuals are better at these activities than others, but there is no occupational specialization in bands. No one makes tools to the exclusion of subsistence activities, or makes leather bags instead of gathering plant foods. These activities are simply integrated into the normal rhythms of daily subsistence activities.

The only activity in most band societies that approaches occupational specialization is the work of shamans, the characteristic medical practitioners of band societies (see Chapter 8). Shamans perform healing and other beneficial work through interacting with supernatural forces. But shamans are not full-time practitioners; like everyone else in their societies, they are primarily involved in acquiring food.

Gender

The most reliable indicator of gender status in all societies seems to be not the level of complexity of organization of the society itself. Rather, (following Friedl's suggestion discussed in the previous chapter) women's status is likely to be highest in those societies in which they participate in primary subsistence as owners or controllers, and especially as public distributors of resources. Certainly, this principle seems to hold true for gender statues in bands. For bands, men as a group usually (but not always) have greater power, authority and prestige than women as a group, and where this is the case, it is apparently the result of men's greater participation in primary subsistence.

TRIBES

With food production, people are tied to land in new ways. Another major consequence of the shift to food production is an increase in population. Denser populations can also result, even without a shift to food production, when subsistence resources are unusually abundant, as with fish and marine mammals on the northwest coast of the United States and the west coast of Canada. And increased population density may also result when hunting groups shift to the use of horses, as was true on the Great Plains of North America. Here, indigenous peoples not only adopted the use of horses after their introduction into the New World by Europeans in the sixteenth century, but they also eventually came to use firearms, which originated from the same source, and which fur-

Figure 5.3   Lakota Sioux "Touch the Clouds" (ca. 1838–1905). Famed as both a warrior and a diplomat in his dealings with Euro Americans, Touch the Clouds was the youngest man ever to lead his band of Lakota.
Photo: James H. Hamilton, 1877.

ther increased hunting success. It must be remembered, however, that Europeans also unwittingly brought in new diseases, and that because Indian peoples had developed no immunities to these diseases, large numbers of them died as a result of contact with European microbes.

When band populations increase, the old systems of communal living cease to work so effectively. It is no longer practical to live in slightly extended, self-sufficient family groups, with ties to a loosely-knit kindred activated by individuals on an ad hoc basis, according to need. Instead, new structures, institutions, and cultural practices develop, and the result is the evolution of tribes. Because the term "tribe" is used by many people in different ways, there may be some confusion as to what, exactly, tribes are, and how they differ from bands. In many ways they are similar. For example, both bands and tribes are acephalous; as with bands, tribal decision making is through consensus and (usually) male seniority; disputes are handled through reparations. Like bands, tribes are characterized by socio-economic equality; there are no social classes; status is achieved rather than ascribed and cannot be transmitted over the generations; and there is no full-time occupational specialization. To anthropologists, the fundamental difference between bands and tribes is size and the new relationships between people and property. All other differences flow from these two.

Lineages

As we have seen, bands usually feature very loosely connected, small, slightly extended family groups. With more people, with the raising of crops, and/or with herds of domesticated animals to conserve, protect, and manage, most tribes develop more elaborate kinship systems that allow them to handle new organizational tasks. As we will see in the next chapter, property-owning peoples assign privileges and responsibilities with respect to this property through chains of related family members. In these societies, groups of related family members also think of themselves as belonging to a named, enduring kinship group, which will continue to exist beyond the lifetime of any individual member. Such on-going groups are referred to as **corporate groups**, and the simplest of all of these is the **lineage**, which is a characteristic unit in tribal societies. Lineages are corporate kinship groups in which membership is traced through specific individuals, usually either the female line or the male line. In the United States, society does not operate on the basis of lineages, but we can see how lineages trace membership if we look at the way in which last names (surnames, or family names) are customarily transmitted in this country. Here, last names are customarily transmitted through the male line only. Both males and females carry their father's last name, though only males transmit it to succeeding generations. Females, though they continue to carry their father's last name, customarily mask it (as a "maiden" name), adopting their husbands' last name upon marriage. Their children carry their own fathers' last names, and women's maiden names will be continued only if they have brothers who have children of their own. Though this system is changing in some segments of United States society, it is a clear inheritance from an earlier European kinship system in which **patrilineages** (lineages traced through the male line) prevailed. Patrilineages are more common among the world's peoples, but **matrilineages** also exist. In matrilineages, membership is traced through female links only.

It is easy to see why lineages would be useful in tribal societies. In a tribal herding society, for example, the animals may belong to the lineages, members of which may be responsible for caring for them, for deciding which animals are to be sacrificed, and for together benefiting from payments of animals as penalties, dowry, or bridewealth. Similarly, in tribes of shifting cultivators, territory is often managed according to lineages, within which all members have rights to cultivate plots and benefit from their harvest.

Lineages may band together to protect their herds or territories, or to raid other groups to increase their holdings. Part of this boundary-defense and raiding may be due to increasing population pressure on limited territory. Part is often due to the fact that expanding herds and improved lands represent investment and potential value that are worth protecting and increasing. And part is due to the fact that the larger population and smaller territory in use (compared to the vast, unpatrollable territories customarily relied upon by foragers) can be patrolled and defended or expanded.

Though lineages are useful institutions, they also have destructive potential. Dividing a population into vertical (or longitudinal) units may cause strife among the units (here, lineages), as they compete for the same fund of limited resources. There are various means that tribal societies employ to limit the threat that lineages pose to the unity of the larger group. One means is the creation of institutions that anthropologists refer to as sodalities, or non kin-based groups organized for a specific purpose (like the religious **sodalities** found in some Christian communities). Though there are many kinds of sodalities, those that occur most frequently in tribes are **age sets**. Age sets consist of persons (usually males) who together occupy an age-based group (called an **age**

grade) for a certain length of time, until together they enter the next ascending age grade. The individuals who enter an age grade together form a continuing group, like members of a high school or college class. Age grades have a variety of purposes and carry out a variety of activities. In many tribal societies, including African cattle-raising groups like the Nuer and Maasai (discussed in the last chapter), young men were initiated into the warrior age grade as adolescents. Subsequent age grades in tribal societies may include categories like "family men" and "elders." Throughout their lives these men maintain loyalties not only to their own lineages, but also to their fellow "alumni" from their age set.

In many tribal societies, initiation into the first tier of an age set takes place every few years, at which time all boys of roughly the same age, usually around puberty, are gathered together and formally initiated. Initiation rituals are extremely variable. Some require boys to endure such hardships as hunger, thirst, or sleep deprivation; some involve learning important spiritual information; and some include ritual body modification, such as scarification, circumcision, or even (as formerly in the northwest part of Australia) **subincision**, the slitting of the underside of the penis. The frequently dramatic and sometimes painful nature of initiation rituals, along with their often visible body alterations, make clear to the community that the individuals involved have been through initiation. They also act as adjuncts to the ritual, itself, maintaining a feeling of solidarity among all the members of the age set, as they go through life, moving from one age grade to another. Thus boys who begin life with loyalty to their own lineages, develop an additional sense of loyalty to the other members of their age sets, which to some extent acts to diffuse kin-based loyalties and thus strengthen the larger group. It is useful to think of lineages as the vertical staves of a barrel, held together and permitting the finished structure of the barrel (society) to exist by the hoops (sodalities) that encircle them horizontally.

Big Men

One specialized role does exist in some tribal communities, particularly in many of the groups in Highland New Guinea, a role that may be considered that of primus inter pares, or a first among equals. This is the role of the big man. The term "big man" is derived from the Neomelanesian creole word (see Chapter 7 for a discussion of creole languages) "bikpela," which refers to an informal, self constituted leader in some Highland New Guinea communities. Big men are not wealthier than others, but they do have high

Figure 5.4   A former "big man," Irian Jaya (West Papua), Indonesia.
Source: Authors' collection.

prestige and influence in their communities. Their influential status is largely derived from their abilities to persuade other people to join with them in organizing prestigious public rituals at which large numbers of pigs are given away (along with other valuables), and many pigs are eaten at a great feast. These pig giveaways may require many months, or even years, to arrange. A big man cannot order people to contribute pigs to his festival; he has no power to enforce anything. Instead, he must urge people to do as he wishes, and he must balance carefully between being friendly and supportive of his neighbors and being forceful. Too friendly, and his neighbors will not feel obliged to follow the big man; too forceful, and they will be alienated from him. In addition, big men are often in competition with rival big men for control of the hearts and minds of community members. Bearing some resemblance to old-fashioned city politicians, and political party bosses, big men do favors for their neighbors so that they can later call in their debts (mostly in terms of pigs for a feast). Wealth is not the goal of big men. Influence and prestige are.

Gender

Gender roles and relations in tribal societies vary. In general, because most tribal societies are engaged in varieties of food production, all typically dominated by men (herding, horticulture, and hunting), women generally occupy a subordinate place. Many women in band-based societies can subsist relatively independently, supporting themselves and their children with the addition of the meat shared with the group by hunters. But this independence is seldom possible for tribal women, who must depend upon men for survival. They may, however, have important roles in decision-making about subsistence activities, in which they are important participants.[2]

Another cultural element that contributes to the determination of gender relations in tribal societies has to do with kinship. Lineages allow much less flexibility to individuals than do the kindreds characteristic of bands. Because lineages are corporate entities, their members may be concerned that the behavior of an individual will have a negative impact on the group. This is particularly true for a woman married into a patrilocal patrilineage. Though she is not technically a member of the lineage into which she marries, her association with it means that her behavior affects its reputation. Thus, birthright members of the lineage (or long-term in-married women, like mothers-in-law) may watch a newly in-married woman (a daughter-in-law or sister-in-law) carefully and try to control her behavior. Women in matrilineal societies usually maintain higher status than those in patrilineal societies. The reason for this is not that women dominate in matrilineal societies; they do not. But they usually do not move at marriage outside their own family settlement, so their interests tend to be protected by coresident family members.

CHIEFDOMS

If tribal populations grow into the thousands and come to occupy large expanses of territory, it becomes increasingly difficult to organize people, property, and rights according to the traditional system of informal leadership through elders or big men. Thus a new role often develops: that of the chief. Unlike big men in tribal societies, chiefs are not self-appointed, charismatic persuaders. Instead, chiefs occupy institutionalized roles that must always be filled, and filled with an individual who, at least ideally, is either automatically eligible for the role or who is chosen according to a specific rule.

Kinship and Inequality

As in bands and tribes, kinship is of vital importance in chiefdoms, providing support and protection in the absence of the kinds of institutional safety nets that residents of modern industrial states take for granted. But in chiefdoms, kinship is important for an additional reason. Lineages in chiefdoms are generally ranked, so that some lineages, and thus their members, have intrinsically higher status than others. In many chiefdoms lineages are grouped into noble and commoner categories, and within each of these two large groupings there may be additional rankings, as well.

This is the beginning of the phenomenon of ascribed status, mentioned earlier, whereby the status of individuals is, to at least some degree, based on factors outside their control, primarily the status of the family into which they were born. By contrast, we have seen that in bands and tribes, status is individually achieved through personal accomplishment. The notion of achieved status accords with what most contemporary people in the United States like to think about themselves, but it is clear, despite our love of legends about self-made men (and now, self-made women, as well) that American culture also recognizes ascribed status. And United States society also features informally—though definitely—ranked families. Consider such families as the du Ponts, the Rockefellers, the Kennedys, and the Fords (which are nearer to abbreviated kindreds than to lineages). Members of these families certainly enjoy higher than average status, simply because of the fact of their kinship affiliation. And in societies in which hereditary nobility and royalty still exist, as in Britain, the phenomenon of lineage ranking is even stronger than it is in the United States. The lineage of a monarch enjoys higher ranking than that of a duke; that of a duke higher than that of an earl; and that of an earl higher than that of a viscount. Or we could consider the ranking of all free lineages of ancient Rome into patricians and plebeians. The patricians, who defined themselves as the descendants of the founders of the Roman Republic, made up only about five percent of the population of Rome. The rest of the free citizen population were relegated to the category of plebeians, and cut off from many of the prestigious roles and political rights of the patricians (Mitchell 1990). This system developed at a time when Roman society could best be described as a chiefdom, and persisted into its existence as a huge state, during which time the rights of plebeians increased, as did the permeability of patrician boundaries.

In any chiefdom, the role of chief is filled by a member of a chiefly lineage, and upon his death it passes to another member, usually a son, brother, or nephew. In matrilineal kin groups, the son or grandson of the deceased chief's sister often inherits the role. Chiefdoms may be extremely large, encompassing several thousand people, and often involving multiple settlements. In such cases there may be several chiefly lineages, spread among different settlements, and producing secondary chiefs who are adjuncts to the primary, or paramount chief.

The ranked lineage system provides a skeletal structure for the organization of chiefdoms, but it does not usually provide an infrastructure upon which the chiefdom can rely for long-term stability (Carneiro 1981, 1991). The chiefs tend to be individual loci of power to whom other individuals compete for access, usually on the basis of kinship links, or against whom they conspire, usually again, on the basis of kinship.

Political Structure and Division of Labor

We have seen in band and tribal societies that though specific individuals may have distinctive abilities for particular kinds of work, there is no formal division of labor, except by age and gender. In chiefdoms this is not the case. While most of the population of any chiefdom is occupied in primary subsistence activities, the chief and members of his lineage usually do not engage in such activities. Instead, the chief, along with some of his kin and assistants, is involved in ensuring the prosperity and security of the group and their own continuing power through the performance and oversight of important religious rituals, political strategizing, and warfare.

Characteristically, chiefs also collect subsistence goods and other valuables as tribute from the population as a whole, and redistribute these goods to the general population, thus promoting the welfare of the whole group. In return for this "service," they are awarded a dispensation from onerous subsistence activity and a disproportionate amount of food and other consumer goods. Unlike big men, who live no better than other members of the tribal community, chiefs definitely live better than other members of their group.

The power of chiefs varies from group to group. In precontact Polynesia, the power of chiefs was relatively high. Here, chiefs were considered to have not only special supernatural qualities, themselves, but also to manifest the diffuse supernatural power known as **mana**, and to be able to control and manipulate mana. Without their special capabilities, fishing, farming, trade, and warfare would not prosper, and the community would decline. This conviction and acquiescence on the part of the mass of the population were, of course, directly related to the ability of the chief and his deputies to maintain their dominance within the society. This is a clear example of the "consent of the governed," which usually has a coerced quality.

But even in Polynesia, the authority exerted by some chiefs and their agents was limited to the collection of tribute for redistribution and the chiefs' use, while in other areas, as in Hawaii, even secondary chiefs could remove families from their customary territories and even kill them if they did not

Figure 5.5   Hawaiian Chief by Rembrandt Peale (American 1778–1860).

perform or produce according to the chief's demands. Since most chiefs, both in Polynesia and elsewhere, were considered to be the conduit between their population and the supernatural world, it was to the benefit of the community to support their chief, as a form of self interest. If, however, the chief appeared to have lost his touch, or to fail in the performance of his duties to protect and sustain the group, the community, organized by rivals for chiefly power, was likely to turn against a chief and withdraw support. Given this context and the lack of a bureaucratic infrastructure to rely upon, it is hardly surprising that the chief's role, and thus the organization of chiefdoms, have been unstable.

Gender

Women's roles in chiefdoms, as in bands and tribes, tend to be quite distinct from those of men. And like women in tribal societies, they tend to be more involved with the processing of the products of subsistence, rather than with primary subsistence, itself, as owners or controllers. This has been the case in Polynesia, where men dominate in the extraction of marine resources and do the heavy labor in the fields. It is the pattern as well in many areas of sub-Saharan Africa, where men own the livestock and are the owners of the agricultural fields. In many chiefdoms of the native New World, including the Mississippian cultures of the precontact southeast United States, men controlled the cornfields.

In addition to their generally subordinate position, women in many chiefdoms have been subject to severe restrictions on their independence and autonomy. This was particularly true of women in highly-ranked lineages, who were actual or potential mates for chiefs. In order to ensure the "purity" of the blood of chiefly offspring, the activities of chiefly consorts were rigidly restricted, even where sexual activity was more permissive for other, lower-ranked women.

As in those tribal societies where matrilineages prevailed, there was often somewhat greater autonomy for females in matrilineal chiefdoms. Still, restrictions on female activities were in all cases greater than those on the behavior of males. There were some exceptions, seen most notably in the roles of two indigenous queens of the short lived kingdom of Hawaii (1795–1893), Queen Ka'ahumanu (1773–1832), who inherited the role from her husband, and Queen Lili'uokalani (1833–1917), the last monarch of Hawaii, who inherited the role from her brother. Though referred to as "queens," these monarchs functioned more like traditional chiefs.

In many Bantu chiefdoms in sub-Saharan Africa, there is a special role reserved for a woman in the chief's household, referred to in English as the "queen mother." This is often the chief's own mother, but if not, she is another senior woman, sometimes another of the late chief's wives. The "queen mother" role has primarily to do with rituals affecting fertility—fertility of women, of the land, and of stock. Her activities are recognized as essential, and great prestige accrues to her. But her occupancy of her role depends upon her connection to chiefs, both past and present, and she has little independence outside her prescribed sphere. Though significant, the queen mother's role, which continues in some West African societies in the present, has limited meaning for the mass of women in Bantu societies.

STATES

A state is a form of social and political organization characterized by a large, occupationally diverse, stratified population integrated through the agency of a central, coercive authority, and with a corporate identity as a state. States are urban-based and operate through bureaucracies and taxation. States include a diversity of forms—from kingdoms to republics, from dictatorships to democracies, from capitalist governments to centrally planned economies.

Not surprisingly, seniority and consensus are much less important in state societies than they are in bands, tribes, and even chiefdoms. Though persons in positions of leadership in states do tend to be elders, this is primarily because it takes considerable time to secure the alliances and credentials needed to assume political power. But unlike more simply organized societies, not all elders have higher status and greater influence than all junior members in a state society. In bands and tribes, elders are repositories of practical informa-

Figure 5.6   The last Hawaiian monarch, Queen Lili'uokalani. For 98 years, from 1795 to 1893, the chiefdoms of the Hawaiian Islands were united into the Kingdom of Hawaii, which was overthrown by the United States in 1893 to protect American commercial interests. The Queen, like all the other monarchs of Hawaii, was part of an old chiefly family.
Source: Wikimedia

tion. Technology and patterns of living change slowly, so that old solutions remain valid for problems that develop generations later. But in state societies technology and cultural patterns change far more rapidly, making old information less useful as time passes. Today, in a state level society like the United States, many people have the notion that they ought to respect elders, but the uncomfortable feeling that elders are tiresome, restrictive, and irrelevant.

Today some peoples of the world live in communities that may be classed as chiefdoms, as tribes, and even as bands. Nevertheless, all people are now firmly entrenched in the era of the state, and have been for several centuries. Though other forms of social organization persist, they now all exist within the confines of state level societies, and at the sufferance of states. Where bands endure, they are constrained by the laws and often the political boundaries of national governments. Where tribal peoples continue to follow cultural patterns of their ancestors, they must now avoid transgressing the laws, limits, and conventions of the countries within which they live. And though there are African chiefdoms that continue to have administrative roles within national political infrastructures, those chiefdoms are now subordinate to the countries within which they exist, rather than existing as the independent political entities they once were.

It is no longer possible to return to simpler varieties of social organization unless a cataclysmic disaster, either human-produced or natural, strikes the earth. This has not always been true. There are sites all over the globe where state-level societies have disintegrated as states and their populations have simply returned to rural living, raising animals and growing crops in small farming settlements. Such locations include the Indus Valley Harappan civilization of Pakistan that dissolved around 1900 B.C.E.; the Mesopotamian civilization of Sumer, now covered in sand, that declined a century later; and the lowlands of Central America, where the Mayan civilization collapsed in the tenth century of the current era.

But there are differences between these ancient state societies and those of today. First, the people who left these urban centers in ancient times were far less numerous than are the populations of today's urban centers. The following estimated world population figures (all but the last taken from Kremer 1993) illustrate the dramatic differences in population between the ancient past and more recent times:

10,000 B.C.E.	4 million
1000 B.C.E.	50 million
1 C.E.	170 million
1000 C.E.	265 million
1500 C.E.	425 million
1750 C.E.	720 million
1900 C.E.	1.8 billion
1950 C.E.	2.5 billion
2013 C.E.	7.2 billion

Second, given this dramatic increase in population, there is far less unoccupied land suitable for farming available today than in ancient times. Third, as we have seen in Chapter 3, today's world is so thoroughly interrelated and mutually dependent that it is nearly impossible to drop out of the urban based, state-level system once one has become a part of it. Even tribal manioc horticulturalists in the Amazon basin and rice farmers in Madagascar are only a few hours' walk from cell phone service, and closer than that to plastic sheeting and imported, packaged "convenience" foods. Fourth, and finally, the numbers of people who live in urban-based or urban-dependent communities are now so large that they cannot possibly all be fed without intensive agriculture.

In short: we cannot go home again. Cities and the state societies they produce are here to stay for the foreseeable future and will in all certainty exist well beyond the lifetime of anyone reading this book. Their controls, restrictions, limitations, and even inequities cannot simply be swept away in some romantic yearning for the past. Our reproductive and technological successes have tethered us, even those of us who live in bands, tribes, and chiefdoms, to dependence upon states.

Kinship

Kinship in states did not disappear. This was especially true in ancient and premodern states, where family affiliation was the greatest single determiner of access to wealth, power, and authority. Kin groups and kinship links not only established rights to thrones and to property, but also continued to provide support and security for individuals. However, as states have become larger and more complex, and as their populations have increased and become more diverse, mobile, and geographically dispersed, reliance upon kinship has declined.

In place of dependence on kin, the state has taken on more of the responsibilities that were previously the obligation of family members. Today, for example, the state provides and regulates education, oversight of births and deaths, regulation of many occupations, and the safety, value, and wholesomeness of such commodities as food, beverages, and manufactured items. The state regulates the use and often the ownership of land and other property. In all but the most impoverished state-based societies, the state is now responsible for providing relief to individuals without resources. Of course, the stratification within states produces a higher proportion of such individuals. Nevertheless, the pervasive sharing that is characteristic of less complex social groupings is virtually absent in states, and in many states, especially the United States, there has developed a cultural value oriented toward individualism. In such societies individuals are responsible only for themselves, or perhaps their own nuclear families, but not for the more distantly related family members or neighbors who are a part of every individual's concern in non-state societies.[3]

Inequality

Stratification is the structural essence of states. It provides an institutional framework and justification for inequality on a scale never experienced by humans before states developed. Even chiefdoms, though their lineages are ranked in terms of prestige, and their chiefs have greater access to wealth than others, seldom maintain social structures according to which groups of participants are denied the necessities of a rewarding life. But in states such groups of nonprivileged persons do exist; they are often quite large; and their poverty and powerlessness are transmitted from generation to generation through institutions of structural inequality.

The term "stratification" is derived from the Latin *stratum*, or "level," and this is the principle upon which the system is based. Basically, the level an individual occupies in a state society determines access to the necessities and benefits of life. If mobility is possible from one level to another, then the levels are referred to as **classes**. If there can be no mobility from one level to another, then the levels are referred to as **castes**. In the past, caste systems were known in many places in the world. In ancient Roman society, as noted earlier, the patricians and the plebeians operated as castes. Caste systems are well known today from the Hindu South Asian countries of India and Nepal, though today caste divisions are no longer officially recognized by the state in either country. Ideas and practices concerning caste do still exist in these societies, however.

Caste is based on a cultural notion of ritual purity or worth, which is generally enacted in daily life by an individual's occupation and other behaviors. Class usually depends upon a combination of factors, including occupation, ethnicity, education, social habits (How do you hold a spoon? What kind of clothing do you wear? Do you chew tobacco?), and income. Both class and caste provide organization for large populations in such a way that variable access to valued commodities and benefits is justified by widely held cultural beliefs. Often the justification is accepted by the very segment of the population who gain the least from it.

In the South Asian caste system, the highest ("clean") castes constitute a majority of the population, while the lowest ("unclean") castes are a minority group. By contrast, class systems have a structure often represented as a pyramid, with the highest status grouping at the top, which involves the fewest people, and progressively lower groupings falling farther down the pyramid, and involving increasing numbers of people. That is, a very few people have high status and the wealth and power that usually go with it, while most of the people have much lower status and much less of the good things of life. In caste systems, too, the majority of the population with the least wealth make up the broad base of the socioeconomic pyramid, while the top of the pyramid, representing those with the greatest wealth and power, is represented by a very small number.

Stratification is usually justified in caste systems by a supernaturally derived principle. In the South Asian (Hindu) caste system, for example, supernatural assignment of caste is considered to depend upon karma, or the cumulative performance of one's obligations in all past lives. Thus whatever slot an individual occupies in life is justified, according to the society's emic view, by his or her own previous actions, and there is no cause for alteration of the system.

Class systems are generally believed by those who occupy their more comfortable slots to be the result of individual skills, abilities, and personal efforts, perhaps helped by the chance of one's birth. People who occupy low positions not surprisingly see the situation somewhat differently. From their perspective, success is blocked by lack of resources, lack of connections, and lack of information on how to get ahead.

Some modern, wealthier state societies devise policies and provide services to help the poorer segments of society gain access to some resources. But the increased access of many people at the bottom of these populations in prosperous countries is often counterbalanced by the increasing poverty in other, poorer countries. The populations in these poor countries provide raw or manufactured goods, or, increasingly, services at low cost to wealthier countries. The pyramid structure of state level societies is thus preserved in the modern world, but the extent of the pyramid's base is transnational.

Division of Labor

In state level societies labor is highly diversified. Even in ancient states, where the majority of the population was still involved in the production of food, occupational specialization had increased to a tremendous extent. Not only did craft and manufacturing specialties develop, but also administrative specialties, which allowed their practitioners to organize and maintain such complex institutions as military organizations, government institutions, and religious structures. Along with these specialties were stratified social categories. That is, some occupations conferred upon their practitioners higher status than did others. These statuses tended to be passed down through the generations, often along with the practice of the occupation, itself. In India, the son of a sweeper will inherit both his father's occupation, as well as his father's extremely low status. Sweepers in India are Untouchables, members of the lowest caste grouping, who deal with cleaning up all sorts of filth. And a contemporary neurosurgeon in the United States will certainly pass his or her relatively high status on to any children, along with accumulated wealth upon death. A disproportionate number of the children of North American doctors become doctors, themselves. Occupational specialization in modern state level societies is much more variable than it has been in the past, though there is still some tendency to carry on an occupation something like that of one's parents, and to maintain their status, whether high, middle, or low. Both the authors of this text, for example, professors of anthropology, are the daughters of professors, one of veterinary medicine and the other of psychology.

Technological intensification has resulted in the elimination of many traditional occupations, and the development of additional new occupations. As we have seen, the mechanization of agriculture has resulted in a tiny fraction of the former agricultural labor force now being involved in agricultural production. The development of the internal combustion engine and mechanized manufacture has put the majority of blacksmiths out of business. And the invention of cheap household machinery, like washing machines, electric irons, and vacuum cleaners, has resulted in a dramatic decline in the army of domestic servants (some of them enslaved) formerly employed by the middle and upper classes in state level societies.

Gender

Of all the categories of state organization we explore in this chapter, gender is probably the most variable. And of all the social groupings we explore with respect to gender, state level societies probably provide the widest range of variation. As we saw in the previous chapter, women in agricultural societies were originally cut out of primary subsistence activities, however essential they were to the processing of the products of subsistence. Since agriculture is the fundamental subsistence base for states, what this means is that in early states, women as a group had lower status and less autonomy than men as a group. As we have also seen, once the possession of property became important to human groups, men in these groups were inclined to restrict the autonomy and mobility of women so as to ensure their sexual fidelity and thus the transmission of their property to children who are their own. These have been characteristics of state level societies for thousands of years. There have, of course, been exceptions to the rule of subordination of women in states. We all know the names of a small number of famous women in ancient states, including Nefertiti, the wife of Pharaoh Tutankhamun of Egypt; Cleopatra, the Hellenistic (that is, Greek) Pharaoh of Egypt; Empress Theodora of the Eastern Roman Empire; and Eleanor of Aquitaine, Queen first of France and subsequently of England. But the fact remains that these famous women are anomalies. Even (or perhaps especially) at the top of the status pyramid in state level societies, women as a group have been subordinate to men.

Today gender roles and relations in state level societies have changed dramatically in some places. In many states traditional gender roles and relations continue to exist. In many others, however, especially in wealthier, developed countries, which include the United States, many women in the last fifty years have increasingly participated in education, assumed new roles, and have entered occupations that were formerly reserved for men. In many of these countries, as well as in some poorer ones, the new options for women have to some extent been countered by an additional phenomenon: the decline of marriage and the increasing fragility of those marriages that do occur. What this means is that more women are solely responsible not only for their own maintenance, but for the maintenance of their children, as well. Though some men who no longer live with their children and former partners provide some support for their children, more do not.

SUMMARY

Having reviewed the varieties of social organization outlined by anthropologists, we can identify four primary variables according to which they differ. The first of these variables seems to drive the second; the second drives the third; and the third drives the fourth.

First is subsistence. Does a group in question produce its own food, or are its members foragers? If they are foragers, their population is likely to remain small. Second is population size. If the group remains small, as is characteristic of most foragers, it will generally be egalitarian. But if the group produces its own food, as pastoralists, horticulturalists, or agriculturalists, the population will grow, and as it grows and relationships among members become more attenuated, inequality is likely to increase.

Third is the nature of authority. As the population increases and as control over productive property (land, livestock etc.) becomes vital, coercive authority and institutions will develop. This brings an intensification of organization of the growing population and the administration of the increasingly complex integrative institutions.

Fourth is social stratification. As population and administrative complexity increase, stratification of the population will increase, with a characteristic pyramidal class structure. There will be a small proportion of the population who occupy the top of the pyramid, and enjoy disproportionate access to wealth, power, and autonomy. As one goes down the pyramid, larger and larger numbers of people are represented, with decreasing access to the good things of life. (This has been mitigated to some extent in some modern states.) The myths that headed this chapter are now clearly debunked.

Myth #1   All societies require a few people who rule (a central, coercive governing authority) and a majority of people who are ruled.

Bands and tribes do not have any official leaders, or any persons or roles that are invested with central, coercive power. Though this may seem incredible to us (because we live in a state-based society that does have a small group of rulers and a large group of ruled), we find that for thousands of years there were no such societies. Originally all human groups were unstratified and had no official rulers. Though this system would not work for modern, state-based societies, in small-scale, egalitarian societies in which people are linked to each other through bonds of descent or marriage, it worked well.

Myth #2   Indeed all societies should have some central coercive authority; otherwise the society would be chaotic and unworkable.

Not all societies in the world have had laws to regulate human behavior. Bands and tribes, both of which have small populations, closely related by ties of blood and/or marriage, do not need explicit laws, and do not have coercive authority to enforce them. Instead, people are kept in line primarily by group opinion and the implicit threat of being shunned if they violate tradition too severely. Thus, chaos does not occur in these groups, as it certainly would in much larger groups, like chiefdoms and states. In these societies, with their enormous populations of unrelated inhabitants, laws and central, coercive authority seem to be a necessity.

Myth #3   It is in the nature of human societies to have social classes that vary according to people's occupations, relative wealth, and prestige.

Although most societies on the earth today do have either classes or castes, this, again, is characteristic of certain kinds of social organization, chiefdoms and states, the latter of which is the norm in the contemporary world. But at one time all societies were egalitarian bands or tribes, in which there were neither classes nor castes. In general, all adult women pursued the same occupation: procuring wild plant foods, tending small domesticated animals and garden plots, and processing plants and animals into food and clothing. All adult men pursued the same occupation, as well: hunting large game, managing domesticated herd animals, and doing the heavy labor of preparing garden plots. There was little variation in wealth and no institutionalized role that would permit the transmission of wealth or status from one generation to the next, thus preventing the development of ascribed status that is the basis of class and caste.

Myth #4   A person born into a low position in society can generally rise above that position through hard work.

Social mobility—the idea that by hard work one can rise in the world—is one of the cherished principles of North American life. But in many societies, even where this is technically possible, such social mobility is rare. In the contemporary United States, for example, most people occupy roughly the same position of wealth, power, and status as their parents. This is true because an individual's expectations and access to education, training, scarce resources, and powerful and influential acquaintances tend to be strongly influenced by his or her upbringing and early experiences. This is often the case in class-based societies, but it is technically absolutely true in caste-based societies.

QUESTIONS FOR THOUGHT AND REFLECTION

1. We have all seen cartoons, like the one included in tis chapter, in which space aliens arrive in unknown territory and ask the people they first meet to "take me to your leader." What is the underlying assumption behind this demand? After having read this chapter, why would you say that the request may make very little sense to the newly encountered population?

2. What are the similarities shared by bands and tribes? In what significant ways do they differ? How do these two kinds of groups differ from chiefdoms and starts?

3. As the term is used by anthropologists, what is a "sodality"? (The word has a slightly different significance within the Catholic Church.) Provide an example of an African tribal sodality and explain how it works. What are the benefits of sodalities such as this in the tribal societies that have them?

4. What are the characteristics shared by chiefdoms and states that set them apart from bands and tribes? How do chiefdoms and states differ from each other? One of the distinctive characteristics of chiefdoms is that they tend to be unstable with respect to the makeup of their group of governing elites. Why do you think this is the case? How do states mange to combat this phenomenon with greater success?

5. Ironically, states include both societies with the greatest inequality in the world, as well as some with very little inequality. Explain how this could possibly be true. How does inequality develop in states, and how can it be eliminated or at least mitigated?. If inequality can be mitigated, why has this not always happened in state-level societies?

6. Using population size as the driving variable, explain how and why population increases are likely to be the most important spur to the development of increasing complexity and stratification in the social organization of bands, tribes, chiefdoms, and states.

ENDNOTES

[1] The meaning of "savage" is obvious; the term "barbarian" is derived from an onomatopoetic word coined by the Greeks. In their ethnocentric view, all people who were not Greek sounded ridiculous speaking their own languages, which the Greeks mimicked as sounding like "bar-bar-bar-bar."

[2] One of the many reasons that European immigrants to the New World and their descendants made such terrible decisions about Native peoples and land tenure had to do with ignorance. Europeans did not understand or accept the reality that many tribal women, especially in the northeast of what is now the United States, made important and binding decisions about land. Often it was women who decided which horticultural land the tribe would use and how it should be allocated. But Europeans were seldom willing to deal with women in those situations in which they bothered to negotiate terms of their takeover of native lands.

[3] Thus the term "family parasitism" (parasitisme familiale) was developed by French social scientists for the phenomenon prevalent in many parts of Africa in which a person who achieves a measure of success in the modern, urban world is then obliged to share his wealth and influence with members of his extended family, who may show up in the city to live with him, and expect him to support them and find them jobs. Though this pattern is directly derived from family obligations that prevail in tribal societies, it works far less well in modern states, and even African political leaders now refer to it as "family parasitism."

REFERENCES CITED

Carneiro, Robert
    1981 "The Chiefdom: Precursor to the State" in *The Transition to Statehood in the New World*,
        Grant D. Jones and Robert R. Kautz, eds., pp 37–79. New York: Cambridge University Press.
    1991 "The Nature of the Chiefdom as Revealed by Evidence from the Cauca Valley of Ecuador"
        in *Profiles in Cultural Evolution: Papers from a Conference in Honor of Elman R. Service*,

A. Terry Rambo and Katheen Gillogly, eds., pp. 167–190. Ann Arbor: University of Michigan Press.

Darwin, Charles
1859 *On the Origin of Species by Means of Natural Selection.* London: John Murry.

Kremer, Michael
1993 "Population Growth and Technological Change: One Milliom BC to 1990." *The Quarterly Journal of Economics* 108 (30): 681–716.

Lee, Richard B.
2012 *The Dobe Ju/'hoansi* (Case Studies in Cultural Anthropology). 4th edition. Stamford, Ct.: Cengage Learning.

Mitchell, Richard E.
1990 *Patricians and Plebeians: The Origins of the Roman State.* Ithaca: Cornell University Press.

Morgan, Lewis Henry
1877 *Ancient Society or Researches in the Lines of Human Progress from Savagery, through Barbarism to Civilization.* New York: Henry Holt.

Service, Elman
1962 *Primitive Social Organization: an Evolutionary Perspective.* New York: Random House.
1963 *Profiles in Ethnology.* New York: Harper and Row.

CHAPTER 6

KINSHIP AND MARRIAGE

How families are structured

For most people, the families they are born into and those they create later in life constitute their primary relationships. Family units are also powerful agents of our socialization, shaping our aptitudes and opportunities as well as our basic political and religious orientations. Nearly everyone holds a curiosity about his or her genealogical ancestry, illustrious or not. Growing numbers of people mail off swabs of their DNA to find their genetic "matches" and deep genetic (**haplotype**) roots. And these days many people seek precise knowledge of their biological connections to others when they are concerned with their possible inheritance of genetic diseases. Kinship is an important feature of human life everywhere, and it has been investigated by anthropology more than by any other discipline. In anthropology, kinship is defined as the recognition of relationships based on descent or marriage. The former, those based on descent, are called **consanguineal** relationships (English uses the metaphor of "blood" relatives for these). Relationships through marriage ("in-laws") are known as **affinal** relationships.

Anthropologists are interested in kinship for a number of reasons. First, kinship is a human universal: All human groups trace and classify consanguineal and affinal relationships. Second, kinship is a fundamental aspect of our species' evolution, as discussed briefly in Chapter 3 and elaborated further in this chapter. Third, in many societies studied by anthropologists, kinship is a crucial feature of social organization. It determines the most important groups to which individuals belong and the social, political, economic, and often spiritual relationships among these groups. Fourth, kinship and ideas about kin relations are in all societies interwoven with cultural ides about personhood, gender, and social identity. In one society we may see debates about "family values" and gay marriage. In another we may see that ancestor worship is the cornerstone of religion. In yet others kinship groupings are also major political groupings. The way that human groups understand and structure kinship varies considerably, but everywhere we look, kinship is central to culture.

A perfectly reasonable but infrequently asked question is: Why do humans have ideas of kinship? That is, why do humans everywhere recognize a wide variety of kin, calculate closeness and distance in their kin relationships and classify their kin? Anthropologists and others have come up with a few ideas. One idea from evolutionary theory is known as **kin selection**. First proposed by W. D. Hamilton (1964), kin selection refers to the idea that individuals can enhance their biological fitness (reproductive success) not only through their own reproduction but also through promoting the survival and reproduction of others who share at least some of their genes, namely their close kin. Thus the process of kin selection is a part of natural selection and it results in kin-favoring behavior. Human kinship systems, then, are mechanisms for the recognition and favoring of kin. Closer kin, in this view, are likely to be favored over more distant ones.[1] Another idea, developed mostly by anthropologists, is that humans live in groups; for their survival they are dependent on the formation of cohesive groups that can be perpetuated over time. However kin recognition came about, kinship became a very handy basis on which humans could form and structure the primary groups in which they live in such a way that the groups could be perpetuated over time. In this chapter we will soon see ethnographic examples of how humans use kinship to form, structure, and perpetuate their primary groups and how kinship assumes primary importance in human societies. Finally, we will discuss kinship in terms of cultural dynamics, with particular reference to Euro-American societies that are currently undergoing profound changes in the domain of kinship and the family. And, of course, we will try in this chapter to dispel some myths of kinship, in particular the following:

Common Myths of Culture
Myth #1   Human societies form descent groups by tracing links through both parents.
Myth #2   All societies use nuclear family units as a basic structure.

Myth #3 Matrilineal societies are matriarchal.

Myth #4 People in all cultures perceive kinship as based on biological reproduction. (kinship relationships are seen as "blood" relationships).

Myth #5 Kin (father, mother, aunt, etc) are called by different terms in different languages but all peoples distinguish kin in identical ways.

To follow some of the material in this chapter it will be necessary for students to know the Kinship Code, a handy device that anthropologists use to construct kinship diagrams. The elements of the code are presented below in Figure 6.1a. Figure 6.1b then shows an example of one type of kinship diagram. This particular diagram is ego-centric; that is, it focuses on one individual (an "ego" shaded in the diagram, in this case Mark Antony of ancient Rome) and traces out ego's kinship relationships or genealogy. Readers might like to construct their own genealogy using the Code to become familiar with it.

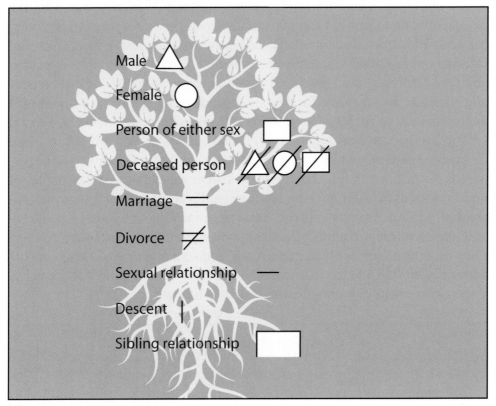

Figure 6.1a   The Kinship Code

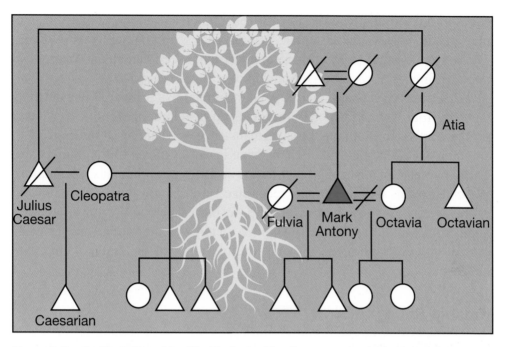

Figure 6.1b   An illustration of the Kinship Code. The diagram shows some kinship and marriage links among rulers of ancient Rome around 31 B.C.E., with a focus on Mark Antony (shaded in the diagram). By this time Mark Antony's parents had passed away. Antony had been married to Fulvia and they had two sons before Fulvia died. Then Antony married Octavia, sister to Octavian (who later became Emperor Augustus), and also the grand niece (sister's daughter's daughter) of Julius Caesar. They had two daughters. Antony eventually divorced her. Meanwhile Antony had a long-term affair with Cleopatra, queen of Egypt, and three children with her. Cleopatra had had an affair with Julius Caesar (assassinated in 44 B.C.E.) and bore him a son, Caesarion.

KINSHIP

We saw in Chapter 3 that kinship is of great significance in many species of nonhuman primates, far more than is commonly known and more than primatologists knew even a few decades ago. This finding shows a strong, fundamental similarity between human and nonhuman primate kinship. Nonhuman and human primates exhibit similar features of kinship in four major ways. First, both nonhuman primates and humans recognize kin, though human recognition is expanded far beyond that of the nonhuman primates. Second, among both human and nonhuman primates, mating and residence patterns are interconnected with kinship. Third, some nonhuman primates and most (but not all) human groups make use of lineages (lines of kin over generations) in their social structure. As we saw earlier, among many kinds of Old World monkeys, there are distinct subgroups of ranked matrilineages, that is, lineages traced through females. Recall from Chapter 3 that these matrilineages may consist of, say, an old female, her daughters, and her daughters' infants. These matrilineages show a fourth similarity between human and many non-human primates: recognition of kinship over the generations.

What, then, do humans have beyond the nonhuman primates? In a nutshell, there are four ways in which human kinship developed beyond that of other primates and is thus unique. First, humans developed and used the concept of common ancestors. Second, humans have in-laws (affines) through marriage. Third, humans linguistically label their kin, and fourth, humans often culturally construct as well as simply "recognize" kin relationships. To see how all of this works and how human kinship developed, we will briefly look at a number of specific features of kinship. We begin with the features most closely shared with other primates, moving to dimensions of the features unique to humans.

Kinship Recognition

Nonhuman primates, as we saw, recognize some kin, but how do they do so? It is now widely agreed that they most probably do so through an association mechanism that builds upon the strong mother-child tie. In other words, an infant primate grows up forming a close bond with the mother and then gradually learns to recognize some others (for example his/ her siblings) as "kin" on the basis of their interaction with the mother and the infant, itself (Bernstein 1991, Silk 2001). Using this mechanism, the range of individuals recognized as kin will vary according to some other factors, most notably residence patterns. Among species where females stay together and young males disperse, there will be a number of maternally related individuals residing together in a group—related to one another as grandmothers, mothers, daughters, grand-daughters, maternal siblings, maternal aunts, and maternal cousins. Kinship recognition in these species will be more extensive than in groups where females disperse out and do not remain together over the generations. In these species where females move out, kinship recognition will be limited to one's mother and maternal siblings; other maternally-related individuals will not be present in the group.

In the species where females stay put, a child will come to recognize its own mother, maternal grandmother, mother's maternal grandmother, and maternal siblings. A female will later recognize her own offspring, daughters' offspring and granddaughter's offspring. It is unclear to what extent maternal aunts and sisters' daughters (nieces) are recognized as kin and it appears that maternal cousins are not distinguished from non-kin (Chapais 2008:39). This pattern marks the fullest extent of primate kin recognition and, of course, it is quite limited compared to that of humans.

For most primates, paternal kin will not be recognized at all because among them there are not close associations of fathers with mothers. And there is no other way (no known innate mechanism, for example) by which individuals in a primate group could know who was a father to whom. Among chimpanzees, for example, fathers and mothers have little association beyond mating, and mating is promiscuous, so that individuals cannot "know" paternity. Chimpanzee females also disperse out at maturity so that communities will not contain individuals who are maternally linked over the generations (grandmothers/ granddaughters etc). What we have in chimpanzee groups are adult males related through paternal links, but these links are not recognized. Maternal brothers (who will stay in the group) recognize each other through their association with their common mother. But paternal half-brothers (who share a common father but have separate mothers) will not recognize one another as kin and will behave toward one another no differently than they would toward non-kin. The same would hold for intergenerational paternal links (fathers sons/grandfathers/grandsons etc.).

Humans, in contrast to nonhuman primates, recognize kin links through both mothers and fathers. Kinship in all human societies is in this way **bilateral**. How could this have happened, or how did the human line develop bilateral kinship? The most likely idea is that it came about with pair-bonding, that is the development of fairly stable mating unions between a male and a female. Some primates are pair-bonded—gibbons, for example—but these pair-bonded primates live in isolated units, not in larger multi-male, multi-female groupings. If young primates in these units "know" their fathers, they know them through their association with the mother and as the only adult male in their unit; they are not able to trace connections *through the father*, that is they are not going to recognize father's kin, because a father's kin are not present in the group.

A probable key to the evolution of human-style kinship is the development of pair-bonding within multi-male, multi-female communities (Chapais 2008). With pair-bonding in this context, a new social structure consisting of multi-family groups emerges. With this structure, there is a "father" (mother's stable mate), and also potential recognition of father's kin—his father, his mother, and his brothers—through their association with one's father. By the same process, a father could recognize his own offspring (his stable mates' children). When this is added to the already existing ability to recognize one's own mother and, through her, one's own maternal siblings and other maternal kin, kinship recognition is considerably expanded and becomes bilateral.

Why and when humans developed pair-bonded mating is not known. The most prominent idea is that pair-bonding came about as a parental strategy. That is, evolving human infants came to require more care than mothers could provide by themselves; their survival came to depend on paternal care and protection as well. Primatologist Bernard Chapais (2008) however, suggests that human pair bonding likely developed earlier, before human infants came to require additional care. He suggests that pair-bonding probably developed instead as a mate-guarding strategy. Here, certain ecological conditions may have led to females foraging in very small groups such that one male could breed with them (pair-bond with each of them) and keep other males away. However it happened, human pair-bonding and the bilateral kinship it allowed changed human life forever.

Reproduction and Residence

All primate species (indeed, all mammals) generally avoid incestuous matings. **Incest** refers to heterosexual intercourse with primary kin, that is an individual's mother, father, sister and brother. There are good reasons for the avoidance of sex with close relatives; most notably, incestuous unions over time will bring about the loss of genetic diversity in a population and the probable accumulation of deleterious genes (Boyd and Silk 2011).

Nonhuman primates have a built-in mechanism of incest avoidance in their dispersal patterns. At puberty either males or females (or both) will disperse away from their natal group to join and mate within other groups. For example, among chimpanzees, males typically stay put and young females migrate out to join other groups. Among macaques, as we saw in Chapter 3, the males leave and the females stay put. Through this dispersal incestuous matings are avoided, although they do sometimes occur before a dispersal or when a dispersal fails to take place.

Human populations show something similar in what are called their postmarital residence norms, that is, conventions or rules about where couples live after marriage. Most cultures of the world follow **patrilocal** residence whereby the bride moves to the place of the groom and the couple lives with or near the groom's kin. Patrilocal residence is widespread throughout Asia, the Middle East and many parts of Africa. On every continent some peoples practice **matrilocal** residence, whereby the groom moves and the couple lives with or near the bride's natal group. In Europe and North America and increasingly in urban areas throughout the world, residence is often **neolocal**: the couple sets up an independent residence away from both the bride's and the groom's families. Much less common is **natolocal** residence whereby husbands and wives each remain with their natal groups and do not live together. Here brothers and sisters reside together for life, raising the sister's children together; husbands go off to visit their wives in other households for purposes of sex and procreation. Natolocal residence was practiced in times past among people of Tory Island off the coast of Ireland (Fox, 1978) and among the Nayar people of India. This pattern still exists in rural western Ireland, especially with last-born children, who have the responsibility to stay with and care for their parents and who stand to inherit the farm. There are a few other rare forms of residence among human cultures. Also, most human groups tolerate some exceptions to their residence norms.

As with the dispersal patterns of nonhuman primates, a consequence of human post-marital residence norms is that incestuous matings are largely averted although they do sometimes occur. But where incest is concerned, humans have gone beyond other primates to construct the nearly universal **incest taboo**, that is, the explicit prohibition of incest. Among humans, incest—where it is known to occur—is usually severely punished and met with attitudes of abhorrence and disgust. There are a few exceptions to the human incest taboo: royal (and some commoner) families in ancient Egypt allowed or encouraged brother-sister marriages and some royal father-daughter marriages occurred, as well. Brother-sister marriages also occurred among royal families of Peru (among the Inca) and Hawaii before the arrival of Euro Americans.

In addition to the nearly universal incest taboo prohibiting sexual activity between primary kin, most cultures also prohibit sexual relations between other people, some close kin but others not biological kin at all. For example, in many Islamic areas, sexual intercourse between a biologically unrelated male and a female who as infants were breast-fed by the same woman is prohibited and considered incestuous. In earlier times the Roman Catholic Church prohibited sex and marriage between godparents and biological parents, between godparents and godchildren, or between an individual and his/ her sibling's widow[er]. Some cultures prohibit sex and marriage between first cousins, while others do not; in some cultures, sex and marriage with a certain kind of cousin (say, a mother's sister's child) is prohibited while marriage with another type of cousin (say, a father's sister's child) is permitted and preferred. In many cases these additionally prohibited sexual unions are locally classified as "incestuous" and are as strongly prohibited, punished, and seen as abhorrent as is sex between primary kin. These additional prohibitions are often called "extensions of the incest taboo." While the incest taboo is nearly universal, these extensions are highly varied across cultures. One of the most uncommon extensions of the incest taboo is the !Kung prohibition on sex or marriage with a person who has the same name as that of a close relative. Since the !Kung have very few personal names, this can make the search for an appropriate mate for one's child quite a challenge.

Anthropologists have spent a large amount of time trying to explain the incest taboo and in particular why incest is usually seen as so abhorrent, but to this day we are not entirely sure. One idea that has helped to clarify the situation is known as the Westermarck Effect, named after Edward Westermarck. Westermarck (1891) proposed that persons who had been raised together in childhood were unlikely to develop sexual attraction for one another later in life. Something about the experience of close childhood associations dampens sexual interest later on. Possibly something similar occurs between adult parents and children that they raise. This idea has held up over time and indeed a lot of evidence supports it. For example, studies of the Israeli *kibbutzim* (communal villages), where groups of children were collectively raised, away from their parents, showed that neither romantic attachments nor marriages occurred among these children when they reached adulthood (Shepher 1983). Recent studies have also shown that a Westermarck effect may be operating among nonhuman primates (Pussey 2002). Still, although the Westermarck Effect may explain why rates of incest are low in human populations, it does not by itself go far to explain the nearly universal incest taboo. It somewhat begs the question: if humans are unlikely to be sexually attracted to their primary kin in the first place, why do we see such strong prohibitions of and sanctions against incest? It also fails to explain why brother-sister incest is more common than father-daughter or mother-son incest in so many societies, including our own.

However incest and the incest taboo are understood, both humans and nonhuman primates generally mate outside their immediate circle of kin and both show a movement of the young away from their natal groups—either a movement of males or females or both—for purposes of mating. Among humans, most reproduction is socially organized through and actually takes places within institutions of marriage. Marriage is, of course, absolutely unique to humans, but it does show interesting parallels with mating patterns of nonhuman primates in terms of form. Some nonhuman primates (e.g., hamadryas baboons) live in one-male, multi-female groups where the single male mates with the several females. Other primates (e.g., chimpanzees) live in multi-male, multi-female groups where mating is largely promiscuous. Others (e.g., for example saddle-back tamarins) live in groups where several males live and mate with a single female. And still others (i.e., gibbons) show a pattern whereby one male and one female form a stable mating unit.

Human marriages take three forms: **monogamy** (a union of two persons, usually a man and a woman), **polygyny** (a union of one man and two or more women at the same time) and **polyandry** (a union of one woman and two or more men at the same time). Polygyny and polyandry may each be referred to as **polygamy.** It appears, then, that humans have largely retained the mating patterns of nonhuman primates, although they have dropped the promiscuous pattern displayed by chimpanzees. Of course, it goes without saying that human sexual intercourse or mating can and does take place outside marriage; similarly, some intercourse and matings among nonhuman primates take place outside the monogamous, polygynous, or polyandrous units that form the dominant patterns of some species. In the present-day United States, as well as some other countries, increasing numbers of children are born outside marriage to women who may never marry the fathers of these children or any other man. In the United States in the early part of the twenty-first century, roughly 40 percent of all children are born to unmarried mothers, who may or may not reside with their children's fathers (Mundy 2012).

Among humans, the vast majority of all marital unions are monogamous. In some places (for example, the United States), only monogamous unions are legally recognized. In many other societies polygyny is permitted, as is the case throughout parts of Asia, the Middle East and Africa. But even in areas that permit polygyny, monogamous unions are more common. In Asia and the Middle East polygynous unions account for only two to four percent of all unions. In parts of Africa it is higher, reaching up to 35 percent of all unions in some areas.

Poyandry is very rare and for this reason it has attracted the attention of anthropologists. It occurs in areas of Tibet, Nepal, and India, and was practiced among some Native American groups. A good example of polyandry is found among the Nyinba people of northwest Nepal, a small group of Tibetan Buddhists who practice agriculture, livestock herding, and long-distance trade (Levine 1988). The Nyinba practice **fraternal polyandry** whereby brothers share a wife. In a Nyinba household, generally the eldest brother marries first; when he does, his younger brothers automatically become husbands of this woman as well, acquiring sexual and procreative rights in her. Sexual jealousy among brothers is culturally discouraged and rarely expressed. Usually the wife spends the night with one husband at a time and she should distribute her time and attention equally among her husbands. The Nyinba show two features that are common among polyandrous societies. One is that in these societies many men are frequently away from their communities for long periods, engaging in, for example, warfare, or, as among the Nyinba, long-distance trading. Thus not all of a woman's husbands are necessarily present at the same time. Second, the Nyinba live in a rugged, challenging environment in which significant growth in the human population would considerably strain resources. In the case of the Nyinba this is a mountainous environment with precarious natural resources. Anthropologists have considered that polyandry in these environments is advantageous because it limits population growth. If several brothers each took a separate wife they would potentially produce more children than if they shared one wife. And in the mountainous region of Nepal, the Nyinba have attained a notably greater prosperity than neighboring groups that do not practice polyandry.

Lineages and Ancestors

One thing humans do with kinship connections is to use them as the basis for important, enduring groups. These groups persist through time and over the gen-

Figure 6.2   A polyandrous family in Tibet.
Photo courtesy of Bill Amoy.

erations. New members may be added through birth and deleted through death, but the group itself lives on, giving some stability and continuity to the human society. As noted before, among some Old World monkeys kinship serves a very similar function—the formation of distinct, ranked matrilineages that constitute subgroups in the primate community. These primates are showing a recognition of maternal kinship over the generations and the use of this recognition for the formation of distinct groups which are important to the social structure of the community. In addition, as we saw in Chapter 3, this lineal structure determines relative rank among the females (and young yet-to-disperse males) of the community. Using the Kinship Code, we can visualize a community of such primate matrilinages as in Figure 6.3 below. This diagram shows four matrilineages. The males within them will move out when they mature. The adult males of this group have migrated in from other communities.

Humans have gone beyond this use of lineages in three significant ways. First, their lineages include both sexes in life-long membership. Second, humans have constructed **patrilineages** as well as matrilineages. And third, humans have developed and used the concept of common ancestors to form

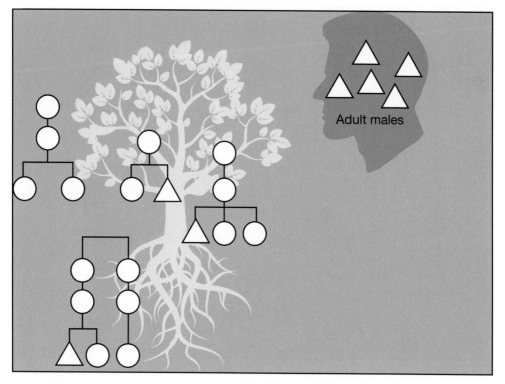

Figure 6.3. A hypothetical community of nonhuman primates with matrilineages. Males born into these units migrate out at maturity; adult males have migrated in from other groups.

groups. We will look first at the inclusion of both sexes in life-long membership in a group. In a nonhuman primate matrilineage, membership in the group
is transmitted to females through mothers. The young yet-to-disperse males
are in a sense temporary members of these groups; they hang out and interact
with others within these units and their rank within their larger community
is set by the rank of their matrilineage. But these males will leave, severing
forever all ties with these matrilineal groupings. Figure 6.4 shows a human
matrilineage, where persons sharing matrilineal descent are shaded. Here we
see something new: males as well as females are members of the group on
a permanent basis. The males are life-long members whether they disperse
out or not. Males assume membership through their mothers but they cannot
transmit this membership to their own children. Only their sisters can do this.
In human communities the children of these males will be members of their
wives' matrilineal units.

From this discussion so far, we can see an important difference between
human and nonhuman primate lineages: only in human lineages are ties maintained with the young members who disperse out. These young persons are

Figure 6.4 A human matrilineal descent construct. Members of the matriline are shaded.
Both males and females are members of their mother's matriline but only females can pass
this membership on to their children.

not temporary members of lineages; they are permanent members. They do not sever ties with their natal kin but maintain those ties for life. Some primatologists have drawn attention to this unique feature of human life, pointing out that the human way of life and kinship entails the capacity to recognize kin even after long periods of separation (Rodseth et al). This, they maintain, likely required the development of human language.

Next we can look at Figure 6.5. This shows a human patrilineage where membership is traced through males only. Males and females are both born into the group but only males can pass this membership on to their children in the next generation. The children of the female members will be members of these females' husband's patrilineal groups. Nothing like this is found in nonhuman primate communities.

Finally, humans, in contrast to nonhuman primates, have developed concepts of common ancestors, which they use to form their matrilinal or patrilineal lineages. Thus some nonhuman primates recognize maternal kin over the

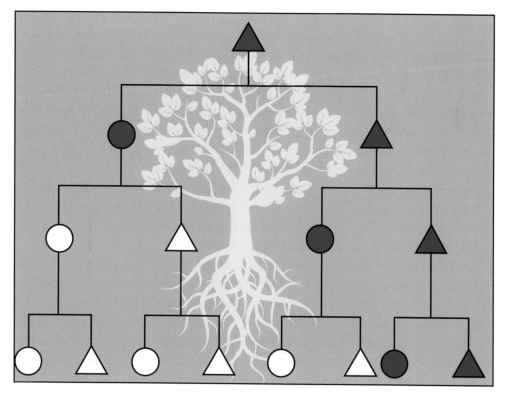

Figure 6.5 A patrilineal descent construct. Persons sharing partilineal descent are shaded. Both males and females are members of their father's patriline but only males can pass this membership on to their children.

generations (which is quite remarkable in itself) but humans can conceptualize their groups in terms of descent from a common ancestor in the remote past. Thus all the descendants of so-and-so (however many generations back) traced through women (for matrilineages) or men (for patrilineages) are members of the descent group. The group is named, and all members inherit the name so that everyone knows from the names which group he/ she belongs to and to which group everyone else belongs. In this way a rather large number of people can be organized into distinct descent groups.

In lineages, members trace their descent to a common ancestor through genealogically known links. Another type of descent group we find in many societies is known as a **clan.** This differs from a lineage in that members of a clan cannot (or can no longer) trace their links with one another through the common ancestor. Usually, too many generations have passed, and the exact links among people have become obscured. Often the founding ancestor of a clan is perceived not as a real person but as a mythological figure, an animal, plant (e.g. bear, lion, sage brush), or a supernatural being, and often this mythological figure is worshipped in common by members of the descent group. This religious worship of a kin group's founding being as a symbol of group identity is called **totemism.** In many societies, lineages are subdivisions of clans; other societies may have clans but no lineages or lineages but no clans.

Aside from matrilineal and patrilineal descent (both of which are **unilineal**, tracing descent through only one sex) there are two other modes of descent in human societies: **cognatic** and **bilateral** (both are *nonunilineal*). In cognatic decent members connect themselves to common ancestors through any combination of male or female links. For example, a member of a cognatic descent group might be a son's son's child of a founding ancestor or he/she might be a son's daughter's child. Both males and females pass on membership in the cognatic descent group. Cognatic decent is or was found among Scottish clans in Europe and the Maori people of New Zealand.

Finally, bilateral descent characterizes societies that trace kin connections over the generations through both male and female links (like cognatic descent) but *without the formation of descent groups*. In these societies decent is conceptualized cognatically but there is no overall organization of people into distinct descent groups. There are no lineages and clans, as such. Euro-American societies are examples of bilateral decent, as are many hunting-gathering groups (although some of the latter do have other modes of descent). Thus it is societies at the ends of a techno-economic spectrum—with foraging at one end and urban, industrial capitalism at the other—where we typically find bilateral descent and lack of descent groups, or at least lack of strong descent groups. But among societies in the middle of this spectrum—rural horticultural or agricultural groups—we see societies with descent groups (whether matrilineal, patrilineal, or cognatic) that are also **corporate decent groups,** and this feature gives them a lot of power. A corporate decent group is one where members own some important assets in common and share rights, privileges, and liabilities. The assets may be valuable property such as land, but can also be more abstract—for example, sacred religious lore or special healing knowledge. If a society's descent groups are corporate, they will likely exert a great deal of power over all individual members, determining, for example, when and who they will marry, their rights to use certain natural resources and their rights to reside in specific territories; they will also determine an individual's most basic identity in the society and will engender a strong sense of solidarity with the descent group.

At this point, it will be helpful to look inside some real human societies to show how descent and descent groups operate, particularly in the case of unilineal descent which is probably less familiar to most readers. But first, a word of caution is in order for matrilineal descent. Many people have mistakenly assumed that matrilineal societies are **matriarchal**, that is, female-dominant or ruled by women. Many scholars of the nineteenth century made a similar mistake. They postulated that the first human societies were matriarchal, ruled by women, but that with time and "advancement" they became patriarchal. When these scholars encountered contemporary matrilineal societies, they saw their form of descent as a remnant or carry-over of a matriarchal past. Today anthropologists stress that matrilineal only means decent through women; it does not suggest what gender relationships are like in the society. In some matrilineal societies women exert a great deal of power (e.g., among the Iroquois of North America); in others (e.g., the Nayar of India), women and children were strictly under the authority of the women's brothers. Anthropologists also point out that we have not found any cases of true matriarchal societies on the planet, past or present. There are plenty of cases of societies that are gender equal or near-equal, such as the Navajo of the southwest United States, the Mosuo of China and the !Kung (or Ju//'hoansi) of southern Africa. And women in all societies play important—sometimes often powerful—roles. But cases of truly female dominant groups, where men are subjugated and do not assume positions of extra-domestic power and authority (or do so only very exceptionally) have not been found.

A good example of a matrilineal society is found among the Hopi Indians of Arizona. The Hopi are divided into matrilineal clans, and each clan is associated with an animal (such as Bear or Snake), plant, or some natural force. Marriages within the clan are forbidden. The Hopi clan is a strong, corporate group that owns land along with ritual knowledge and paraphernalia. Male clan members are obliged to perform certain religious ceremonies within Hopi culture; female clan members are in charge of the preparations for these ceremonies. The Hopi are well-known for their elaborate religious rituals, which are interwoven with their kinship organization. The Hopi clans are subdivided into matrilineages which are headed by senior women, although these women's brothers or mother's brothers assume official roles in lineage affairs. The Hopi are also matrilocal. Men move into their wives' households and farm the land of their wives' matrilineal groups. Men have considerable authority over their sisters' children but very little authority over their own children. As in many matrilineal societies the tie between brothers and sisters among the Hopi is strong, and that between husbands and wives is relatively weak. Divorce is easy: women may simply kick out their husbands or husbands may simply leave their wives.

Patrilineal societies are far more prevalent than matrilineal ones; they cover large areas of Asia, the Middle East and many parts of Africa. Patrilineal descent is in fact the most prevalent form of descent among human societies. To see how some of them work we can take a look at patrilineal descent in pre-Revolutionary China (before 1949), using the ethnography of Martin Yang (1945), an anthropologist who studied the village of his birth. Here the primary kinship group was the patrilineage, a corporate descent group which spanned five or more generations. Within lineages, inheritance of property (land and other valuables) passed from fathers to sons (women did not usually inherit). Each lineage also had its own ancestral shrine, and worship of ancestors was extremely important; for one thing, unplaced ancestors could cause considerable harm to their living patrilineal descendants. Within lineages, relationships were strongly hierarchical. Sons were to be strictly subservient to their fathers and all senior male lineage kin. It was also the duty of all males to marry and have sons to reproduce the lineage. Women at marriage were rather fully incorporated into the patrilineages of their husbands (retaining very few rights in their natal patrilineages) but they were culturally seen as marginal to these groups. Even though women bore children for their husbands' patrilineages, Chinese people perceived their lineages as pure lines of males extending back in time and into the future. Marriages were arranged by parents, and brides and grooms were often strangers to one another. A bride moved patrilocally into her husband's home where she assumed a low status and was seen as an untrustworthy outsider. She was to be subservient to her husband and especially to her mother-in-law. Gradually her status in the household rose when she bore sons for the lineage and eventually, when her own sons married, she could become a powerful mother-in-law herself. If she failed to bear children, her husband would likely take a secondary wife. In Yang's village, the patrilineage was the core of society and patrilineal kin relationships affected every aspect of people's lives, determining economic relationships, marriages, and interpersonal authority; lineages connected the living with the dead, and everywhere engendered a sense of lineage honor incumbent on all members to protect.

China has seen many changes since 1949, but a great deal of its patrilineal ideology and practice, including ancestor worship, is still evident today in rural areas. In broad outline this patrilineal kinship system, with cultural variations, also obtains throughout South Asia—India, Nepal and Sri Lanka. Clearly it is a kinship structure and supporting ideology that impacts gender relationships. The emphasis on a pure line of male descent, the importance of male reproduction, the concern to protect patrilineage honor—these features have been referred to as a culturally construed "lineal masculinity" and have been highly important in specifying a favoring of sons and a subservient status of women in these regions (King and Stone (2010).

MARRIAGE, AFFINES AND ALLIANCE

Nonhuman primates have mating patterns; humans have marriage. Among humans, marriage is a cultural universal. That is, marriage occurs in all societies, though not all humans are married, and mating also occurs outside marriage. There is only one case to our knowledge of a culture that might be said to not have (or not to have had) marriage at all, and even this case is uncertain. This is the Mosuo of southwest China, a matrilineal group of rural agriculturists who speak a Tibeto-Burman language and practice a form of Tibetan Buddhism. The Mosuo lived natolocally, where brothers and sisters remained together for life. Men and women formed sexual relationships called *tisese* ("walking back and forth") whereby men went to visit their lovers at night in the women's homes, leaving early the next morning (Cai 2008, Shih 2010). Women and men each had any number of *tisese* relationships. These could be initiated or broken off at any time by either party and they involved no obligations of any kind between the man and the woman or between their families; they entailed no ritual celebrations, no financial transactions, nothing. Children were members of their mother's matrilineal groups. Men had no rights in or authority over their own biological children; they had little interest in knowing which children might be their own. These *tisese* relations cannot be considered "marriage" in any sense of the term, but the Mosuo also did have actual marriage (a contractual union involving rights and obligations) as an option although, at least in 1989, only about 14 percent of adults in one village entered this type of union (Shih 2010). Still, according to Cai Hua (2008), the Chinese Quig Dynasty imposed this actual marriage on the upper levels of Mosuo society, particularly on the family of the Mosuo chief, in 1644. If this is true, then prior to 1644 the Mosuo would have been a culture without marriage.

Marriages often involve transfers of wealth from one family to another. A common form of marriage payment is known as **bridewealth**, that is, a transfer of wealth from the kin of the groom to the kin of the bride at marriage. In many areas this bridewealth is seen as compensation to the bride's family for the loss of the bride and her labor, and/ or as a wealth transfer that secures the rights over the bride's fertility to the husband's group. Another form of marriage payment is **dowry**, or wealth given by kin of the bride that accompanies the bride at marriage. The ultimate destination of dowry wealth varies. Commonly it goes to the marrying couple to be used by them and to be inherited by their children, but in some cases (as throughout north India today) most of the dowry wealth ends up with the kin of the groom. Dowry is common in Asia (and formerly in Europe) while bridewealth is widespread in sub-Saharan Africa (Goody 1976). In very general terms dowry is associated with stratified societies where female contributions to subsistence are minor and where women are subordinate to men. Here, dowry is used to match a bride's family's wealth with the wealth and status of the groom's family and so ensure that marriages and wealth remain within class boundaries. In this way upper-class wealth does not seep out to lower orders through inappropriate marriages. In these systems there are sharp restrictions on female sexual behavior to prevent premarital pregnancy; otherwise a lower-class male might impregnate a woman and then claim rights to her and her dowry wealth (Stone 2014a).

Marriages are formal institutionalized unions, usually celebrated with elaborate rituals, and, depending on the society in question, often have numerous functions, for example, legitimizing children or signifying adult status of those entering into the union. The form, nature, and meaning of marriages vary widely cross-culturally, but one thing marriages do in virtually all societies is unite two separate groups of people; they create affinal relationships (in-laws). Nothing comparable to this is found in the nonhuman primate world. Among nonhuman primates, relationships among separate local communities are either non-existent or hostile. Young nonhuman primates disperse out and join new local groups, but the groups themselves do not become allied to one another in this process.

Figure 6.6   A Nepalese wedding.
Source: Authors' collection.

Anthropologists have long considered that this is precisely what human marriages do and why they developed in our species: marriages create inter-group *alliances*. They potentially establish peace between groups. No doubt this was a good thing, given that over the Paleolithic period humans were becoming increasingly armed and dangerous, developing ever more effective weapons. As one anthropologist of the nineteenth century put it: "Again and again in the world's history, savage tribes must have had before them the simple practical alternative between marrying out or being killed out" (Tylor 1889:267). Marriage, then, was a way of linking groups in non-hostile, potentially cooperative associations, paving the way for higher levels of organization beyond the local community—that is, organization into bands, tribes, chiefdoms etc.

The human way of insuring that marriages would establish inter-group alliances was to institute rules of **exogamy**; that is, a rules specifying that one must marry *outside* particular categories or groups—for example, outside one's village or outside one's lineage, clan etc. For the most part, unilineal decent groups (patrilineal or matrilineal lineages and clans) are exogamous (exceptions will be noted shortly), and it is presumed that early human groups practiced descent group exogamy. In addition, many cultures have marriage rules that ensure *perpetual* alliances between descent groups. Claude Lévi-Strauss (1969) was among the first anthropologists to analyze this situation. He noted that while some peoples merely have a rule of descent group exogamy, some others have in addition a rule that one must marry not only outside one's own group but also *into* a specific other group (he called these "elementary systems"). In its simplest form, such a system specifies that people of Group A must marry people of Group B and vice versa. Groups A and B are then not just marrying out, they are *exchanging spouses*; in the process they are perpetually linked together; they are dependent on one another for spouses. A slightly more complicated arrangement is where descent groups marry "in a circle." Here, women of Group A marry men of Group B; women of Group B marry men of Group C and women of Group C marry men of group A. More than three groups can be involved in such a system. In this kind of circle system, all of the participating groups are perpetually linked together. In Levi-Strauss' view, human marriage began as a spouse exchange that produced alliances between and among groups. Marriage began as a means of inter-group alliance. Whatever the origin, it is clear that throughout many different places and times, marriage has been used strategically to create or cement political alliances, to ally one's own family with wealthy or powerful in-laws, or to acquire affines who will be dependent on and loyal to one's own family. It is only fairly recently and in a few places (notably Euro-American areas) that marriages have been seen as primarily enacted for the happiness of the couple involved.

At this point it might be interesting to point out a variety of exogamy that is different from the rest: the rule or law that one must marry outside one's sex or gender category. While this regulation is extremely common, it is far from universal. Woman-woman marriages are known, primarily in sub-Saharan Africa. Here, a barren woman may marry another woman, who then conceives a child with a man. This child will belong to the infertile woman (and will address her as "father") and be a member of the woman's natal patrilineage. The woman then has a child to help her as she ages and inherit her property when she dies. Cases of male-male marriages are known, for example, among Native American groups. In these situations a male wife (individuals originally described as *berdaches* by anthropologists, and now more often called "two spirit" persons, following some Native preferences) is a gynomimetic, a man who takes the role, dress, and demeanor of a woman. This male wife almost always is one of several wives, so that the husband can have children. But the relationship provides sexual variety for the husband.

Marriages may also be governed by **endogamy rules**, or rules that one must marry *within* a particular category or group. For example some societies divided into castes have rules of caste endogamy. In the United States we see a strong pattern of class endogamy, although there is no explicit rule about this. And there are also cases where there is a rule, a pattern or a preference for descent group endogamy—one must or in any case should, if possible, marry within one's lineage or clan. In a patrilineal system for example, a man would be permitted or encouraged to marry his father's brother's daughter, who is a member of his patrilineage. Patrilineal descent group endogamous marriages are common and often encouraged in Arabic cultures of the Middle East. In many cases one is not marrying a first cousin but a person classified as a patrilineal cousin, say, a man marrying his father's father's brother's son's son's daughter (a second cousin once removed). Kin group endogamous marriages lose the advantage of reaching outward and forming alliances with outsiders, but they have other advantages. Where the group involved has considerable wealth or power, descent group endogamy ensures that the wealth and power stay within the descent group over time. In other words, young people will not take their inherited wealth or position of power with them into another group at marriage. This is the main reason that peoples practicing descent group endogamy give for the practice. We do not know but presume that descent group endogamous marriages came later in the human scene and first developed among the wealthier, more powerful segments of stratified societies. If we look at the rise of powerful empires (for example the Roman Empire), we often see that the power-seekers start out with rigorous use of kin group exogamous marriages to gain and consolidate alliances. Then, once secure in power they or their descendants switch to kin group endogamous marriages to maintain their power and wealth and ensure that it not seep out to other groups (Stone 2014a).

KINSHIP TERMINOLOGY

All human groups linguistically classify their kin, but they distinguish kin in quite different ways. Thus in English "cousin" can mean one's mother's brother's child, one's mother's sister's child, one's father's brother's child or one's father's sister's child. In some other classification systems these kin are covered by four different terms. In English one's mother is distinguished from one's mother's sister by a separate term (aunt) whereas in another system, these two kin are called by the same term.

Anthropologists determine the system of kinship terminology for any cultural group by placing an ego (the person from whose perspective the kinship terms are applied) at the center of a diagram, tracing out various kin from ego and then labeling what term ego uses for each of his/her kin. When this is done, different systems can be compared and some distinctive features of each system can be noted. For example, if we do this for an English kinship terminology system we will quickly see that kin terms here highlight a core nuclear family set of relationships by giving a distinctive term for each possible member—mother, father, brother sister, son, daughter. Beyond that core grouping, many kin are merged together—for example "cousins" as noted above but also father's brother and mother's brother are merged (uncle) as are mother's sister and father's sister (aunt). Grandparents all are merged together and only distinguished by sex. This kinship terminology system reflects the cultural importance of the nuclear family to the people who use the system. It also reflects the bilateral nature of decent in this system; that is, relatives traced through the father are not distinguished from relatives traced through the mother. By contrast, in unilineal descent systems these relatives have a very different relationship to ego. For example in a patrilineal system, father's brother belongs to ego's own descent group whereas mother's brother does not. Normally in unilineal systems, these two relatives are called by different terms.

With this in mind, take a look at the system in Figure 6.7. This is known as the Hawaiian system and was in use among indigenous Hawaiians before 1800 in pre-contact times It is also currently used in other parts of Polynesia and in Melanesia. Here kin are distinguished only on the basis of generation and sex. Hence there are very few terms in the whole system. Notice that a nuclear family is not linguistically carved out and that ego's terms for primary kin are the same as terms used for collateral kin. Hawaiian kinship terminology is associated with societies that lack corporate descent groups or that have cognatic decent.

While cultures vary in how they classify kin, all classification systems in the world can be grouped into a few basic types. The Hawaiian system is one such type. The English kin terminology discussed above belongs to the Eskimo system (named for the Inuit, who were once called Eskimos). Each system as it is actually used may have its little quirks, but no known system is unique in its basic form. We are unsure why this is so, but it is interesting that there appear to be limitations on the cultural variation of kinship classification. There are some ideas that early humans developed one system (most think it was a system called Dravidian) from which the others were later transformations (Godeleir 1998, Allen 2008). In a Davidian system, one's father's

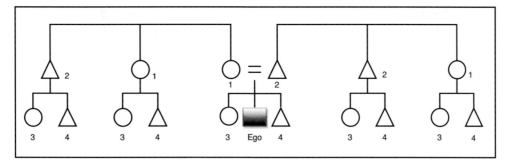

Figure 6.7   Hawaiian kinship terminology. Kin who are designated by the same term are labeled with the same number. In this system, kin are terminologically distinguished only on the basis of sex and generation.

brother's children and one's mother's sister's children are classed as one's siblings and marriage with them is prohibited. One's father's sister's children and one's mother's brother's children are distinguished from siblings and marriage with them is allowed.

THE CULTURAL CONSTRUCTION OF KINSHIP

The final kinship contrast between human and nonhuman primates is that humans not only recognize and calculate their kinship connections, they also culturally construct them. We are all aware of practices such as adoption, blood-brotherhood, god-parenthood, and so on, that create strong and lasting kin-like bonds among people. We do not see this among nonhuman primates although there is one primate behavior that possibly shows a glimmer of this capacity. It often has been reported among chimpanzees and other primate species (and even among other mammals) that an adult female will raise her dead sister's orphaned infant as if, for all practical purposes, it were her own.

In any event, humans are extremely creative with kinship, showing the unique flexibility afforded them by their elaborate cultural capacities. In a nutshell, humans are able to *make* kin as well as grow their own. This occurs in two ways. One is the institution of practices like adoption which are often seen by the people themselves as "as if" kin relationships; that is, people understand them as *like* kinship or *modeled on* kinship but different from actual kinship. In anthropology these relationships are sometimes referred to as **fictive kinship**. Another way that many peoples create kin is through non-biological cultural constructions of kinship itself. Here, kinship is locally understood to be based on common residence, certain rituals, food sharing and/ or other behaviors (Schneider 1984). This is not fictive kinship; the bonds created are locally understood to be as strong as, if not stronger than, bonds of "blood." In some parts of New Guinea for instance, some kin groupings are formed through common residence rather than through presumed biological relationships. For another example, Janet Carsten (1995), has shown how among Malays on the island of Langkawi, kinship emerges over time through acts of receiving and giving food and through sharing of hearth space. These actions can create kinship between people who are known not to be biological kin. In turn, if these acts are discontinued or reduced over time, even among biologically related people, the sense of kinship between them is likewise seen to lessen or cease. The work of Carsten and others has demonstrated that among many peoples kinship is *a process* that is constructed gradually over time, and not necessarily established once and for all through acts of birth.

Clearly, a presumed biological connection between people is not the only basis for human kinship construction, although worldwide it is the most common basis. Biogenetic kinship is also central to Euro-American constructions of kinship as pointed out long ago by David Schneider (1968). Americans perceive kinship as based on blood relationships, whereby practices like adoption *are* cases of fictive kinship. But it cannot be presumed that other peoples perceive their kinship in this strong and exclusive biogenetic way.

Non-biological constructions of kinship exist in all societies and for good reason: human groups can apply kinship flexibly to link up with and/or incorporate outsiders as well as to organize actual or presumed biological kin. This flexible use of kinship is then similar to the use of exogamous marriage to forge interpersonal and inter-group alliances. Humans can thus extend kinship terms to outsiders or use rituals, acts of feeding, and so on, to establish kinship with non-kin or even strangers (Rodseth and Wrangham 2004:390, Stone 2014b, Stone and Lurquin 2007:225). Over time, the bonds of kinship so created may be even stronger and more durable than affinal bonds formed through intermarriage. In any event, the essence of human kinship is not only the ability to recognize (presumably real) kin but also to make kin, all in one system.

Many cultural anthropologists, probably the majority, see kinship as a purely cultural construction (Sahlins 2013). In this view, ideas and practices concerning kinship vary widely from culture to culture such that kinship can only be understood within each culture separately. These anthropologists deny that kin selection theory applies to humans, that there is a biological basis for human construction and use of kinship systems, and that perceived biological or genetic connections are universally understood in all cultures to constitute kinship. Another view, the one emphasized here, is that kinship is both biological and cultural. It is biological in the sense that it emerged in human society through our bio-cultural evolution; it is a part of our primate heritage. In this view, kin recognition and kin-favoring behavior likely arose in humans, as in many other species, through a process of kin selection. This view of kinship grants that non-biological bases for kinship are found in many cultures and that in some cases these are locally understood as more significant than perceived biological connections. These non-biological bases for kinship reflect the distinctively human capacity to create kin, or extend kinship status to non-biological kin, as well as recognize or presume biological connections between people. What humans evolved is a "capacity for kinship" comparable to a capacity for language. Like the many languages humans speak, kinship systems vary widely; yet these are variations on common themes of descent, marriage, residence, and classification of relatives.

Kinship and Culture Change

We are now in a position to roughly characterize any kinship system in the world simply by noting its mode of descent, post-marital residence pattern, and marriage forms. Thus we can say that most people in the contemporary United States and Europe are bilateral, neolocal, and monogamous. We could add that they use Eskimo kinship terminology. The Nuer of Africa were patrilineal, patrilocal, and polygynous-monogamous while the Nayar of India were matrilineal, natolocal, and polygynous-polyandrous. These different dimensions of kinship systems do not necessarily vary together. Thus, whereas most parilineal societies are also patrilocal, this is not always the case. The Mundurucú of Brazil for example are patrilineal-matrilocal. Here men move to the villages of their wives upon marriage, but there they live together in a men's house. Their wives live in separate houses with their own mothers, sisters, own children and sisters' children. In these households members belong to different descent groups—that of their fathers.

The combinations of the different dimensions of kinship systems result in considerable cross-cultural variation, but what accounts for this diversity? Why, for example, are some groups matrilineal and others patrilineal? Why are some monogamous while others permit or prefer polygyny? We cannot precisely answer this question, but anthropologists have come up with some clues. Many of these concern ecological considerations. We have already seen the argument that polyandry fosters lower population growth and that this is advantageous in rugged, challenging physical environments. Some anthropologists have suggested that as humans evolved and spread across the globe, modes of descent followed from patterns of residence, which in turn were fostered by ecological constraints and modes of subsistence. So, for example, groups in which women collectively performed the major subsistence tasks (as in hoe-based horticulturte) would benefit from matrilocal residence as this would keep kin-related, potentially cooperative groups of women together. Societies where cooperative groups of males were needed for major subsistence tasks (such as hunting or plow-based agriculture) would benefit from patrilocal residence. Patterns of descent would follow accordingly. However, the ethnographic evidence does not support this line of argument; we do not see strong correlations between residence forms and the division of labor by sex.[2] Some anthropologists have postulated that kinship systems, like language, are relatively slow to change, possibly because many aspects of kinship systems are learned early in life and so are resistant to modification. In this view a patrilineal/patrilocal system could develop under certain ecological conditions and then remain intact through cultural transmission even when ecological conditions and mode of subsistence change (Hewlett, Silvestri, and Gugliemino 2002).

But for all the stability of kinship systems, we are seeing profound changes in kinship around the world at the present time. Many of these changes are being acutely felt in the United States and Europe, but some are also having an impact nearly everywhere. One important change concerns the development of New Reproductive Technologies (NRTs)—surrogate motherhood, artificial insemination through sperm donation, in-virto fertilization, and many others. These technologies assist couples to have a child, but they have also fragmented motherhood. The genetic mother, the birth mother and the legal mother of a child may be three different people. These technologies also permit gay and lesbian couples to reproduce children genetically related to both of them. For example, a woman could undergo artificial insemination using the sperm of her lesbian partner's brother. Different cultures are responding in different and very interesting ways to these technologies. In Israel, for example, some people are concerned that use of donor sperm could result in a kind of "adultery" of sperm and egg where the women undergoing the procedure is married and the donor a Jewish man. Adultery in this Jewish state is defined as sexual intercourse between a Jewish man and a married Jewish woman not married to that man As a result of this, some rabbis encourage the use of non-Jewish sperm for married Jewish women seeking a child through artificial insemination (Kahn 2000). Of course, in Jewish traditional law, Jewish identity is passed through the mother, so that a Jewish woman's children will be Jewish regardless of who the biological father may be.

Another important kinship change in Europe and the United States concerns the form of the family. In the United States a nuclear family consisting of a neolocal heterosexual couple with their own biological children was for long a cultural ideal. In the 1960s about 45 percent of American households took this form; today under 20 percent do, and today, as mentioned earlier in this chapter, about 40 percent of children are born to unmarried mothers. Far more common these days than in the past are single-person households, single-parent households and so-called "blended family" households consisting of parent/child units along with step-parents and step-siblings. Also significant are the growing numbers of "never-married mothers," unmarried women who elect to keep their extranuptial (or out-of-wedlock) children and remain single (McKee and Stone 2007).

Today the divorce rate in the United States is around 50 percent (and has been since the 1960s). On the whole, marriage is in decline. For one thing, it is occurring at later ages; the average age of marriage in the United States for women is now 26 and for males is 29 (up from 20 and 23, respectively, in the 1960s). For another, remarriage after divorce is declining (Coontz, 2006), and more couples are choosing to co-habit rather than marry. Meanwhile, women in the workforce are not only out-numbering men but are finally closing the wage gap. Today nearly 40 percent of wives out-earn their husbands (Mundy 2012:6). Other changes include an increase in the number of persons who live alone (now a quarter of all households in the United States are single-person households, Coontz 2006), an increase in married or co-habiting couples who choose to remain childless, and in general a shrinking family size. Altogether we are seeing diversification of family forms and domestic living, a rising tolerance of this diversity, and an opening of options concerning sex, marriage, and family (Coontz, 2006).

While many young adults are retreating from or considerably delaying marriage, one group—gay/lesbian rights activists—seeks to legalize same sex marriage and, where legalized, significant numbers of gay and lesbian couples are getting married (Stone 2004a). Same sex marriage is now the law of the land in the United States as well as in many European countries. Today many same-sex couples are raising children, acquired either through new reproductive technologies or from previous heterosexual unions of one or both partners. Those opposed to same-sex marriage have voiced concerns that these unions are in some way detrimental to the welfare of children. This is emphatically not the case, as innumerable studies have by now shown. (Mezey, 2015). Children of same-sex unions do as well in school, are as suc-

Figure 6.8   A same-sex wedding ceremony.
Photo: John Jiao, Flickr (Yahoo.com).

cessful later in life, and enjoy as much stability and well being as children of heterosexual unions.

Now in the twenty-first century, we are seeing a new landscape of marriage and the family, new options and choices, new stresses and strains. What do all of these changes mean? Perhaps it is too early to offer any coherent interpretation, but there are a few ideas that may shed light on some of the trends. One is that the changes seem to be bringing a shift in the United States and Europe from biogenetic-based kinship to choice-based kinship (Stone 2001, 2004b). Many step-parents, step-children and step-siblings, for example, emphasize that they have real and meaningful kinship with people to whom they are not biologically connected; they *choose* their kinship and make a personal commitment to that choice. The same emphasis on choice is seen among women whose children are born of a surrogate mother (Ragone 1994) and among many who adopt children. Another idea is that marriage has become outmoded, partly because of techno-economic changes and the impact of these on gender relationships. Women no longer need husbands for economic survival—they can survive and support children on their own earnings, even if these earnings are low—and, given fast foods, permanent press clothing, cleaning services etc., men no longer need wives for domestic services (McKee and Stone 2007).

Some people in the United States see these changes in marriage and family form as a "breakdown" of *the* family, a threat to family stability. Others see some of these changes as positive, allowing more choice and flexibility in domestic life. We have certainly seen throughout this book and especially in this chapter that cross-culturally there is no *one* family form; a variety of arrangements allow for the meeting of human needs and aspirations, some benefiting certain people and their interests over others. Finally, it is always helpful to see change, as such, in a long-term perspective. In the Middle Ages there were laws all over Europe safeguarding men's right to beat their wives (Gottlieb 1993). In the nineteenth century in the United States, courts automatically assumed that custody of children should be given to husbands in cases of marital separation, and at that time the legal age of sexual consent for girls was 10 to 12 years old in most states (Coontz 2006)! Astounding as it may seem in hindsight, many objected to changes in these laws and assumptions and saw them as threats to the proper order of men, women and families.

SUMMARY

This chapter has explored the topics of kinship and marriage by contrasting human patterns with comparable features among nonhuman primates. The comparison has shown that humans are unique in their tracing of kinship bilaterally, their recognition of common ancestors, their use of marriage to form inter-group alliances, their recognition of in-laws, their use of kinship terminology and their cultural construction of kinship. We have also discussed how human kinship may have developed from a primate baseline during our evolution. Table 6.1 on the next page summarizes the difference between humans and nonhuman primates according to several aspects of kinship listed on the right of the table.

The table makes clear that many aspects of human kinship (the first four on the table) are rooted in our primate heritage. The last four, unique to our species, are more complex features that may have emerged primarily through human pair-bonding and the development of language.

TABLE 6.1

Kinship aspects	Nonhuman Primates	Humans
1. Reproduction	a. Incest avoidance	a. Incest taboo
	b. Mating patterns	b. Marriage forms
2. Residence	Dispersal patterns	Post-marital residence
3. Kinship recognition	Limited	Expanded
4. Lineages	Yes	Yes, varied
	(matrilineages among some species)	
5. Common ancestors	No	Yes
6. Inter-group alliances	No	Yes
7. Kinship terminology	No	Yes
8. Cultural construction of kinship	No	Yes

We have also seen in this chapter how kinship and marriage are currently undergoing profound changes in many areas of the world, particularly in the United States and Europe. To highlight some major points of this chapter we return to the myths of kinship and marriage mentioned in the beginning.

> **Myth #1**   Human societies form descent groups by tracing links through both parents.
>
> Euro-American societies conceptualize descent in this bilateral way, but in fact most cultures of the world do not. Descent groupings are more often formed unilineally and the most common form of descent is patrilineal, or descent traced through men only. It is true that most (but not all) societies trace kin links through both mothers and fathers, but consider themselves members of *descent groups* only through their link to one parent.
>
> **Myth #2**   All societies use nuclear family units as a basic structure.
>
> As we have seen, there is quite a variety of residence patterns in human societies. Nuclear families are common, although in many cases they are residentially buried within larger extended groupings of kin. Additionally, some societies practice natolocal residence whereby brothers and sisters remain together for life and husbands and wives merely visit one another, usually in the household of the wife. In other cases female kin stay together in households and husbands of the women reside in a separate men's house.

Myth #3   Matrilineal societies are matriarchal.

The term "matrilineal" means decent through women, and does not imply matriarchy or rule by women. There are no truly matriarchal human societies—that is, societies where men do not or only very rarely exercise extra-domestic authority or where men are subjugated to women. In some matrilineal societies women do exercise a great deal of power and authority; in others they are under the firm authority of their brothers and senior matrilineal male kin.

Myth #4   People in all cultures perceive kinship as based on biological reproduction (kinship relationships are seen as "blood" relationships).

This idea was once taken for granted, even among anthropologists. It is now understood that many cultures of the word employ non-biological bases for kinship construction such as feeding, sharing house space, sharing territorial residence, and/ or performing certain rituals. A perceived biological connection is but one basis for kinship construction, but it is the most common worldwide. Most cultures of the world use both biological and non-biological bases in their constructions of kinship.

Myth #5   Kin (father, mother, aunt, etc.) are called by different terms in different languages but all peoples distinguish kin in identical ways.

On the contrary, peoples of the world linguistically distinguish kin in very different ways. For example some have separate terms for primary kin while others linguistically merge these kin with other collateral kin. There are, however, only a limited number of overall patterns in kinship terminology systems.

QUESTIONS FOR THOUGHT AND REFLECTION

1. What are some of the specific similarities between the ways kinship operates among nonhuman primates and among human primates? What are some of the differences? What can you suggest as reasons for both the similarities and differences?

2. What do anthropologists mean by the "incest taboo"? What kinds of biological functions does the incest taboo have, and what kinds of social functions?

3. All societies have some rules of exogamy and other rules of endogamy. Sometimes these rules are explicit and are even laws; other rules are implicit and informal, though still culturally important. What are some of the rules of exogamy and endogamy that prevail in the contemporary United States? What functions do they seem to serve? How have some older rules changed recently? Why?

4. For the last one hundred years or so there has been an increasing trend, especially in developed, urban-based societies, toward marriages in which the husband and wife choose their own partners for the purpose of their own happiness. But for most of human history marriages have been arranged by parents and other kin primarily to benefit their larger kin groups. Why do you think this shift is taking place? What does it say about the changing nature of marriage?

5. Marriage, as explained in this chapter, is a virtual cultural universal, though it takes varied forms. But in the United States and in some other countries, marriage is declining. Of those who do marry, roughly the same proportion will continue to get divorced as in the last 50 years (roughly 50 percent). And a vastly increased number of children will be born to unmarried mothers. What do you think accounts for these changes? What do you see as their consequences, both positive and negative? Why do you think these changes did not happen a hundred or a thousand years ago?

NOTES

[1] Kin selection theory was put forth to account for altruistic behavior in organisms, that is, behavior that enhances others' fitness while putting one's own life or fitness at considerable risk—for example some animals' alarm calls that warn others of danger but that also expose the alarm-calling animal to predators. If altruistic behaviors favor close kin then they also enhance one's own fitness. There is an actual formula (known as Hamilton's Rule) for kin selection theory: altruistic behavior will be favored by selection if $rb>c$, where r = the coefficient of genetic relatedness between the actor and recipients, b = the sum of fitness benefit to recipients, and c = the fitness costs to the actor.

[2] Some anthropologists then proposed other explanations for these different patterns in residence. For example, some proposed that these residential forms were related to different patterns of human warfare (Harris 1997).

REFERENCES CITED

Allen, Nicholas J.
  2008 " Tetradic Theory and the Origin of Human Kinship Systems." In Allen, Nicholas J., Hilary Callan, Robin Dunbar Allen, Nicholas J. and Wendy James, *Early Human Kinship: From Sex to Social Reproduction*, pp. 96–112, Malden, MA: Blackwell Publishing.

Boyd, Robert and Joan B. Silk
  2011. *How Humans Evolved.* 6th ed. New York: W.W. Norton & Company.

Cai Hua
  2008. *A Society without Husbands or Fathers: The Na of China* (translated by Asti Hustvedt). New York: Zone Books.

Carsten, Janet
  1995. The Substance of Kinship and the Heat of the Hearth: Feeding, Personhood, and Relatedness among Malays in Pulau Langkawi. *American Ethnologist* 22: 223–241.

Chapais, Bernard
  2008. *Primeval Kinship: How Pair-Bonding Gave Birth to Human Society.* Cambridge, MA: Harvard University Press.

Coontz, Stephanie
  2006. *Marriage, A History: How Love Conquered Marriage.* New York: Penguin Boooks.

Fox, Robin
  1978 The Tory Islanders. Cambridge: Cambridge University Press.

Godelier, Maurice
  1998 "Afterword: Transformations and Lines of Evolution." In Godelier, Maurice, Thomas R. Trautmann, and Franklin E. Tjon Sie Fat,eds., *Transformations of Kinship*, pp. 386–413, Washington, DC: Smithsonian Institution Press.

Gottlieb, Beatrice
  1993. *The Family in the Western World from the Black Death to the Industrial Age.* New York: Oxford University Press.

Hamilton, W. D.
  1964. The Genetical Evolution of Social Behavior. *Journal of Theoretical Biology* 7: 1–51.

Harris, Marvin
  1997. *Culture, People, Nature: An Introduction to General Anthropology*, 7th ed. New York: Longman.

Hewlett, Barry S., A. De Silvestri, and C.R. Gugliemino
  2002. Semes and Genes in Africa. *Current Anthropology* 43:313–321.

Kahn, Susan Martha
  2000. *Reproducing Jews: A Cultural Account of Assisted Conception in Israel.* Durham, NC: Duke University Press.

King, Diane E. and Linda Stone
  2010. Lineal Masculinity: Gendered Memory within Patriiny. *American Ethnologist* 37(2):323–336

Levine, Nancy E.
   1988. *The Dynamics of Polyandry: Kinship, Domesticity, and Population on the Tibetan Border*. Chicago: University of Chicago Press.

Lévi-Strauss, Claude
   1969 [orig. 1949]. *The Elementary Structures of Kinship*. Translated by James Harle Bell, John Richard von Strurmer, and Rodney Needham; edited by Rodney Needham. Boston: Beacon Press.

McKee, Nancy P., and Linda Stone
   2007. *Gender and Culture in America*, 3rd ed. Cornwall-on-Hudson, NY: Sloan Publishing.

Money, Nancy J.

2015 LGBT Families (*Contemporary Framimly Perspectives*). Thousand Oaks CA: Sage.

Mundy, Liza
   2012. *The Richer Sex*. New York: Simon & Schuster

Pusey, Anne E.
   2002. Of Genes and Apes: Chimpanzee Social Organization and Reproduction. In Frans de Waal, ed., *Tree of Origin: What Primate Behavior Can Tell Us about Human Social Evolution*, pp.9–37. Cambridge, MA: Harvard University Press.

Ragoné, Helena
   1994. *Surrogate Motherhood: Conception in the Heart*. Boulder, CO: Westview Press.

Rodseth, Lars, Richard W. Wrangham, Alisa M. Harrigan, and Barbara B. Smuts
   1991. The Human Community As a Primate Society. *Current Anthropology* 32(3): 221–241.

Rodseth, Lars and Richard Wrangham
   2004. Human Kinship: A Continuation of Politics by Other Means? In Bernard Chapais and Carol M. Berman, eds*., Kinship and Behavior in Primates*, pp. 389–419. New York: Oxford University Press.

Schneider, David M.
   1968. *American Kinship: A Cultural Account*. Englewood Cliffs, NJ: Prentice-Hall.
   1984. *A Critique of the Study of Kinship*. Ann Arbor: University of Michigan Press.

Shepher, Joseph
   1983. *Incest: A Biosocial View*. New York: Academic Press.

Shih, Chaun-kang
   2010. *Quest for harmony: The Mosuo Tradition of Sexual Union and Family Life*. Stanford, CA: Stanford University Press.

Stone, Linda
   2001. Theoretical Implications of New Directions in Anthropological Kinship. IN Stone, Linda, ed. *New Directions in Anthropological Kinship*, pp. 1–20. Boulder, CO: Rowman and Littlefield Publ.
   2004a. Anthropology and Gay Marriage. *American Anthropology Newsletter* Vol 45(5):10.
   2004b. Has the World Turned? Kinship in the Contemporary American Soap Opera. In Parkin, Robert and Linda Stone eds. *Family and Kinship*. Malden, MA: Blackwell Publishing
   2014a. *Kinship and Gender: An Introduction*. 5th ed. Boulder, CO: Westview Press.

2014b. Kinship Constructed Us: The Implications of Primate Studies for Cultural Anthropology. In Michael Egan, ed. *The Character of Human Institutions: Robin Fox and the Rise of Biosocial Science*. pp. 135–159. New Brunswick, NJ: Transaction Press.

Stone, Linda, and Paul F. Lurquin
  2007. *Genes, Culture, and Human Evolution*: *A Synthesis*. Malden, MA: Blackwell Publishing.

Tylor, Edward B.
  1889. On a Method of Investigating the Development of Institutions: Applied to Laws of Marriage and Descent. *Journal of the Royal Anthropological Institute* 18: 245–269.

Westermarck, Edward A.
  1891. *The History of Human Marriage*. London: Macmillan.

Yang, Martin C.
  1945. *A Chinese Village: Taitou, Shantung Province*. New York: Columbia University Press.

CHAPTER 7

HUMAN COMMUNICATION

Language and other ways
we transmit information

Language is a major aspect of human culture. In many ways language is a window on other dimensions of culture, reflecting shared social thought, worldviews, and gender assumptions, to name a few, often without the speakers' awareness. Unfortunately, though, linguistics can become very technical very fast. This ensures that non-specialists rarely get to enjoy the fascinating world of language. In this chapter we will avoid technicalities and open the linguistic door wide enough to make sure everyone is welcome.

Language is one of the aspects of human culture and behavior about which most people have the least information, and yet ironically some of the strongest opinions. To help students think about the material presented in this chapter, we will start with some of the myths that lurk in the corners of many people's minds.

Common Myths of Culture
Myth #1   Language is an all or nothing proposition. Either you have it or you do not.
Myth #2   Some languages are better than others; they are more logical, or better able to express complex ideas.

> **Myth #3** Dialects spoken by people of low socioeconomic status are inherently inferior to dialects spoken by people with high socioeconomic status.
>
> **Myth #4** Speaking multiple languages impairs learning and contributes to psychological stress.

HUMAN COMMUNICATION

Like all animals, humans communicate with each other. And though humans have a range of different communication systems to draw upon, one system appears to be unique to humans. This is language, which is not only the most useful and flexible system of communication at our disposal, but which most anthropologists believe to be a defining characteristic of humans. That is, anthropologists generally contend that no other species presently alive possesses a communication system in scope or power like laanguage. At what time human ancestors began to use language and the extent to which contemporry nonhuman animals can make use of human language are controversial issues, as has already been suggested in chapter 3. But for now, it is important to make two points about the development of language.

1. Communication systems of all species can best be considered as forming a **continuum** (a chain of related elements) of communicative phenomena of increasing power, complexity, and flexibility. At the simplest extreme, this continuum may be seen as having something like the involuntary chemical signaling of slime mold cells and, at the most complex extreme, the voluntary linguistic signaling of human speech. Viewed from this perspective, human language, though unique, is merely the endpoint of a chain of evolutionarily related systems of animal communication.

2. All contemporary languages and dialects of languages are equally developed and equally capable of expressing complex human thought. This is the principle of **linguistic relativity**, which states that no language is superior to or more advanced than any other language. It is true that some languages may possess specialized **lexicons**, or vocabularies, that allow them to refer to particular phenomena with easily available words or terms. But if speakers of another language develop the need for such words, they quickly produce a solution. A well-known example of this phenomenon is the Navajo development of terms for automobile parts. The Navajo of Arizona and New Mexico are locally famed for their

resourcefulness as auto mechanics, but their language lacked indigenous, or native, words for automobile parts. The Navajo might have borrowed English terms for words like "carburetor," "brakes," "headlights," and "engine." Speakers of many languages use this strategy. What the Navajo did, however, was to use Navajo words for body parts as metaphors for car parts, a strategy that also works just fine. Thus, an automobile's headlights are called "eyes" in Navajo; its carburetor is called "lungs;" and its engine is its "heart" (Witherspoon 1977).

LANGUAGE DEFINED

There have been many definitions proposed for language, each one with a slightly different twist. Some definitions stress linguistic structure, some stress historical development, and some stress the social and cultural aspects of language use. The definition of language presented below focuses on language as a uniquely human phenomenon but with roots in ancestral, nonhuman communication systems and with elements that are organized into an interrelated whole. Each numbered and underlined word or phrase will be explored following the definition.

> **Language is a (1) learned (2) system of (3) intentional communication based on (4) orally produced, (5) arbitrary symbols in which there is a (6) fixed, one-to-one correspondence between symbol and (7) referent.**

1. learned   Although all normal humans have an innate capacity to *acquire* language, a capability that is a part of their genetic makeup, they will not be able to speak unless they specifically *learn* to do so. Whether a kitten is raised outdoors on a farm or inside a New York City high-rise apartment building, it will still meow and hiss, or flatten its ears and swish its tail when angry or afraid. These communicative behaviors are not learned; they are *genetically encoded* in the kitten's DNA and develop naturally as it matures into a cat. A human, by contrast, will not learn to speak unless she or he is exposed to interactive language use. That is, though a human does not have to be *taught* to speak, she or he must *learn* to do so.

One may well ask how we know this, because it would seem that all children *would* be exposed to interactive language use. But there are abusive households in which children do *not* have this experience. The best known example is that of a child known as Genie, who came to the attention of authorities in Southern California at the age of 13 in 1970. She had spent the previous nine years tied to a potty chair in an empty room, released only at night, when she was confined to a sleeping bag in a crib-like bed covered with a screen. Her father forbade anyone in the family to speak to her, and when she was finally discovered, she could not speak. There was no evidence that Genie was physically impaired, and she did acquire many words after she came to the attention of authorities and received psychological care. She did not, however, assemble the words she learned into adult-like sentences, and she never acquired normal language use. There is still disagreement as to how much of Genie's linguistic deficit is due to the severe psychological trauma of her upbringing and how much is due to the fact that she did not learn to speak during the so-called "critical period" for language acquisition in early childhood (Curtiss, 1977; Rymer, 1994). Today Genie lives in a group home for developmentally disabled adults. Genie's story, like those of several other individuals discovered in similar circumstances, is a tragedy, but it is also a demonstration of the validity of the contention that humans must *learn* to speak.

2. system   Language is made up of multiple, interrelated parts that together form a unified whole, developed for the conveyance of meaning. As with all systems, any alteration in one element is likely to have an effect on the overall functioning of the entire network. If one linguistic element is altered, the meaning a speaker wishes to convey is likewise altered. For example, suppose the **phonetic**, or sound, makeup of a word is changed when a speaker pronounces the first sound in "pat" by vibrating the vocal cords as the sound is being produced. Even though all other vocal activities remain the same, the word "pat" now comes out as "bat." And thus the meaning of the sentence "I gave the baby a pat on the head" changes from a report of an affectionate gesture to a statement of harm. Similarly, in the English language, "The woman sang to the horse," while a little peculiar, is at least plausible. "The horse sang to the woman," however, is a fantasy, produced when the positions of the two nouns, "woman" and "horse," are reversed. Every language has its own method of conveying meaning, and all methods involve elements linked together in a system.

3. intentional communication   The conscious goal of language is communication. The reason this point is worth making is that for many nonhuman animals, communication is never or only sometimes the conscious goal of the users of the system that conveys it. For example, when a chimpanzee acquires a desirable food item, it becomes agitated and produces a characteristic screeching and hooting vocalization. These sounds alert other chimpanzees to the presence of food, thus introducing competition for it. This probably has a beneficial effect for the group as a whole, but not such a great effect for the animal who found the food in the first place. The first chimpanzee to locate the food did not *intend* to communicate the presence of the food; s/he had no control over the sounds produced. Chimpanzees are genetically programmed to communicate in such situations, whether they want to or not. In much the same way, a human who steps on a tack is likely to vocalize involuntarily (and often in rather strong language). Thus the human who is a victim of a tack attack communicates whether s/he wishes to or not. This is the result of the activation of the **limbic region** of the brain, an evolutionarily ancient area, and one over which humans have little conscious control. But in humans such communication amounts to a tiny fraction of our use of language; the overwhelming majority of what we say is voluntary and intentional.

4. orally produced   Language manifests itself in speech, and speech is orally produced. That is, it is produced by the vocal apparatus in and around the mouth. Humans do have other signaling systems, like body position, hand and other body movement, proximity to other speakers, and facial expressions. These characteristics, however, are vastly less productive and flexible than speech, and they are not necessary for communication. If they *were* necessary, then visually impaired people would not be able to communicate with each other, and telephones would not work for transmitting messages.

By contrast with humans, the primary communication systems of nonhuman animals often rely on elements that are not orally produced. For example, there are the visually based messages of dogs and their relatives (like wolves), which tuck their tails under their bodies, and hunch their backs to appear smaller than they are, to indicate subordination and a nonthreatening demeanor. Many mammals, including dogs, cats, and some primates, make themselves look as large as possible when they want to assert dominance and demonstrate aggressiveness. They extend themselves to their full height, and their fur stands up on end, a phenomenon technically called "piloerection." Another non-vocal animal communicative device not used by humans is scent. This includes the scent produced by some nonhuman females when they are in estrus (or "in heat"), signaling sexual receptivity, or the scent produced in the urine or other body fluids of males of many species that serve to mark their territory or signal their dominance. In both these cases the communication is involuntarily triggered and genetically programmed.

There is one exception to the statement that language is orally produced, and this has to do with the sign languages of the deaf. Today most linguists agree that such developed signing systems as American Sign Language (also known as ASL or Ameslan) and British Sign Language (which is somewhat different from ASL), as well as several other well-developed systems elsewhere in the world, have all the elements of any other natural language except for sound and do permit the communication of the full range of human expressive needs.

5. arbitrary symbol At its most basic level, a symbol is something that stands for something else. Linguistic symbols are words or pieces of words, and the connection they have to what they refer to is *arbitrary,* rather than *necessary.* That is, there is nothing fundamentally "doglike" about the English word "dog," any more than there is about the French word "*chien,*" the Spanish word "*perro,*" or the German word "*hund,*" to give examples from just four closely related Indo-European languages. There is nothing shiny about the word "silver," or yellowish about the word "yellow." The only reason these words mean what they do is that over thousands of years humans have agreed upon the convention that certain words and pieces of words (like "-ing" or "-ed" in English) will stand for certain things, qualities, or relationships. No one is sure how these conventions developed, though it seems highly unlikely that a committee of early proto-humans got together and officially decided on words and their meanings!

There are a few exceptions to the rule of arbitrariness in language. One is words that are clearly onomatopoetic; that is, they sound like what they mean. Animal sounds make up a big part of this group, like "meow," "cockadoodle-doo," and even "screech" and "twitter." Every language has some onomatopoetic words.

There is another group of words that are apparently not entirely arbitrary, but this one is harder to explain. These words contain elements, designated as **phonesthemes** by British linguist J.R. Firth when he first described them in 1930. Phonesthemes are combinations of sounds that appear in a collection of words that seem to share some common referential connection, but are not "genetically" related to each other. Thus, the words "gleam," "glow," "glisten," and "glitter," (can you think of others?) all seem to have something to do with light. Yet the words do not derive from a common ancestor word, and it is impossible to describe a connection that the sound "gl" has with light.

Of course, there are plenty of words beginning with "gl" that have nothing to do with light (such as "glad," "glamor," and "globe"). Many (and perhaps all) languages have phonesthemes, but they account for only a tiny fraction of words in any language.

6. fixed, one-to-one correspondence   Words and pieces of words (called "morphemes," as we will discuss shortly) mean only what speakers of the languages in which they occur have agreed that they mean. At first, this seems so obvious as to be worthless. But consider a dog's bark or a cat's meow. By barking, a dog may convey a greeting, an indication of excitement, a desire to go out or come in, an inclination to eat a dog biscuit, or annoyance at someone trespassing on his/her territory. Although every dog has different styles of barking, some of which are fairly easy for humans to decode, the fact remains that a single barking style can have quite a repertoire of meanings. By contrast, "flower/flour" (remember that words are fundamentally collections of *sounds*, not *letters)* can refer to pretty things that grow out of plants or white powdery stuff. It can be a verb that means to develop pretty plant elements or to apply white powdery stuff to something. And it can be used metaphorically, as in "the flower of Greek youth." But that is it. Humans cannot use language to mean something that other speakers of the language have not agreed to. If they did, human language would not work.

Despite their fixed significance at a single point in time, the meanings of words and expressions gradually shift over time, causing minor confusion. Thus, it is difficult for many contemporary English speakers to understand Shakespeare (who died in 1616) or the King James Version of the Bible (which was first published in 1611), because many of the words used have changed in meaning or have disappeared from use. Despite such changes, and the fact that many words have a range of meanings at any given time, words do not vary randomly, or at the whim of the speaker. A brief excerpt from Lewis Carroll's *Through the Looking Glass* (1972 [1871]), the sequel to *Alice in Wonderland*, illustrates the importance of limits to variation in meaning in human language. Alice is talking to the obnoxious Humpty Dumpty:

> "But 'glory' doesn't mean 'a nice knock-down argument,'" Alice objected. "When *I* use a word," Humpty Dumpty said in rather a scornful tone, "it means exactly what I choose it to mean—neither more nor less."

Figure 7.1 Humpty Dumpty and Alice.
Sir John Tenneil, 19th century.

Of course, Humpty Dumpty is an insane egg, who soon falls to his death off a wall. So much for his misconceptions about shared meaning in language.

7. referent In the context of language, a referent is what a word (or more properly, a morpheme) refers to. This is easy to understand if we consider such nouns as "book," or "highway," or "Mississippi River." But what about nouns like "love" or "faith" or "sin"? We cannot point to concrete objects that correspond to these nouns, but we can certainly point to situations in which love, faith, and sin are reflected. Similarly, with verbs, we cannot usually point to a concrete referent for them, but again we can point to situations that illustrate them.

There are more interesting kinds of referents to explore, though. What is the referent for "the?" For such pieces of words as "-ing" or "-ly?" These referents are relatively abstract notions or ideas that humans carry around in their heads, but they have no other, independent existence. The fact that speakers of a given language all use words and pieces of words to mean roughly the same thing, however, is a convincing demonstration that even where there are no independently existing entities to which a word or morpheme may refer, every word or morpheme has a referent. To explore this idea, spend a little time trying to come up with a description of the referent for "of." It is possible, but not easy. Such morphemes can probably be most usefully thought of as referring to certain kinds of qualities or relationships, like specificity or connectedness.

THE VARIETIES OF LINGUISTICS

When humans talk they are usually unaware of the structure or history of the languages they speak, the ways in which these languages are related to other languages, or to the communication systems of other animals. Generally, we just open our mouths and let the words flow out. But linguists, for whom language is an object of professional study (people who speak multiple languages are properly called "polyglots" rather than "linguists"), have divided the study of language into several categories, which we discuss briefly below.

Descriptive linguistics

Descriptive linguistics explores, categorizes, and analyzes the basic structural organization of language. It divides language into three interrelated systems: **phonology** (the sound system), **morphology** (the system of meaningful sequences of sounds, that is, words and pieces of words), and **syntax** (the system by which words are assembled into meaningful sequences, or sentences).

THE INTERNATIONAL PHONETIC ALPHABET (revised to 2005)

CONSONANTS (PULMONIC)   © 2005 IPA

	Bilabial	Labiodental	Dental	Alveolar	Post alveolar	Retroflex	Palatal	Velar	Uvular	Pharyngeal	Glottal
Plosive	p b			t d		ʈ ɖ	c ɟ	k g	q ɢ		ʔ
Nasal	m	ɱ		n		ɳ	ɲ	ŋ	N		
Trill	B			r					R		
Tap or Flap		ⱱ		ɾ		ɽ					
Fricative	ɸ β	f v	θ ð	s z	ʃ ʒ	ʂ ʐ	ç ʝ	x ɣ	χ ʁ	ħ ʕ	h ɦ
Lateral fricative				ɬ ɮ							
Approximant		ʋ		ɹ		ɻ	j	ɰ			
Lateral approximant				l		ɭ	ʎ	L			

Where symbols appear in pairs, the one to the right represents a voiced consonant. Shaded areas denote articulations judged impossible.

CONSONANTS (NON-PULMONIC)

Clicks		Voiced implosives		Ejectives	
ʘ	Bilabial	ɓ	Bilabial	'	Examples:
ǀ	Dental	ɗ	Dental/alveolar	p'	Bilabial
ǃ	(Post)alveolar	ʄ	Palatal	t'	Dental/alveolar
ǂ	Palatoalveolar	ɠ	Velar	k'	Velar
ǁ	Alveolar lateral	ʛ	Uvular	s'	Alveolar fricative

VOWELS

Where symbols appear in pairs, the one to the right represents a rounded vowel.

OTHER SYMBOLS

ʍ Voiceless labial-velar fricative
w Voiced labial-velar approximant
ɥ Voiced labial-palatal approximant
ʜ Voiceless epiglottal fricative
ʢ Voiced epiglottal fricative
ʡ Epiglottal plosive

ɕ ʑ Alveolo-palatal fricatives
ɺ Voiced alveolar lateral flap
ɧ Simultaneous ʃ and x

Affricates and double articulations can be represented by two symbols joined by a tie bar if necessary.

k͡p t͡s

SUPRASEGMENTALS

ˈ Primary stress
ˌ Secondary stress   ˌfoʊnəˈtɪʃən
ː Long   eː
ˑ Half-long   eˑ
˘ Extra-short   ĕ
| Minor (foot) group
‖ Major (intonation) group
. Syllable break   ɹi.ækt
‿ Linking (absence of a break)

DIACRITICS   Diacritics may be placed above a symbol with a descender, e.g. ŋ̊

	Voiceless	n̥ d̥		Breathy voiced	b̤ a̤		Dental	t̪ d̪
	Voiced	s̬ t̬		Creaky voiced	b̰ a̰		Apical	t̺ d̺
	Aspirated	tʰ dʰ		Linguolabial	t̼ d̼		Laminal	t̻ d̻
	More rounded	ɔ̹		Labialized	tʷ dʷ		Nasalized	ẽ
	Less rounded	ɔ̜		Palatalized	tʲ dʲ		Nasal release	dⁿ
	Advanced	u̟		Velarized	tˠ dˠ		Lateral release	dˡ
	Retracted	e̠		Pharyngealized	tˤ dˤ		No audible release	d̚
	Centralized	ë		Velarized or pharyngealized	ɫ			
	Mid-centralized	ɘ̽		Raised	e̝	(ɹ̝ = voiced alveolar fricative)		
	Syllabic	n̩		Lowered	e̞	(β̞ = voiced bilabial approximant)		
	Non-syllabic	e̯		Advanced Tongue Root	e̘			
	Rhoticity	ɚ a˞		Retracted Tongue Root	e̙			

TONES AND WORD ACCENTS

LEVEL			CONTOUR		
e̋ or ˥	Extra high		ě or ˄	Rising	
é ˦	High		ê ˅	Falling	
ē ˧	Mid		e᷄ ˄	High rising	
è ˨	Low		e᷅ ˄	Low rising	
ȅ ˩	Extra low		e᷈ ˄	Rising-falling	
↓	Downstep		↗	Global rise	
↑	Upstep		↘	Global fall	

Figure 7.2   IPA chart. This chart shows all the symbols used by linguists to represent every speech sound that occurs in every one of the word's languages.

Phonology

In representing speech sounds, linguists make use of the **International Phonetic Alphabet (IPA)**. This is an alphabet that includes a separate symbol for every speech sound that appears in every language spoken by any person in the world. It includes some symbols that are the same as English letters, and many that are not, as you can see by looking at the chart. The difference, however, is that each symbol in the IPA has only a single pronunciation. Thus anyone who knows the IPA can instantly write down a word s/he hears in any language, regardless of whether s/he knows the meaning of the word or not. In this way, the IPA is clearly superior to any other writing system on the planet, in terms of clarity and simplicity.

Although different languages have different repertoires of sounds, there is a lot of overlap in the sounds they use. Some languages, like those of Polynesia, use relatively few different sounds, usually fewer than 20, in the construction of their words. Other languages, like the Khoisan languages spoken in southwestern Africa by a variety of peoples, including the !Kung, may contain more than 90 different speech sounds. Among the sounds used in Khoisan languages are the distinctive "click" sounds, which linguists refer to as "implosives," and which many people may have heard in the 1980 film *The Gods Must Be Crazy.* They are produced by drawing air *into* the vocal tract, rather than expelling it *out of* the lungs, which is the usual method of producing speech. English has around 40 different speech sounds (depending on the dialect and how the analysis is done), which puts it somewhere in the middle of the world's languages for variety of sounds used. It is important to note that the *number* of distinctive speech sounds a language possesses has nothing to do with the complexity of thought or expression of speakers of that language.

The distinctive sounds that make a difference in meaning in a particular language are called **phonemes**. In our discussion of speech sounds in the preceding paragraph, what we were really talking about was phonemes. All languages have variations in their phonemes of which their speakers are seldom aware. In English, for example, the "p" at the beginning of a word sounds a bit different from the "p" at the end of a word, and both sound different from the "p" in the middle of a word. Try saying "pat," "tap," and "spat" for yourself. You will notice that the "p" in "pat" is aspirated, or pronounced with a little puff of air, while the "p" in "tap" is suppressed or "checked;" that is, it is not aspirated at all. And the "p" in "spat" is relatively unaspirated. Native speakers of English make these adjustments in pronouncing "p" without even thinking about them; to native speakers, they are insignificant variations in one sound, rather than distinctive, separate sounds. But in some languages, like many spoken in South Asia, a word beginning with an aspirated "p" means something different from the same word beginning with an *unaspirated* "p." For example, in Nepali (a language closely related to Hindi) the word "pakaunu" (no aspirated "p") means "to cook," whereas the word "phakaunu" (with an aspirated "p" written here as "ph") means "to seduce." One can imagine the inappropriate things native English speakers might unwittingly say when first learning Nepali! What is important to note here is that in Nepali, an aspirated "p" and unaspirated "p" are two separate phonemes. In English, by contrast, variations in the pronunciation of "p" are *not* separate phonemes, and they do *not* make a difference in meaning. If a child or a nonnative speaker uses the "wrong" kind of "p" in a word, it just sounds a little strange, but it does not make the word mean something else.

We can look at this same phenomenon from the other side by considering the sounds of "r" and "l." In some Asian languages "r" and "l" are merely alternate ways of pronouncing the same sound—just like the various kinds of "p" in English. But in English, "r" and "l" are perceived as two completely separate sounds; they are separate phonemes. Of course, it is nearly impossible for an English speaker to imagine that anyone could consider "r" and "l" essentially the same sound, a phenomenon that led the American linguist **Edward Sapir** to refer to "the psychological reality of the phoneme" in an article of the same name (1949). What this means is that people tend to believe, consciously or unconsciously, that the phonemes of their own language are *genuinely* different from each other, while phonemic distinctions not represented in their own language are insignificant.

Morphology

Morphology is the study of the structure of words and meaningful segments of words. Just as phonemes are the basic units of analysis of phonology, morphemes are the basic units of analysis of morphology. A morpheme is an irreducible unit of sound that has specific meaning. That is, you cannot break the sequence of sounds down any further and still have them mean anything specific. Thus, the word "book" is a morpheme, because it has specific meaning, and it cannot be broken down into any constituent meaningful parts.. By contrast, the word "books" is made up of two morphemes: one is the noun, "book," and the other is the plural morpheme, "–s." "Book" is a *free* morpheme; that is, it can exist on its own as a separate word. But "–s" is a *bound* morpheme; that is, it *cannot* exist on its own, but must be bound or attached to another morpheme. Similarly, the word "able" contains a single free morpheme, an adjective indicating competence. The word "unable" contains two morphemes, the free one we just mentioned, and another, bound, morpheme that negates it.

In English bound morphemes exist as prefixes or suffixes. Among English suffixes, many contain grammatical information, such as plural markers, tense markers, markers of grammatical person or number, and the like. But English does not use a lot of bound morphological markers to convey grammatical information, as anyone who has learned other European languages has found out. For example, consider the present tense of the English verb, "to go":

I go	we go
you (sing) go	you (pl) go
he goes	they go

Then consider the way the same verb looks in the present tense in Spanish:

yo voy	nosotros vamos
tú vas	vosotros vais
él va	ellos van

In the case of English, a suffix added to the verb occurs only in the third person singular, while in Spanish each form of the verb has a different suffix.

This example shows that compared with many other languages such as Spaish, English includes very little grammatical information in its words. We would say that English is less **inflected** than Spanish. An example of an even more highly inflected language is Latin, where different suffixes added to root words correspond to different **cases** and numbers. Cases are grammatical categories of nouns, pronouns, and adjectives that indicate the role the word plays in a sentence.

English, as noted, uses few grammatical morphemes, but English is far from the least inflected language in the world. Chinese languages[1] are well known for their lack of inflection and grammatical morphemes. In both English and Chinese languages, speakers must rely on rigid word order to ensure that their meaning is conveyed, because such information as which word is the subject of a sentence is not indicated by a bound morpheme. In English the sentence "The boy loves the girl" can be expressed only in this way. To say "The girl loves the boy" means something quite different. In Latin, however, *"Puer puellam amat"* means the same thing ("The boy loves the girl"), no matter what order the words are arranged in. The morpheme "–am" identifies *"puellam"* ("girl") as the direct object of the sentence no matter where the word appears. Similarly, the fact that *"puer"* ("boy") has no other morpheme attached to it identifies it as the subject of the sentence, no matter where it occurs in the sentence. *"Puellam puer amat"* or *"Amat puer puellam"*—or any other arrangement of words—still means the same thing in Latin.

Syntax

Word order is the basic focus of syntax, the third major element of descriptive linguistics. Today many linguists, including the distinguished American linguist, **Noam Chomsky**, consider syntax, or the organization of words in sentences, as the most basic characteristic of language. Many such scholars contend that linguistic structure or organization is a reflection of universal, innate, though unconscious human intellectual capabilities that develop in normal humans as they mature. These underlying structures, referred to as "deep structures" or "logical forms," represent the underlying basis of the actual utterances humans produce. Linguists refer to the organization of what people actually say as "surface structures" or "phonological forms."

Different languages have different ways of stringing words together to form sentences, as well as different ways of altering these strings of words to form questions, or to make passive voice constructions, commands, or subordinate clauses. That is, syntax varies from language to language, and within any given language syntactic variation permits flexibility of expression. For example, in English, a basic declarative sentence like "Horses eat hay" can be altered syntactically to ask a question ("Do horses eat hay?"), to be expressed in the passive voice ("Hay is eaten by horses"), to be transformed into a command ("Horses, eat hay!"), or to become part of a larger sentence ("He says that horses eat hay"). All languages have syntactic devices for accomplishing the same kinds of changes or transformations, but there may be substantial variation in how they do it.

Different languages have different characteristic word orders. English is referred to as a SVO language, because the syntactic elements in declarative sentences are usually arranged as Subject, Verb, Object. Latin (like Japanese and Turkish) is usually described as a SOV language, though as we have seen, Latin word order is extremely flexible. English shares its SOV word order with French, Spanish, and many Chinese languages. And Austronesian languages, which include Malagasy (spoken in Madagascar), Polynesian languages, and Formosan (originally and to some extent still spoken by the indigenous population of Taiwan), usually employ a VSO or VOS word order. In fact, all six of the possible word orders that mathematically *could* exist in fact *do* exist. Klingon, for example, the language created for *Star Trek* by linguist Marc Okrand, is an OVS language—very rare!

Evolutionary Linguistics

Though there was substantial interest in the origin and development of language in earlier centuries, what we now call "evolutionary linguistics" is primarily a product of the late twentieth and early twenty-first centuries. This late start is largely the result of the 1866 prohibition of the Linguistic Society of Paris against discussion of language origins, on the grounds that such discussions were irresponsibly speculative. More recently, and with new modes of analysis, interest in language origins has revived, along with renewed interest in the origins of other cultural phenomena such as religion and kinship.

One may think of evolutionary linguistics as the archaeology of language. But in this respect linguistics faces a special problem: until the development of writing, which began in Sumer, in Western Asia, only about than 5,000 years ago, there are virtually no concrete remnants of language, itself. Phonemes leave no fossils; there are no fossil words! There are, however, fossil remains of early human ancestors, which can give us some clues about when these ancestors developed the organic structures that would have allowed them to speak, a topic touched upon briefly in Chapter 3. For example, fragments of a brain case can be reassembled, allowing scientists to make casts of the interior of the skull (called *endocasts*) and gain some idea of the shape of the brain once contained there. These endocasts allow an estimate of whether areas of the brain associated with language in modern humans existed in a fossil ancestor.

Another approach used to throw light on language origins, is work done with living nonhuman primates, especially chimpanzees, but also with gorillas and orangutans. Many people are familiar with **Washoe**, the first chimpanzee to be taught American Sign Language, who was part of a project initiated by Beatrice and Allen Gardner at the University of Nevada, Reno, in 1967. Washoe later moved to Central Washington University, where Roget Fouts continues the research begun by the Gardners. Washoe died in 2007, but today several other chimpanzees are part of Fouts's experimental community of signing chimpamzees. The gorilla, Koko, who has been featured in numerous publications and television programs, and the orangutan, Chantek, have also been taught American Sign Language, as have a number of other apes.

Scientists chose a gestural communication system, rather than a spoken medium, as a linguistic medium for apes for two reasons. First, the vocal apparatus of nonhuman primates is different from that of humans, and may not permit a range of sounds adequate for a human language. Second, and more important, nonhuman primates do not have much conscious cortical control over vocal output; rather, the sounds that come out of the mouths of nonhuman primates are the result of the emotions produced by external circumstances, as we discussed earlier. By contrast, apes *can* consciously control hand movements, making sign language a possibility for them. For this same reason, some nonhuman primates (primarily chimpanzees) have been successfully trained to communicate via computers fitted with abstract graphic symbols for morphemes and syntactic structures.

The results of nonhuman language experiments remain controversial, and they are still ongoing. On one side of the controversy are those scholars who say that though nonhuman language experiments have resulted in apes learning the signs in a human communication system, this cannot reasonably be called language acquisition. Herbert S. Terrace (who conducted experiments with the chimpanzee Nim Chimpsky—whose name is a parody of that of Noam Chomsky, the distinguished American linguist) contends that the animals have learned very few signs, that they have had to be taught each sign through rigorous training, and that they do not generate lengthy or interesting sentences or have a mastery of complex syntax (Terrace 1979). On the other side of the controversy are researchers like Roger Fouts (1997) who say that some nonhuman primates *are* able to acquire some elements of language. Fouts agrees that while chimpanzees and gorillas do not generate humanlike complexity with their borrowed communication system, they *have* done some significant things with it. Thus, many of these apes have acquired well over a hundred signs, have used these signs in both conventional and novel ways, have coined new terms (like "cry-hurt fruit" for "radish"), and have passed the signs on to new generations.

At this point it is helpful to return to the idea presented at the beginning of this chapter, that all communication systems are best thought of as existing on a continuum. With this view, is possible to derive some evolutionary insight from the achievements of nonhuman primates in their use of a human communication system. True, Washoe, Koko, Chantek, and the other signing and computer-using apes, did not invent the systems they have adopted.

True, they do not use these systems with the same flexibility and virtuosity with which humans use them. But the fact that they can use them at all is remarkable. It also suggests that the cognitive capabilities on which human language is based may have developed earlier than once believed, and that a rudimentary form of language may have been employed by human ancestors hundreds of thousands of years ago, before the development of anatomically modern humans.

Nonhuman language experiments are exciting and have been carried out not only with primates, but with sea mammals like dolphins and seals, and even with birds. Yet another type of investigation into the evolutionary development of language explores existing (and extinct but recorded) languages. These investigations can address the question of whether all human languages are derived from a single ancestor language, or whether there are multiple parent (usually called "mother") languages. Some researchers are pursuing clues to a language family they call "Nostratic," which they believe originated in northeastern Africa and may have been ancestral to many European, Asian, and African languages (Bomhard 2008). More generally accepted research, such as that conducted by the linguist Joseph Greenberg (1970, 1987) has explored relationships among related languages in large "macrofamilies" of languages in Africa and others in the Americas. All of these studies attempt to generate information on elements of large groups of related languages to determine what elements were likely to have existed in the earliest languages or proto languages spoken by the ancestors of living speakers.

Another tack is taken by linguists such as Derek Bickerton (1981, 2009), who looks at **pidgin** and **creole** languages for clues to language origins. Pidgins are reduced linguistic systems made up of elements from three or more constituent languages that develop when speakers of these languages come together and have no common language by which to communicate. Pidgins are no one's first language, and are used only when necessary in trading situations, or when people are forced to work with or for those with whom they share no other language. Usually, pidgins die out when the situations in which they develop change, and there is no longer a need for them. But sometimes pidgins become entrenched within a population, and are taught to a new generation as a first language, in which case they become known as creole languages. Some widely spoken creole languages include Kiswahili (often called "Swahili" by English speakers), spoken in East Africa, Bahasa Indonesia and Bahasa Malay, very similar languages spoken in Malaysia and Indonesia, and Tok Pisin, or Neo Melanesian, spoken in Papua New Guinea.

The Lord's Prayer (Tok Pisin)

Papa bilong mipela, Yu stap long heven. Nem bilong yu i mas i stap holi, Kingdom bilong yu i mas i kam, strongim mipela long bihainim laik bilong yu long graun, olsem ol i bihainim long heven. Givim mipela kaikai inap long tude. Pogivim rong bilong mipela,olsem mipela i pogivim ol arapela i mekim rong long mipela. Sambai long mipela long taim bilong traim. Na rausim olgeta samting nogut long mipela. Kingdom na strong na
glori, em i bilong yu tasol oltaim oltaim. Tru.

The Lord's Prayer (English)

Our father, who art in heaven, hallowed be thy name. Thy kingdom come, thy will be done on earth as it is in heaven. Give us this day our daily bread, and forgive us our trespasses as, we forgive those who trespass against us. Lead us not into temptation, but deliver us from evil, for thine is the kingdom, the power, and the glory, now and forever. Amen

Figure 7.3 Neo Melanesian (an English-based creole). This example of the Lord's Prayer demonstrates how a creole language, in this case Tok Pisin (also called Neo Melanesian), contains recognizable elements of the constituent languages, though they may be spelled and pronounced somewhat differently and used in very different ways. Thus, in the Lord's Prayer, the opening phrase "Papa bilong mipela" is derived from the English words "papa," "belong," "me," and " fellow," but it means "Our [or "my"] father." This is not "bad" or distorted English, any more than the many French words and structures in English make English "bad French." Tok Pisin (derived from "Talk Pidgin") is simply another language.

Bickerton and others have noted that there are structural characteristics of pidgin and creole languages that appear very similar to each other, regardless of the constituent languages involved. They suggest that these similarities may have something to do with fundamental human cognitive capabilities. They contend that these similarities are easier to see in pidgins and creoles because these languages are relatively recent in origin, and have not yet acquired the linguistic accretions that have obscured these structures in older languages. That is, their "skeletons" are more apparent than are the skeletons of older languages. Like other speculations on language origins, however, such ideas remain controversial.

Psycholinguistics

Psycholinguistics has primarily to do with issues relating language and the brain. Among these, one of the most fundamental is language acquisition, particularly the acquisition of first languages by small children. For thousands of years people have marveled at the remarkable facility with which toddlers acquire language without apparent effort, and with far greater speed than adults acquire second or any subsequent languages. How do they do it? How do children figure out how to break up the sentences and phrases they hear into pieces and reorganize those pieces into new sentences of their own? Linguists and cognitive psychologists are still working on these questions, but the following presents some of the currently most influential ideas.

All normal humans are born with the cognitive capability to acquire language (just as they are born with the physiological capability to acquire upright posture and bipedal locomotion). American linguist Noam Chomsky has famously called this cognitive capability the Language Acquisition Device (LAD, which unfortunately makes it seem like a *thing—which it is not,* rather than an innate *capacity—which is what he intended).* As children hear language around them, especially language directed to them, they unconsciously construct strategies (or rules) for breaking up strings of words they hear and putting them back together. At first these constructions concern just single words: "Up," "More," "In," and every parent's favorite, "No." Later, children start combining words into pairs: "Bye-bye Daddy?" "More juice," and "All-gone milk." From there on, the sky is the limit and children's language comes to resemble the language of adults, as they refine their provisional "rules" to reflect the speech they hear around them. At first, children overgeneralize from the language structures that they have internalized, but eventually they learn the quirks and exceptions of their mother tongue(s). You can witness children's language learning strategies at work when you hear American children saying things like "The sheeps are in the road," which is ungrammatical. The children have never actually heard such a sentence, so they are not imitating it. What they *are* doing is using structures and words they *have* heard, and assembling them according to models that are *usually* correct, but not in particular cases (as in the plural of "sheep," which is the same as its singular.).

As discussed earlier, with the tragic story of Genie as an example, children who do not learn to speak early in their lives generally will never attain adult competence. But how late is too late? Linguist Eric Lenneberg (1967) advanced the "critical period hypothesis" for language learning, which states

Figure 7.4   Egyptian Hieroglyphs.

Figure 7.5   Mayan Hieroglyphs. Museo de Siti Palenque, Mexico.

that language not learned by the age of twelve will not be learned with native adult competence. Alas, in the United States, where second and third languages are formally taught in school to native English speakers, this process almost universally begins *after* the age of twelve.

Historical Linguistics

Historical linguistics covers the development of languages through time by tracing the diversification of one language into many "daughter" languages. It also reconstructs earlier, ancestral languages using clues from existing related languages and from ancient written records. There are numerous mysteries left to solve in the world of ancient writing systems, including Linear A (used to write the language of Crete before the fifteenth century B.C.E.), Etruscan (used for the language of the same name in the pre-Roman northern area of

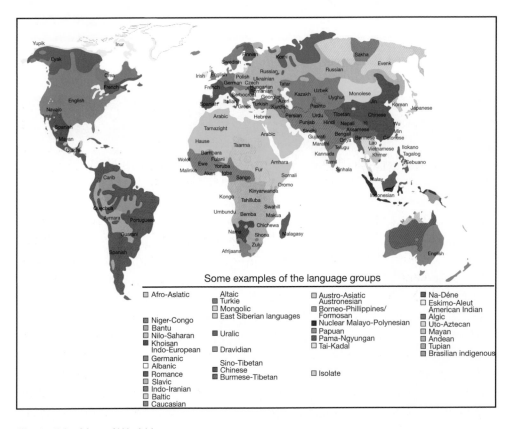

Figure 7.6   Map of World Languages.
Courtesy of Merritt Ruhlen

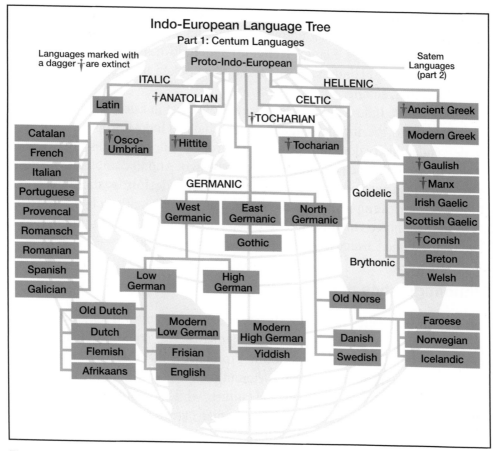

Figure 7.7 Chart of Indo-European Family of Languages. This chart shows many of the current and extinct languages and language sub-families of the Indo European family.

Italy known formerly as Etruria and now as Tuscany), and the writing system of the Harappan civilization of the Indus Valley in India and Pakistan from 3000 to 1500 B.C.E. Considering that Egyptian hieroglyphs were decoded only about 200 years ago, and that Linear B (the writing system of the Mycenaean Greeks) and Mayan hieroglyphs were decoded only after World War II, it is clear that enormously important work has been done quite recently.

In general, the languages of the world have been broken up into a number of large groups of related languages, known as "language families." Though linguists sometimes disagree about where exactly to draw the boundaries, the languages in each family are believed to be descended from a single ancestral language. English, for example, is part of the Germanic branch of the Indo-European language family. The Germanic branch includes languages such as Dutch, German, and Swedish, while the Romance languages include French,

Italian, Spanish, and other languages descended from Latin, the *Roman* language. "Romance" here has nothing to do with love! Other subfamilies of Indo-European include Slavic, Hellenic, and Indo-Iranian (including Farsi, spoken in Iran, and Hindi, Bengali, and Urdu, spoken in India and Pakistan), as well as other, smaller subfamilies.

Though more Indo-European languages now exist in Europe than anywhere else in the world, the original language from which all Indo-European languages are descended likely does not come from Europe at all, but from somewhere in western or central Asia, several thousand years ago. And to complicate matters, there are languages spoken in Europe that are *not* Indo-European. Finnish and Hungarian, for example, are Uralic languages, and distantly related to Turkish. And then there is the mysterious Basque language, known to linguists as a "language isolate," because it has no known relatives at all.

Ethnolinguistics and Sociolinguistics

The area of linguistics most closely associated with cultural anthropology is the double-barreled category of ethnolinguistics and sociolinguistics. What ethnolinguists and sociolinguists both explore are the roles of language in social life, each from a somewhat different perspective. Ethnolinguists study the connections between language and culture, while sociolinguists study connections between language and certain social categories, such as class and gender. We will consider ethnolinguistics first.

Ethnolinguistics

In 1939 the American linguist, Edward Sapir, died at the age of 55. In 1941 his student and colleague, **Benjamin Lee Whorf** (an amateur linguist and professional chemical engineer), died at the age of 44. Though their lives were short, they were enormously influential in the world of anthropological linguistics. Sapir wrote and lectured prolifically and is widely considered the most brilliant and influential American anthropological linguist. With his undergraduate and master's degrees in Germanic languages and linguistics, Sapir was steeped in the linguistic and philosophical work of German scholars who stressed the value and intellectual equivalence of all languages. This view was also shared by German-born Franz Boas (see Chapter 1) who served as Sapir's mentor during his doctoral studies at Columbia University. From these German influences Sapir also incorporated an additional perspective, namely that an individual's native language has a powerful effect on his or her world view, and indirectly, on the culture in which he/she lives. This idea was the germ for what became the **Sapir-Whorf hypothesis**.

1) The Sapir-Whorf Hypothesis

When Whorf began to take courses with Sapir, the two men found that their outlooks on the relationships among language, thought, and culture had much in common. The result of their collaboration, the Sapir-Whorf Hypothesis, is not really a scientific hypothesis, nor did Sapir and Whorf intend it as such. Instead, the term developed largely through the work of their students, and shortly after the end of World War II it had become entrenched in the academic world.

Sapir and Whorf posited that language strongly influences culture and perception. Whorf, for example, discussed how time is dealt with differently in the languages of English and Hopi (spoken by the Hopi people of the southwestern United States). In English, time is marked out in sharp, discrete categories—past, present and future. But in Hopi, time is presented as an ongoing process of manifestation with no sharp breakages. As a result, Whorf argued, English and Hopi speakers perceive the world differently with regard to the fundamental dimension of time.

Sapir and Whorf's statements relating language, culture, and thought varied from bland assertions that the three phenomena are generally interrelated to dramatic statements that a person's language *determines* his or her thought patterns and important elements of specific cultures. Not only were there many, often conflicting, formulations of the language-thought-culture relationship, but unlike a scientific hypothesis, this one was difficult to prove, and impossible to falsify (both defining characteristics of genuine, scientific hypotheses). How can one know if a particular language was responsible for its speakers' values, or if the values are responsible for elements in the language? For example, do ethnic slurs within a language *cause* oppression and discrimination, or do they merely reflect and reinforce it? Or both?

The contribution of the Sapir-Whorf "hypothesis" is probably best appreciated by avoiding its extreme formulations and staying with the middle ground. We could phrase it as something like this: **"Language encodes and so reinforces thought (and thus cultural values)."** By using this formulation of the Sapir-Whorf Hypothesis it is possible to gain an understanding of an issue like that of ethnic slurs. Certainly, a particular culture, as a result of specific historical circumstances, may create an environment in which some participants in the cultural group have taken to using hateful ethnic terms. Through use, these terms may become a common part of the language, and thus will reinforce in the minds of some speakers the notion that the people referred to by those terms *really are* contemptible, stupid, ugly, lazy, and so on. The words, themselves, have not *created* these ideas, but by being linguistically encoded (that is, put into words and grammar), these ethnic slurs have reinforced the ideas over time and over the generations.

If we cease to use such language do we thereby eliminate discrimination and oppression? Of course not. But ceasing to use such language *does* make racism, sexism, and ethnocentrism less culturally acceptable and less easy to activate. It is hardly the whole solution to a complex and destructive social problem, but it is certainly a part of the solution.

2) Classifying the universe

The Sapir-Whorf Hypothesis captured the imaginations of many anthropological linguists, who began to wonder if there were any limits to the ways in which languages carved up the universe, creating different cultural worlds of time, space, color and so on. One way of exploring this question was to look at specific domains, or categories, of phenomena, to see how much variation there was in the ways in which various languages classified the elements within them. The first large study of this kind had to do with color classification, and was published in 1969 by Brent Berlin and Paul Kay. This study demonstrated that out of the enormous variety of possible ways in which human languages *could* classify colors, there were very few ways in which they actually *did* classify them. Berlin and Kay confined their study to what they called "basic color terms." These are terms that are not constructed by analogy with something else (like "orange," for example), and that apply to all phenomena, rather than just to one or two (like "blonde" for hair or "palomino" for horses). Berlin and Kay found that every known language had at least two of these basic color terms: black and white (or dark and light). If there were three, the color added was always red. Other terms were added in a fairly regular order, up to a total of eleven. Subsequent studies of other phenomena, especially of plants and animals, show similar results: though different languages classify the world somewhat differently (variation certainly exists), they all seem to follow similar underlying principles (uniformity exists, as well).

This information is all very interesting—fascinating, even. Who would ever have imagined that such definite patterns could exist within the thousands of mutually unintelligible languages in the world? But what does it all mean? Is it just a curiosity, like a rock in the shape of a unicorn, or does it have some significance? The answer is that these regularities point to a single creative force

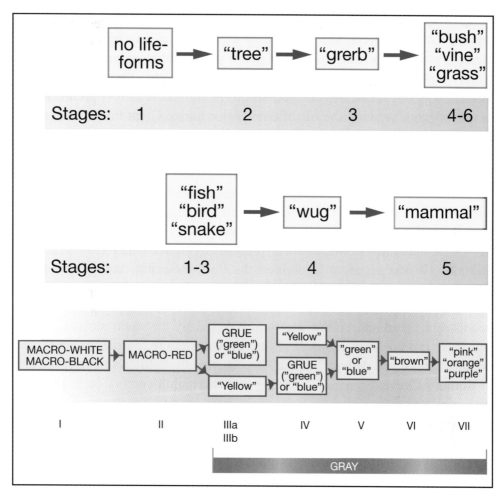

[Figure 7.8a, b, and c. Lexical Universals.

These three figures represent a synthesis of the findings of linguists who explored the limits of language variation. Their results provide a corollary to the most profound discovery of anthropology: in language, as in all other areas of culture, people are both very different in some specifics and profoundly the same in basic human qualities. Though languages vary, they do not vary without constraint. (Witkowski and Brown 1978(7):427–451)

in their construction: the human brain. However different the world's environments and languages may be, and whatever ethnic diversity exists among human populations, human brains all have the same structural components, and they all operate the same way. Faced with a mass of colors, for examples, humans approach this "buzzing, blooming confusion" by initially dividing it into two parts: dark and light (or black and white). These terms have to do with *light* (brightness), rather than *hue* (color). But if a human group adds another basic color term to its language, one color (a real hue, this time), stands out: red, the color of blood, and thus vitally significant to any population. From there, it is not surprising that either green or yellow is added, both of them widely represented and significant in the natural world. Then, whichever of the two was not added before. And so on, though there is less predictability as one progresses along the list of basic color terms. Great minds (that is, all human ones) clearly do think alike!

It would, of course, be wrong to think that languages with fewer color terms are less developed or sophisticated than those with more, or that speakers of the former are less intelligent than speakers of the latter languages. We need only take a look at Homeric Greek to see an example of this aspect of linguistic relativity. The *Iliad* and the *Odyssey* were orally composed around 1200 B.C.E., and fixed in written form, possibly by a poet named Homer, around 800 B.C.E. It was apparent to eighteenth- and nineteenth-century readers of these works that there was a shortage of what Berlin and Kay would later call "basic color terms" in both epics. Black, white, and red exist in Homer's poems, but green and yellow are both covered by the same term (*chloros*), and there are no basic terms for blue, brown, orange, purple, or gray. The famous "gray-eyed Athena" of the *Iliad* is literally "glittering-eyed Athena" in Homeric Greek. So what was going on? Did eighth-century (B.C.E.) Greeks have impaired color vision, as some nineteenth-century classicists speculated? No. They merely spoke a language that had few basic color terms. It was a language that, according to Berlin and Kay, tends to go along with a fairly simple technology and a society organized along tribal lines. In general, the more complicated a society's social organization and technology, the more likely it is to have a lot of basic color terms (though there are exceptions). Fortunately, given the significance of the Greek classics in Western cultures, no one is likely to make the mistake of thinking that the early Greeks' small number of basic color terms indicates a simple understanding of life or a lack of cognitive power!

What these examples show us is that applying ethnolinguistic analysis to classification systems can illuminate how language is a window into human thought and culture. We can see regularities in classification systems, and we can see differences. The regularities are most likely to be the result of human biological universals. The differences are generally caused by specific social phenomena and cultural practices. And once these factors are linguistically encoded, they reinforce the cultural phenomena they encode and make them seem objectively *real* to speakers of the languages in question.

Sociolinguistics

Sociolinguistics refers to the study of the interaction of language and such social categories as gender, social class, race, and ethnicity. It is particularly appealing to many students of cultural anthropology because it is the area of linguistics most directly tied to their special focus.

1) Language and gender An interesting area within sociolinguistics examines the intersection of language and gender. In most societies there are distinctive differences between the ways in which men and women speak. In some small-scale societies of times past, men and women actually spoke different languages, because, as mentioned in Chapter 6, men obtained wives from different ethnic groups, who often spoke different languages. In such societies both boys and girls were raised by their mothers to speak the women's language, but as boys grew older, they abandoned their mothers' (women's) language, and spoke the language of their fathers and other men. This was true of the native Carib and Arawak peoples of the Caribbean area in the

Figure 7.9 Arawak Indians. 1880. Tropenmuseum, Amsterdam, The Netherlands. Wikimedia. CC BY-SA 3.0.

fifteenth and sixteenth centuries. Though the Caribs usually killed Arawak men when they conquered an Arawak group (which is how they gained access to Arawak women), it was the Carib language that ironically died out first: the mixed Carib-Arawak boys eventually gave up switching to speaking Carib as they grew older.

In other places linguists have reported that men and women speak the same language but speak it differently, sometimes so differently that their speech amounts to two separate **dialects** (varieties of a language mutually comprehensible with other dialects). This is true of the Yayuwa speaking Aborigines of Australia (Bradley 1998), and was reported of the Koasati Native Americans of the United States Southeast (Haas 1944). [2]

In many contemporary, state-based societies the differences between male and female language use is not one of language or dialect, but of oral style, or **register**. Early studies of women's language use, especially in the United States, developed the concept of the "**female register**" (Robin Lakoff 1975). The female register was originally described as making use of mitigating, or softening, expressions, deferential conversational strategies, and dramatic adjectives. The reasons suggested for these traits had primarily to do with women's greater sense of insecurity and consequent unwillingness to assert themselves. More recent studies of gender and language in America have stressed that men and women grow up and live in somewhat different cultural spheres and that the styles and content of their speech reflect these differences. So, for example, girls tend to play in small, intimate groups where talking is frequent, while boys play in larger groups where intimate talk is not important, but physical displays of status are. Additionally, we find that as adults men are more comfortable than women in speaking publically in large groups; women are far more likely to ask for directions than men; when hearing of others' troubles, women tend to offer understanding while men offer solutions, and so on (Tannen 1986, 1990).

Data for the fascinating study of gendered language are, fortunately, all around us. Try paying attention to the difference in men's and women's language use in classrooms, on television, in grocery stores, or in personal interactions.[3] You will definitely notice some interesting contrasts.

2) Language and social class The ways in which language is used in such social groupings as class, race, and ethnicity are also of interest to sociolinguists. Americans are very uncomfortable about the issue of social class; many of us even deny that we recognize class divisions and are unwilling to discuss the topic. The American linguist, **William Labov**, however, has explored differences in language use, especially in pronunciation, of different social classes in New York City and Philadelphia. One of Labov's early findings was that in New York, the higher the social class, the more likely speakers were to pronounce the "r" after vowels. Thus, these speakers would pronounce the "r" in "car" rather than saying "cah," as speakers of lower social classes would be likely to do. It is the latter pronunciation that most Americans recognize as part of a "New York accent" (1966, 2006).[4]

In Britain, social class is a less tabooed topic (it seems central to most British TV series), and social class variations in speech are much more distinctive than they are in the United States. One of the best known studies of the interaction of language and social class in English comes from the British researcher, Basil Bernstein (1971). Bernstein concentrated not on phonology (or the way speech *sounds*), but on *what* people said. He concluded that working class speakers in England were less likely than middle-class speakers to be explicit and detailed in their speech. They were more likely to rely upon brief, stereotyped statements when speaking to each other. Middle class speakers, by contrast, were more likely to be explicit and detailed in their speech, and to lay out the implications of their propositions. Bernstein's assessment was that this was due not only to upbringing in families in which such language use was expected, but also to the fact that middle class people were more likely to interact verbally with a wide variety of people. Bernstein's work also helps to explain why middle-class students tend to do better in school than working class students in England. Most schools are, after all, middle class institutions, with middle-class linguistic expectations. In this context, regardless of their intellectual capacity, working class students will appear less academically acute when they follow the linguistic conventions of their own social class.

3) Bidialectalism: Black English Vernacular   Another area of sociolinguistics is the topic of bilingual and bidialectal societies. In the United States, one of the most thoroughly investigated dialects is African American English, also referred to as Black English Vernacular (BEV), and sometimes Ebonics. Thanks to the work of J. L. Dillard (1972) and subsequent scholars, it is now universally accepted by linguists that BEV is a decreolized creole. That is, it is a creole language, originally formed from a variety of African languages spoken by African slaves from different ethnic groups. Other elements of this creole included the European languages spoken by these slaves' captors, including English, Dutch, French, Spanish, and Portuguese. According to our current understanding, first a largely African-base pidgin system developed out of necessity, so that people of different mother tongues could speak to each other. The pidgin then creolized as it became the first language of the children and grandchildren of imported slaves. As generations passed, the creole languages of these slaves, and later of their free descendants, decreolized, or became more like the dominant language around them. In the United States and in such countries as Jamaica, Bermuda, and Belize, this dominant language was English. In Haiti it was French. And in Curacao and Aruba (where the creole language is called Papiamento) it was Portuguese.

Though linguists are aware of the origins of BEV, many speakers of the standard dialect of English in the United States continue to believe that BEV is merely "bad" English, and that it is incapable of complex expression. Linguists have demonstrated that the structure of BEV is as regular and rule governed as the structure of any other dialect or language, and is not merely a random collection of broken standard conventions. The use of double negatives, for example, regularly employed in BEV, parallels similar usage in the standard English of centuries ago, and in many standard European languages, including French, Spanish, and Italian, as they are presently spoken.

Other characteristics of BEV, such as the absence of the verb "to be" (also called the "copula") in some kinds of statements, are similarly predictable and rule governed. This absence of forms of the verb "to be" occurs primarily in statements of habitual existence, such as "She my sister," or "He really smart," as well as before present participles, as in "They going to catch the bus." And lest we imagine that it is only BEV and other Creole languages that do not always use the verb "to be," we should remember that there are plenty of other languages in the world that drop the copula in many situations, and that Latin was one of them. As for the utility of BEV in expressing logical or philosophical thought, William Labov (in a classic article entitled "The Logic of Nonstandard English" [1969]) conclusively demonstrated that BEV is perfectly capable of any kind of argument.

Certainly, it is true that BEV has low status among speakers of standard English, and it is also true that the ability to speak standard English is therefore a very useful skill, especially when it comes to academic success and employment. But it is important to remember that this is not because of some intrinsic defect in BEV, itself. It is due purely to the preference of speakers of standard English for their own dialect and to the social and economic superiority they enjoy that allows them to enforce their preference. Similar situations exist in other countries with speakers of low status dialects of other languages.

4) Multilingualism   The United States early developed an emphasis on monolingualism. In order to weld a common culture and community from its diverse immigrants, the importance of speaking English has been stressed for centuries. "Real" Americans were and are supposed to speak English. Not only were Americans supposed to speak English, but, partly because of the lack of other countries nearby, there developed the idea that speaking *only* one language was normal and desirable.

Many Americans believe that speaking more than one language will have a negative impact on academic success, and they point to the difficulties that some immigrant children have in school. Certainly, these struggles are real, but they are not intrinsic to bilingualism. Instead, they have to do with socioeconomic hardship and with lack of sufficient fluency in the language of instruction. Ironically, however underemphasized the teaching of foreign languages may be in American schools, no one suggests that learning a second or third language is detrimental to academic achievement for native speakers of English who learn additional languages in academic settings.

In many parts of the world, it is normal for the majority of people to speak more than one language. A common estimate is that roughly two-thirds of the world's population speak at least two languages. This is true not only in places in which students learn foreign languages in school, but more commonly, in places where people may speak one language at home and another outside the home. It also occurs where there are people from numerous ethnic and linguistic groups living near each other, where women from a tribal group routinely marry men from another group, and where, as is increasingly common, people must move across national borders in search of work. The Arabic-speaking Gulf states, for example, currently employ both men and women from non-Arabic-speaking countries, including the Philippines, Bangladesh, and Pakistan. Similarly, countries in northern and western Europe, like France, Italy, Germany, and Sweden have for years hosted "guest workers" from North Africa, Turkey, Greece, and eastern Europe, among other places. All of these guest workers, as well as most of their families, if they accompany them, will become fully or partially bilingual, at a minimum. In sum, among the world's peoples it has long been and is now both common and useful to speak more than one language.

SUMMARY

Humans, like many complex organisms, communicate in a variety of ways, including scent, body positioning, and facial expression. But the most flexible and productive medium through which humans communicate is language.

Language may be defined as a learned system of intentional communication based on orally produced, arbitrary symbols in which there is a fixed, one-to-one correspondence between symbol and referent.

All animals have a communication system by which they transmit information, either intentionally or unintentionally, both to individuals of their species and to members of other species. This communication, however, cannot be referred to as language. While some nonhuman animals do transmit relatively complicated information, their communication always lacks significant elements of human language. The most important missing elements are complexity and specificity. For example, a dog can communicate dominance, submission, or the desire to go outdoors, but not the idea that canines deserve the same rights and privileges as humans. Of course, dogs cannot formulate that idea in the first place. Not only is human language more complex than other kinds of animal communication, it is also more flexible. It allows humans to discuss what has happened in the past, what may happen in the future, and what can never happen at all. It lets us lie. An opossum may lie motionless on the ground to deceive a predator into believing that it is dead ("playing possum"), but this hardwired "behavioral lying" is quite different from a human telling his wife that the lipstick on his collar is really just ketchup from the hamburger he had at lunch. In sum, all language is communication but not all communication is language.

To review our discussion of linguistics in this chapter, we can return to the myths about language that began this chapter.

Myth #1.   Language is an all or nothing proposition. Either you have it or you do not.

While contemporary nonhuman animals do not have language, there is plenty of research that suggests it is best to think of communication as a continuum, with contemporary human language at the complex end. Experiments over the last fifty years involving apes using human-devised communications systems, including sign language, have shown that these animals *can* use these systems, though at a rudimentary level. No ape will ever compose the *Gettysburg Address,* but then, no dog or chicken will ever sign "Where is Roger?" as the chimpanzee, Washoe, was known to do. The ape language experiments suggest that if apes have the ability to make limited use of a human communication system, then many of our extinct ancestors, whose brains were substantially larger than those of apes, probably used a communication system somewhere between contemporary human language and natural ape communication.

Myth #2. Some languages are better than others; they are more logical or better able to explain complex ideas.

The lexicon of any language is strongly affected by the environment in which its speakers live, by their technology, and by other elements of their culture. Thus the language of a cattle raising people (whether in Wyoming or in East Africa) will probably have a lot of terms for various kinds of cattle, while the language of people whose society focuses heavily upon electronic technology will have an extensive collection of terms for computers and their functions. But all societies can borrow or develop new terms for new elements that come into their culture, and no society has more difficulty in expressing complicated ideas or emotions than another. Latin, for example, had no single word for "yes" or "no," nor did it have any definite or indefinite articles. But this did not cause the Romans any problems in expressing themselves. And no language is more "logical" or more "emotional" or "romantic" than any other. Italian is sometimes characterized as a romantic language by people who forget it was also the language of Mussolini and Machiavelli. Languages serve to encode the values and interests of their speakers, and in doing this they may reinforce some patterns of thought and behavior. But, as indicated by the principle of linguistic relativity, no language has any intrinsic superiority or inferiority when compared to any other. Linguist Edward Sapir summed up the equality of languages in 1921 when he famously wrote, "When it comes to linguistic form, Plato walks with the Macedonian swineherd and Confucius with the head-hunting [native] of Assam."

Myth #3 Dialects spoken by people of low socioeconomic status are inherently inferior to dialects spoken by people with high socioeconomic status.

Dialects are subdivisions of a language that are mutually intelligible with other dialects of the same language. Thus, what is true of a language is necessarily also true of its constituent dialects: no dialect is intrinsically superior to any other dialect. Certainly some dialects have greater prestige than other dialects, because of the prestige of their speakers. But as Labov and others have shown conclusively, the low status of a dialect has nothing to do with its fundamental intellectual or affective power. In short, it is no more defensible to claim superiority of a high-status dialect over a low-status dialect than it is to claim the superiority of one language over another.

Myth #4 Speaking multiple languages impairs learning and contributes to psychological stress.

Throughout the world there are many communities, including entire countries, in which it is normal for all or most people to speak more than one language. This does not interfere with the speakers' academic or intellectual success, and in fact it may enhance it. In the United States, which has a history of extensive immigration, bilingualism has often been associated with recent immigrant groups who may suffer from low status and low incomes. They may also have difficulty in school because of poor teaching, frequent moves, and chronic absence, all of which impair their ability to learn any subject matter well, including English. When the social and economic circumstances of second- and third-language learners are adequate to ensure well-being, these languages serve to enhance—not detract from—the experiences and life chances of these learners.

QUESTIONS FOR THOUGHT AND REFLECTION

1. If chimpanzees can be taught to use human sign language and other human communicative systems, why have they not developed such systems for themselves?

2. Since the International Phonetic Alphabet (IPA) can precisely render any and all languages in the world, why have not the world's people adopted the IPA as a universal writing system?

3. Throughout time and space there have been societies in which men and women have spoken very differently, using different words, pronunciations, and even different languages. How have some of these practices developed?

4. Why can it be said that the Sapir-Whorf Hypothesis is not a hypothesis? If it is not a hypothesis, then what is it? Even though it is not a hypothesis in the strict sense of the word, it does not seem to disappear from the pages of anthropology textbooks or from the imaginations of anthropology students and scholars. Why do you think this is?

5. The principle of linguistic relativity establishes that no language or dialect is superior to any other in its ability to express the full range of human thought, emotion, and experience. Why, then, do you think some people insist that certain languages are "more emotional" or "more logical" than others? In some eras and in some places and institutions speakers have been penalized for and/or prohibited from using certain languages or dialects. What are some of the reasons for why this has occurred and continues to occur? Can you think of any contemporary situations in which American students continue to be penalized for using a nonstandard dialect in writing? Describe these situations. Do you think they are justified? Why or why not?

6. Linguists are not usually considered very humorous people, but they do like to tell one joke: What do you call a person who speaks two languages? Answer: bilingual. What do you call a person who speaks one language? Answer: American. Why do you think so many non-immigrants in the United States speak only English? What are some of the advantages to learning to use additional languages? When should second- (or third- or fourth-) language learning begin? Why?

NOTES

[1]We should note that no such language as "Chinese" exists. To refer to Mandarin or Hokkien as "Chinese" is a lot like referring to English as "European." There are many related Chinese languages, which are no more mutually comprehensible than English and German.

[2]Another example of language with male and female forms is the native California Yana language, spoken by the famous Ishi, the last speaker of the language, and the last member of the Yana group (Kroeber, Theodora 2011). Interestingly, because Ishi had lived in isolation with his wife and mother-in-law before they died and he was forced to join white society, he used female Yana forms.

[3]Perspectives on gender and language vary widely, with lively debate (see Lakoff and Buchholz 2004 and Cameron 2007 for two quite different views).

[4]See Labov (2001) for his continuing study of language variation in class and ethnicity and the changes that occur in this variation through time.

REFERENCES CITED

Berlin, Brent and Paul Kay
    1969 *Basic Color Terms: Their Universality and Evolution.* Berkeley: University of California Press.

Bernstein, Basil
1971 *Class, Code and Control: Volume 1, Theoretical Studies towards a Sociology of Language.* London: Routledge and Kegan Paul.

Bickerton, Derek
1981 Roots of Language. Ann Arbor: Karona Publishers.
2009 *Adam's Tongue.* New York: Hill and Wang.

Bomhard, Allan R.
2008 *Reconstructing Proto-Nostratic: Comparative Phonology, Morphology, and Vocabulary.* Leiden and Boston: Brill. 2 volumes.

Cameron, Deborah
2007 *The Myth of Mars and Venus: Do Men and Women Really Speak Different Languages?* Oxford: Oxford University Press.

Carroll, Lewis (Charles Lutwidge Dodgson)
1999 (1872) Through the Looking Glass and What Alice Found There. New York: Dover Publications.

Curtiss, Susan
1977 *Genie: A Psycholinguistic Study of a Modern-Day "Wild Child."* Boston: Academic Press.

Dillard, J.L.
1972 *Black English: Its History and Usage in the United States.* New York: Random House.

Firth, John Rupert
1930 *Speech.* London: Benn's Sixpence Library.

Fitch, William Tecumseh Sherman
2010 *The Evolution of Language.* Cambridge: Cambridge University Press.

Fouts, Roger with Stephen Tukel Mills
1997 *Next of Kin: What What Chimpanzees Have Taught Us About Who We Are.* New York: William Morrow.

Greengerg, Joseph
1970 *The Languages of Africa.* 3d edition. Bloomington: Indiana University Press.
1987 *Language in the Americas.* Stanford: Stanford University Press.

Haas, Mary R.
1944 Men's and Womrn's Speech in Koasati. *Language* 20: 142-149.

Labov, William
1966/2006 *The Social Stratification of English in New York City.* Washington, D.C.: Center for Applied Linguistics (2d edition: 2006).
1969 The Logic of Nonstandsrd English. *Georgetown Monographs on Language and Linguistics* 22:1-31.
1970 *The Study of Non-Standard English.* Champaign, Illionois: National Council of Teachers of English.
2001 *Principles of Linguistic Change. Volume III: Cognitive and Cultural Change.* Oxford: Wiley Blackwell.

Lakoff, Robin Toulmach
1975 *Language and Woman's Place.* New York: Harper and Row.

Lakoff, Robin Toulmach and Mary Buchholtz

2004 *Language and Woman;s Place: Text and Commentary.* New York: Oxford University Press, USA.

Lenneberg, Eric H.
  1967 *Biological Foundations of Language.* Hoboken, New Jersey: Wiley.

Linton, Ralph
  1967 Why is the Cassowary not a Bird? A Problem in Zoological Taxonomy among the Karam of the New Guinea Highlands. *Man* (NS) Vol. 2, No. 1: 5-25.

Rymer, Russ
  1994 *Genie: A Scientific Tragedy.* New York: Harper Perennial.

Sapir, Edward
  1949 The Psychological Reality of the Phoneme *in Selected Writings of Edward Sapir in Language, Culture, and Personality*, ed.: David G. Mandelbaum. Berkeley: University of California Press.

Tannen, Deborah
  1986 *That's Not What I Mean! How Conversational Styles Make or Break Relationships.* New York: Morrow..
  1990 *You Just Don't Understand: Women and Men in Conversation.* New York: Ballentine.

Terrace, Herbert
  1979 *Nim.* New York: Knopf.

Witherspoon, Gary
  Language and Art in the Navajo Universe. Ann Arbor: University of Michigan Press.

Witkowski, Stanley R. and Cecil H. Brown
  1978 Lexical Universals. *Annual Review of Anthropology* 7:427-451.

CHAPTER 8

RELIGION

Patterns of belief and their enactment

Religion refers to beliefs and practices concerning supernatural forces. Religion exists in all cultures, although not all individuals profess the dominant beliefs or follow the majority practices of their particular culture. By this point in your reading, it will come as no surprise to learn that anthropology does not address the truth or falsity of religious beliefs and cannot by its professional principles consider any one religion to be superior to another. Rather, anthropology is interested in the origin of religion, cultural similarities and variations in religious belief and practice, and how religion intersects with other aspects of culture.

Anthropologists sometimes distinguish religion from **magic**, following Sir James Frazer, author of the popular and influential book, *The Golden Bough,* mentioned in Chapter 2. Frazer considered magic to be an attempt to make supernatural forces or beings act in certain ways, with a detached, utilitarian attitude. By contrast, he saw religion as an attempt to placate or please supernatural beings, with an attitude of reverence and humility. Although this distinction is sometimes applicable, there are too many ethnographic cases where a sharp division cannot really be made, or where, for example, utilitarian "magical spells" are included with prayers of supplication to gods. For example, when the Hopi people of northern Arizona perform their famous Snake Dance, they are engaged in both a religious ritual and a magical performance. Here they dance with snakes that they then release. The snakes, according to

Hopi belief, carry the group's reverent prayers for rain to supernatural beings. But if the dance is not performed correctly, the **ritual** (a patterned behavioral enactment of beliefs) will not work; the supernaturals will not be pleased and the rains will not come.

Religions are characterized by a set of beliefs about the supernatural (for example, that there is only one god), mythology, ritual, and taboos (prohibitions). The **tenets** (or prescriptive statements of belief) of a religion, when viewed together, typically form a coherent, integrated whole that expresses a people's worldview and most basic values about what is right and wrong— that is, morality. Religious mythology covers accounts of how the universe was created and how natural and supernatural forces came to be. Such narratives usually contain or imply moral messages within them. Note the difference (as mentioned also in the introduction to this book) between this use of the idea of "**myth**" and the popular sense of "myth" as "mistaken belief." Both mythology and the rituals that embody them are full of symbols that anthropologists analyze to uncover the deeper meanings of a people's religious lives and thought. Finally, as anthropologists use the term, taboos are supernaturally prescribed avoidances or prohibitions. These usually cover food restrictions (for example the prohibition of pork consumption in Islam and Judaism or beef consumption in Hinduism) and contact with certain people, places or objects to guard against danger or impurity.

This chapter explores a variety of religious beliefs and practices, discusses the origins and possible functions of religion, shows how religion moves us emotionally and considers the relation of religion to other spheres of life such as politics and ecological relationships. In the process we will dispel the following myths (a term that in this case refers to misconceptions) about religion:

Common Myths of Culture

Myth #1 Religion-based treatments of illness are ineffective quackery.

Myth #2 People are attracted and attached to a religion primarily because of its set of beliefs.

Myth #3 Religion is the opiate of the masses (that is, it pacifies the ignorant masses and makes them accept the status quo).

Myth #4 Religious ritual has no practical impact on the environment.

ORIGINS OF RELIGION

Religion is a "cultural universal." That is, it is an element in every human culture on earth. Thus, we can presume that religion was expressed in the cultures of the earliest human societies. We also know from the archaeological record that by some 60,000 years ago people buried their dead and placed grave goods inside the burials—food and other objects that were probably thought necessary in an afterlife. There is also evidence that Neanderthals had religious beliefs and practices, as evidenced by their intentional burials with flowers placed on the corpse, although this evidence remains controversial. We unfortunately do not know why religion is a human cultural universal or how it came to be so. One common idea is that religion helps us to cope with death, both our own and that of others, through ritual and through ideas about an afterlife or a larger purpose to life. We are not the only animals to be disturbed by the deaths of others, but we are, as far as is known, the only animals to contemplate and fear our own death.

Despite our uncertain knowledge of the origin of religion, anthropologists and others have come up with some very interesting ideas on this topic. An early theory was put forth in the nineteenth century by Sir Edward Tylor (1871) who suggested that religion grew out of the human development of the concept of the soul. Humans, he felt, devised the soul concept to help explain some otherwise puzzling observations, such as the unnerving difference between the living and the dead, or the difference between an animated body and a lifeless corpse. To account for this observable difference, they developed the idea that a soul exists in all living things, leaving the body at death. Similarly, the idea of the mobile soul could account for the experience of dreams—the feeling that we travel to other places while dreaming but wake up where we went to sleep—and could account for why deceased people can appear in our dreams. Souls temporarily leave the body during dreams and permanently leave at death, becoming ghosts that can visit the living in their dreams. For Tylor, it was only a small step then to attribute souls to other natural phenomena such as plants, animals, geological features, the wind and so on. Tylor called this attribution of souls to natural phenomena **animism.** Animism, he said, was the earliest form of religion; later, the idea of souls was extended to human-like deities.

A later nineteenth century scholar, **Robert R. Marett**, a student of Tylor, objected to Tylor's implication that religion arose as a way to satisfy human intellectual needs, or to answer questions about life, death and dreams. He felt that the earliest expressions of religion were instead brought about through human experiences of wonderment and awe in the face of what seemed to them extraordinary and powerful. In his view, prior to animism was a stage of **animatism**, the belief that the entire world is animated by an impersonal force manifest in living and non-living entities. Marrett adopted the Melanesian word **mana** for this force or special power, as introduced briefly in Chapter 5. A charismatic person or a skilled warrior has mana. Objects, too, such as a special arrow that somehow brings down more game than ordinary arrows, can have mana. Marvin Harris (1997: 369) also noted that while not religious, many ideas in Western culture express a belief in mana. Thus, for example, "[v]itamin pills are consumed by many millions of people in the expectation that they will exert a powerful effect on health and well being. Soaps and detergents are said to clean because of 'cleaning power,' gasolines provide engines with 'starting power' or 'go power.'"

Also influenced by Tylor was Sir James Frazer who, as we saw earlier, distinguished religion from magic. In Frazer's view, magic came first in human development, with religion originating as people perceived the failure of magic.

Figure 8.1 Rows of "powerful" vitamins in a supermarket in Oregon. In the United States, attraction to the power of vitamins is an example of belief in mana.
Source: Authors' collection.

Thus magical practices addressed vaguely to supernatural forces did not consistently bring rain, cure illness, or increase hunting success. Early humans then developed ideas about gods or spirits controlling these forces and humans potentially influencing these gods or spirits through prayer and supplication.

Later in the nineteenth century psychiatrist **Sigmund Freud** wrote of religion as adult projections of childhood anxieties and needs. Because children are dependent on their parents for so long, they come to see them as all-powerful. As adults, and especially in times of stress and uncertainty, according to Freud's argument, people often revert to their childhood feelings, but now they construct supernatural beings who will take care of their needs. Religion is then a human quest for powerful parental figures. In this light Freud also saw religion as generalized neurosis, drawing parallels between religious thinking and behavior on the one hand and neurotic behavior on the other. The neurotic individual engages in compulsive, obsessive behavior, strikingly similar to repetitive religious rituals. For Freud, the roots of both individual neurosis and generalized religion are human anxiety and fear. Many of these ideas of Freud are still popular in some circles.

In the early twentieth century French sociologist **Emile Durkheim** theorized that an early form of human religion, one that captured its very essence, was totemism. We can recall from our earlier chapter on kinship that totemism is the ritual worship of an animal, plant, or natural object that is considered the mythological ancestor of a clan or other kinship grouping. For Durkheim, religion, as expressed initially in totemism, is society worshipping itself. Individual humans feel the power of the social group with which they so closely identify. This positive feeling of social solidarity was expressed by early humans through the clan totem and the associated symbols and rituals required to honor the mythological ancestor of the group. Worship of other objects or supernatural beings came later, but in the beginning it was totemism that integrated individuals in kin groups through totemic symbols and group rituals. In this way religion serves society because it enhances solidarity and gives cohesion to social groups.

In the later twentieth and early twenty-first centuries, interest in the origin of religion waned. The ideas of previous scholars were seen as too speculative, and solid evidence for their proposals was lacking. More recently, however, new ideas about the origin of religion have been proposed by evolutionary anthropologists. Among these is the suggestion put forward by primatologist Frans de Waal (2013) who proposes that one basis for religion—morality— has its roots in our evolutionary past. The building blocks of human morality are found in many mammals, most notably in primates. De Waal refers here to examples of altruism and compassion in the animal world. For example, apes will open doors to give other apes access to food, even if they lose some of the food for themselves. Chimpanzees console one another in times of distress. And in one very interesting experiment, capuchin monkeys exhibited a concern with fairness and equity. Here, pairs of monkeys were put in cages, visible to one another. They were trained to perform simple tasks that were rewarded with slices of cucumber. These monkeys like cucumbers but much prefer grapes. Then, when one of the monkeys was suddenly rewarded with grapes and the other left with cucumbers, the cucumber-rewarded monkey would become very agitated, throw down the cucumbers and refuse to perform the tasks (to see a video of this very interesting sequence of behavior go to the following website: www.youtube.com/watch?v=1KhAd0Tyny0). The monkeys are expressing what is known as "inequity aversion." De Waal notes that "[t]he underlying motivation is not so different from human street protests against unemployment or low wages" (2013:300). For de Waal, these primate signs of inequity aversion and other examples of animal empathy or compassion suggest that morality antedates religion and that the roots of human morality reside within our animal heritage. Religion, which is uniquely human, is merely the expression of this ingrained morality on an abstract level. Of course, not all religious systems are focused on equity, let alone morality. Supernaturals themselves can be capricious or downright evil. Thus de Waal's analysis is not universally accepted as the answer to religious origins although his work is very pertinent to the origins of human morality.

Whatever the form of humankind's first religion, it diversified through time and space. Religion, like culture generally, changes. We presume that our hunter-gatherer ancestors did not have full-time religious specialists or religious architecture because hunter-gatherers in historic times have not had them. On the other hand, what may be the world's first temple has been partially excavated at Gobekli Tepe, a site in southeast Turkey. The structure dates to 11,000 years ago and consists of huge pillars reaching 16 feet high and weighing several tons. The pillars are arranged in circles and carved with images of lions, foxes, scorpions and vultures. People of the surrounding region were hunter-gatherers and had yet to take up horticulture or animal husbandry, though they were to do so about 500 years later. Some archaeologists consider the site a place of religious pilgrimage. If correct, this may modify our views of the organizational and building capacities of hunter-gatherer cultures in human prehistory and the form of their religious life. Elsewhere, it is only with agriculture and the development of early states that we see monumental temples, sacred texts and belief in all-powerful gods that sanction the power of the ruling classes.

Many contemporary states have separated religion and the state, although countries like Iran and Israel remain exceptions, and such countries as Thailand, where the King must be Buddhist, or the United Kingdom, where the monarch must be Anglican, are partial exceptions. Even in secular countries many of the prevailing laws are to a great extent derived from current or former religious principles and practices. Countries that are majority Christian prohibit plural marriage, for example, based on Christian teachings, while majority Muslim countries permit polygyny, though not polyandry, in compliance with the Koran. And when same-sex marriage was prohibited, in the United States and elsewhere, the objections voiced were usually religious.

Another feature of religious transformation is that religions tend to branch out from one another. Thus both Christianity and Islam developed out of an earlier monotheistic Judaism. Christianity split into Catholicism, Eastern Orthodoxy, and Protestantism, with the last further diversifying into dozens of different denominations. Hinduism, Buddhism, Jainism and Sikhism all developed out of an earlier Vedic tradition, originating 3,500 years ago in northwestern India. In this way, religions tend to develop a life and evolution of their own. Finally, some religious change is found when one religion is blended in with one or more others, a process called religious **syncretism**. In many cases religious syncretisms were formed when indigenous peoples colonized by Western powers blended their earlier religion with whatever form of Christianity was brought by missionaries and other colonists. Another example of religious syncretism is the Rastafarian religious movement in the Caribbean, which combines elements of Christianity, African religions and Hinduism. A later section of this chapter details two other cases of syncretism—Cargo cults and the Native American Ghost Dance. Many scholars of religion would argue that Christianity and Islam are also syncretic, having developed not only out of Judaism (and Christianity, in the case of Islam), but also from Zoroastrianism, local animistic beliefs, and Greco-Roman spiritual cults and ethical sects.

We may not know how religion originally came about or what form it first took, but we can be sure that early in human existence religious notions were expressed through the beliefs and practices of shamanism, the subject of the next section. Shamanism persists worldwide to this day as a part of or alongside broader religious thought and practice.

SHAMANISM

A shaman, as noted in Chapter 5, is a part-time religious specialist who intercedes between humans and the supernatural world. Usually this intercession is undertaken for the purpose of treating a person for an illness, but shamans can also be called upon to assist humans in other ways, say, to find a lost object or to rid a new house of the influence of harmful spirits. Shamans, as opposed to **priests** or other religious practitioners, acquire their religious status directly through their own experiences and abilities in navigating the spiritual world. They are not ordained by any organized religious authorities. Their legitimacy comes from becoming recognized by a broader community for their power to reach and influence supernatural beings and forces.

Shamans are found everywhere throughout the globe and show remarkable similarities from one region to another. Usually shamans are male, but in many cultures women may become shamans, as well, and in a few areas (for example, Korea) shamans are mostly women. Worldwide, shamans are also frequently characterized by the use of elaborate costumes and masks, often including symbols of flight, such as feathers. Anthropologists point out the connection between these kinds of flight symbols and the notion that a shaman, unlike an ordinary person, is able to undertake "soul travel"; that is, the shaman can transport his or her soul to the supernatural world and return it safely back again. The shaman is in control of this process. Also characteristic of shamans is that this soul travel, or ability to communicate effectively with spirits, is achieved through trance or an altered state of consciousness. In trance the shaman visits spirits or is possessed by one of them. These trance states are typically achieved through the use of rhythmic drums, rattles, and vigorous physical activity such as dancing. In some cultures, but not all, shamans also use drugs to help induce a trance state. Persons may choose to become shamans in some cultures; in others, they are chosen by spirits; that is, they respond to a spiritual "calling" that comes to them in dreams or through spontaneously falling into a trance state. In still other cultures, it may happen either way. Usually a shaman undergoes a period of training with a senior shaman, a process that may take many years and involve higher and higher levels of expertise. Shamans are usually paid for their services, but nowhere is shamanism a path to riches, and shamans in general are not wealthy.

Most of the work of shamans is focused on healing sick patients who seek them out for treatment. By invoking supernatural forces, the shaman may determine the cause of an illness (an unwitting offense to a spirit, sorcery [see below] on the part of an enemy, a neglected family ghost, and so on) and will

Figure 8.2   A Shaman in Nepal.
Source: Authors' collection.

likely recommend ritual action to effect a cure, along with other changes in a patient's diet and behavior. In this role, shamans are a type of indigenous medical practitioner; that is, a person who works in the healing profession using knowledge and practice outside the field of biomedicine. Depending on the culture or region, other such indigenous practitioners may include local herbalists, midwives, or any persons skilled in home remedies. But shamans—although they, too, may be knowledgeable about herbal, dietary, and other naturalistic treatments of illness—are distinctive for their use of supernatural intercession in their treatment of patients.

Many people who lack experience with shamans are apt to think of the healing work they do as quackery and imagine that positive health outcomes of their patients are very rare or only coincidental. Many people also consider that shamanism probably thrives only where modern biomedical treatments are not available. Neither of these impressions is accurate. Of course it is true that shamanic treatments are unlikely to cure cases of advanced cancer or rabies (disorders against which modern medicine is also unlikely to be effective). But what the shaman, unlike many biomedical doctors, *is* able to do is relieve patients of considerable stress, a result that is now known in biomedical circles to have positive impacts on health and to be beneficial in nearly any illness recovery. Shamanic treatments use powerful rituals that incorporate the patient's religious belief system and use this to instill hope and a sense of well-being in the patient.

In addition, and through this same process, shamans are particularly effective in treating patients with psychological disorders. Many obserevers consider that shamans are as effective in treating psychological and psychosomatic disorders as are Western biomedical practitioners (Torrey 1987). Through their skilled use of religious symbols, and through their intimate knowledge of a patient's personal and social life, shamans are in fact able to recommend beneficial changes in a patient's behavior that may involve reducing social and interpersonal tensions for the patient.

True, some shamans have admitted to anthropologists that they sometimes use "sleigh of hand" techniques in their ceremonies, for example, hiding a harmful-looking substance in their mouths, which they later pretend to magically suck out of a patient's body. But shamans do not see this kind of technique as fraudulent. It is merely "something with which to impress the audience" or is meant as a symbolic gesture for those patients who need material proof of the shaman's spiritual powers.

There is some similarity between shamans and so-called "faith healers" in Euro-American societies. Both claim to intercede with the supernatural in an effort to cure illness, and both may achieve some success through psychological mechanisms. However, some of the spectacular televised performances of faith healers where blind people suddenly gain sight and paralyzed people suddenly walk, do seem rather contrived and profit-driven, far beyond what is found with shamanism elsewhere.

It is a mistake to see shamanism as conflicting with biomedicine. Certainly shamans do not see it that way, and indeed many shamans are increasingly aware of and themselves incorporate biomedical options in their treatments of patients. And patients who summon shamans quite easily combine shamanic treatments with resort to over-the-counter medicines as well as biomedical clinics, doctors, and hospitals, taking an attitude of "whatever works." Along the United States-Mexico border, traditional healers in the Mexican American community, referred to as *curanderas* (or *curanderos*, if they are men), combine the functions of herbalists, shamans, and practical, self-taught lay doctors. In one case, a local man, Miguel, suffered from chronic stomach pains. He had tried over-the-counter remedies, but without relief. He was then convinced by his relatives to consult a *curandera*. The *curander,* a married middle-aged woman who lived in a working class neighborhood, had Miguel take off all his clothing but his underwear and lie down on a bed. She listened intently to his belly and then swept his entire torso with branches of the *pirul* tree, to remove any *aires,* or supernatural vapors. While she swept, she recited prayers. Then she told Miguel that he had *empacho*, a blockage of the intestine that can be either physical or spiritual in nature, and produced by either physical or spiritual causes, including *mal de ojo,* or the "evil eye." In addition to praying several times a day, the *curandera* prescribed a small bottle of Pompeian olive oil (an inexpensive, locally sold brand), to be drunk once a day, every day. Miguel got up, got dressed, and paid the *curandera* a fee. He bought several bottles of Pompeian olive oil, which he drank daily, and said his prayers. For a time his stomach pains subsided, but eventually they returned. Miguel then tried other biomedical doctors. He was variously diagnosed as having diverticulitis and then ulcers, and each time new medicines and a change in eating habits were prescribed. Most recently, a new biomedical doctor told Miguel he was stressed and depressed, and prescribed both anti-anxiety and antidepressant medications. Miguel now reports that at least so far, the most recent cures seem to be successful. His case illustrates not only how shamanistic practitioners make use of a variety of techniques, including modern biomedical approaches, but also that their patients see shamanic healing as integrated into a variety of cure-seeking strategies by patients who have access to several options.

For decades, Westerners who sought to bring modern biomedicine to remote rural areas of developing countries saw shamans and shamanism as the enemy, as a constraint founded on ignorance and superstition. But today, many health development programs in developing countries recruit shamans as "barefoot doctors" who travel the countryside, now trained in preventive health care and equipped with simple biomedicines and even condoms to help address the health needs of the population. In many cases, these programs have been quite successful.

THE DARK ARTS

The dark side of shamanic healing power is, of course, the power to harm, to cause physical pain, illness or death. In some cultures shamans are not considered to use this kind of harmful power; in others it is thought that they can and do use their power for either help or harm; so while they are respected and summoned in times of illness, they are also slightly feared. But it is not only shamans who can practice the "dark arts;" nearly all cultures have ideas about **sorcery** and **witchcraft** conducted wittingly or unwittingly by ordinary people. The terms "sorcery" and "witchcraft" are often used interchangeably but technically speaking, there is a difference. A sorcerer uses objects or substances to deliberately harm another. A witch merely uses thoughts and emotions and may not even be aware that he/she is inflicting harm. For example, a jealous person may cast an "evil eye" on another, causing illness without even being aware of it. As for sorcery, Sir James Frazer long ago detected two common principles at work in many different cultures. One he called "**contagious magic**" which operates on the principle that objects once in contact with a person continue to affect that person. So, for example, if you can acquire a piece of another person's hair, fingernail, tooth, or other substance you can inflict harm on that person by performing certain acts on the hair, nail, etc. The other principle he called "**imitative magic**," where actions undertaken on an object that represents a person can have an effect on that person. One example is voodoo practice, which may involve such activities as the sticking of pins into a doll representing a person. Of course, imitative and contagious magic can alternatively be used to help or cure a person.

HOW RELIGION MOVES US: THE POWER OF RITUAL

One might think that people are deeply committed to and participate in religion largely because of the attraction of particular religious tenets or belief systems. It is, after all, comforting to consider notions of a loving God, or even whimsical, indifferent spirits who can be influenced by one's offerings. Ideas about a divine purpose to life and a blissful afterlife are likewise compelling, though they are not elements in all religious systems. While there may be some truth to this idea that religions move us through their tenets, anthropological studies have suggested that a great deal of the magnetic force that ties persons to religions lies not in teachings but in ritual. Ritual (which, as we saw earlier, is a set of prescribed, ceremonial acts) can be a transformative process; it grabs us from one place or state and moves us to another and, equally important, it does so through powerful, compelling symbols, symbols that speak to us more poignantly and more movingly than mere words.

One of the first anthropologists to analyze the power of rituals was Arnold van Gennep (1960 [orig. 1908]) with his discussion of **rites of passage**. According to van Gennep, rites of passage, that is, ritualized transitions such as initiations into adulthood, weddings, and funerals, are in all cultures marked by three stages: 1) separation of the individual from a previous status, 2) a period of **liminality** or "in-betweenness," and 3) integration of the individual into his or her new status or social state. Accordingly, transition rites can be studied through decoding their processes and symbols of separation, liminality and integration. It is the second stage, liminality, that is the most important. Here the individual is suspended between normal categories, and is ambiguous, neither fully one thing nor the other, on the verge of a transition. It is a period of both promise and danger (Douglass 1966), a period often permeated with safeguards and taboos to symbolically protect the individual from harm. Traditionally in America and Europe for example, grooms and brides were forbidden to see one another on the eve of their wedding, and it was considered unlucky for the groom to see the bride's wedding dress before the ceremony.

British anthropologist Victor Turner (1969, 1974) took van Gennep's ideas a little further, noting that what is special about the ritual period of liminality is that this ambiguous, "betwixt and between" state can generate what he called **communitas.** Communitas is a feeling of abandoning one's individuality and merging into a wholeness with others in a spirit of unity and equality. Although he did not put it quite this way, Turner's writings suggest that to experience communitas, at least occasionally, is a deep human need. So much of our ordinary lives are bound up with "structure," which for Turner was the opposite of communitas. Structure refers to the official, legal, and political norms of social life, to the patterned roles that individuals play and the differentiated social statuses they occupy, to the normative institutions of society. But humans cannot (or at least do not) live by structure alone; everywhere there will be expressions of communitas. There are many examples of communitas, not all of them religious in nature. A simple one is the celebration of New Year's Eve in Euro-American culture. Note that New Year's Eve is itself liminal, betwix and between the old year and the new. To celebrate the transition people gather together, often imbibe champagne, abandon their differentiated statuses and come together in a spirit of equality and oneness. Behaviors normally disapproved may be excused or overlooked on this night.

Another example of communitas in the new year is the pre-Columbian Mayan period of five days at the end of one year and the beginning of the new one, which was called *Wayeb'*. During this time the normal barriers between the secular world and the sacred world were absent so that malevolent supernaturals could harm the living (Foster 2002). In contrast to Euro-Americans on New Year's Eve, who go out together in a spirit of revelry, pre-Columbian Mayan families gathered together in their houses during Wayeb' in defensive communitas. They ventured out only if they had to, and then banged on pots to scare away dangerous spirits, while religious practitioners performed rituals to protect the community.

Turner gave the counterculture movement in American in the 1960s as an example of communitas. This movement sought to challenge "the establishment" (structure) with displays of communitas; the dress and behavior of the "hippies" was full of symbols of equality and social holism; even normative gender distinctions were downplayed in dress and hair styles.

Anthropologists Edmund Leach (1964) and Mary Douglass (1966) long ago noted the great symbolic power of so-called "anomalous creatures" in religious myth and ritual. These are beings that embody a contradiction or are simultaneously two opposing things at once. For example, in Christianity the figure of Christ is somehow both man and God. Similarly, Mary is both Virgin and Mother. In Christ's being both divine and human, and in Mary's embodiment of a contradiction, lies their power to mediate between the human and the supernatural realms (Leach 1964:39). Turner further noted the common presence of such anomalous beings in liminal contexts, where these beings have not only meditative power but also the power through their anomaly to enhance communitas.

Religious ritual, then, moves us in part because it provides a vehicle that can generate communitas. A good illustration of how it does so is found in the Good Friday processions carried out each year throughout the Sorrentine Peninsula in Southern Italy. These dramatic processions express a major cultural concern in the region: the preparation for death (Stone 2013). In local cathedrals individuals post prayers for "a good death," which by definition is a death well prepared, both in a spiritual and a secular sense. A good death includes the securing of a proper burial place. Most people of the region already know where they will be buried or speak with anxiety about the necessity of securing a proper place for themselves and their family members. In this area there is also the practice of secondary burial. After death a corpse is first buried in a common ground for a period of ten years. This is followed by exhumation and drying of the bones which are then kept in a small box and replaced within a common wall of the cemetery or in a family burial house, which is often large and opulent. Reburial is accompanied by a gathering of relatives and a final Benediction Mass performed by a Catholic priest. In these and other ways, Catholicism in Southern Italy, along with many other religions (Hertz 1960), shows a connection between the fate of the soul and the ritual treatment of the corpse. The concern with preparing for death extends, of course, beyond preparations of the body to preparations of the soul as well, to concepts of sin, penitence and redemption. A "good death" in one in which the person has confessed his or her sins, performed penance, and sought redemption.

The Good Friday processions are a ritual enactment of this process. On one level the processions reenact the passage from Jesus' crucifixion to his resurrection, or the transformation of Jesus from martyr to redeemer. But on another implicit level, the ritual drama is a movement in sacred time between the anticipation of and preparation for ordinary human death. The processions are performed by members of Catholic lay brotherhoods (confraternities).

These brotherhoods have served as death preparers for their members and the community of Catholics in general for hundreds of years, acting as burial societies, performing masses for the dead and, in times past, conducting prisoners to their places of execution.[1]

In the Southern Italian town of Sorrento, the Good Friday procession begins at dawn, a liminal period between night and morning, with a "white" procession conducted by the Confraternity of St. Monica.[2] The town of Sorrento becomes a kind of sacred space through which confraternity males, dressed in white robes with hoods, meander, stopping at churches along the way. At the head of the procession is a small band playing funeral marches. Next is a group of robed and hooded men carrying crosses. These are followed by a larger group where each individual carries a symbol of the passion, or suffering, of Christ. For example, one carries a crown of thorns, another carries a Veronica cloth (a reproduction of a cloth said to bear the image of the face of Jesus after a woman named Veronica wiped it of blood and sweat when she met him on the way to his crucifixion). Next comes a choir singing the *Miserere* (a Latin translation of one of the psalms attributed to David[3]) in four tones. And finally, a group of eight men carry on poles a statue of the Madonna in Pain, a life-size statue of a suffering Mary, dressed in blue, with a dagger in her chest. The theme of this first, white procession is the anguished Virgin Mary "searching for her lost son" sometime between Christ's capture and the crucifixion.

At dusk on Good Friday a parallel "black" procession takes place, conducted by the Confraternity of Death. It is very similar to the white procession, with a band, choir and so on, except that those in the procession wear black robes with hoods and members carry two statues. The first statue to appear in procession is the Dead Christ, a delicately carved, life-size wooden statue realistically showing an anguished face with blood dripping down the head from a crown of thorns. Following the Dead Christ is another Madonna in Pain, though this one is dressed in black. In this concluding procession the Madonna has found her crucified son. Throughout both processions townspeople gather along the streets to observe the procession in somber silence. People of the region say that during the procession they are filled with thoughts of the suffering of Christ and also filled with thoughts of their own sins and the need for God's forgiveness of them through Christ, the Redeemer. The whole procession itself is an act of penitence for participants and audience.

It is easy to see in the processions a rich use of symbols (crosses, crowns of thorns, etc.) arrayed into a three-fold opposition marking time, color, and theme. In the beginning is dawn/ white/ Mary searching for her son. At the end is dusk/ black/ son found. A transition has been made. The processions mark

Figure 8.3   The Confaternity of St. Monica conducts its Good Friday procession at dawn. Sorrento, Italy.

Source: Authors' collection.

a liminal period between these two poles that engenders communitas. We can see this in the emphasis on equality and anonymity in the wearing of the robes and hoods that equalize those in procession and mask their individuality or status distinctions. A sense of communitas is also clearly felt when the entire ceremony is over and the participants of the Black procession return to their church. The somber mood that dominated both processions is rather suddenly broken as confraternity brothers throw off their robes and hoods, tossing them into a disorganized heap in a corner. They then shake hands and embrace one another, in a joyous mood but with tears in their eyes. They similarly greet members of the audience who have followed them into the church. A relieved festive mood prevails, a mood which is carried out into the streets of Sorrento and continues for the rest of the night.

Clearly, death is a central focus of the procession ritual and it is one that is played out on two levels. The ritual shows the movement of Christ from capture through crucifixion, with Mary also moving from an anguished "searching" for Jesus through her finding and following of his dead body. At the same time on a human plane, through the ritual creation of communitas, procession participants and their audience take a journey through sacred time that moves them from the anticipation of their own death to preparation for it. Underlying the journey of both Christ and Mary is a parallel journey of the human soul, one focused on the concepts of sin and penitence. The confraternity brothers in procession are mediators between human life and the supernatural. In this role they gain symbolic power through their hoods, which transform them from individualized, differentiated confraternity members (a matter of structure) into equal, anonymous figures (a matter of communitas). The procession itself is an act of penitence, and so directly addresses the question of Catholic preparation for death. Through the carrying of the symbols of the passion of Christ, the singing of the *Miserere*, and the carrying of crosses and statues, this theme is extended further. For audience and participants alike, the procession is in a larger view a mass penitence for the sin of humankind, but at the same time a powerful reminder that recognition of sins and receiving of grace are the path to Catholic preparation for a good death.

Within the sacred journey of Good Friday, Christ is already dead, but this is not quite yet known by the searching Mary in the opening dawn/white phase of the ritual. It is only through the second dusk/black procession that the closure comes and exit from the liminal time is carried through. We can, then, see in the Good Friday processions of Sorrento how religion moves us (truly transforms us and takes us on sacred journeys) through the power to generate our human need of communitas.

RELIGION AS RESISTANCE

Karl Marx (1843) famously wrote a phrase that is often translated as "religion is the opiate of the masses." The masses are oppressed by those elites who hold social, political, and economic power over them. In their suffering the masses turn to religion to dull the pain of their poverty, despair, and hopelessness, much as one might turn to opium to dull the pain of a broken limb. They cling especially to the idea of a better life after death (as in "Blessed are the meek, for they will inherit the earth," from Christ's Sermon on the Mount). According to this line of thinking, oppressed people need the illusion of religion to mask the pain of the reality of their oppressed conditions. In this way religion is also useful to the oppressors because it keeps the masses quietly "on opium" and so unlikely to present any serious challenge to their fate.

There may be some validity to the view of religion as social sedative. But in fact, religion is more often the springboard or framework for social protest and resistance to oppression. Most, if not all large-scale religions begin as a protest against undesirable conditions and often against some prior established religion (Robbins 2011). Thus Buddhism began in part as a reform of Hinduism and a protest against the Hindu caste hierarchy; Christianity began as a protest against then-current Jewish practice; Protestantism began as a protest against Catholic corruptions of the time, and so on. Even more importantly, religious movements give voice to oppression and can instigate and organize political activism.

Anthropologists refer to organized religious expressions of resistance, protest, or dissatisfaction with the status quo as **revitalization movements.** These are deliberate attempts by members of a society to construct a more satisfying culture (Wallace 1966). Such movements (sometimes referred to as millenarian movements) tend to take place in times of extreme social stress and cultural disruption caused, for example, by conquest and colonization of indigenous groups. Good examples of these movements are the **Cargo Cults** in Melanesia and New Zealand in the late nineteenth and early twentieth centuries. Here, the culture of indigenous peoples was severely disrupted by colonization and the rapid culture change that it brought. In particular, the old economy based on exchanges of shells and pigs was replaced by the acquisition and trade of new Western goods. Local people saw that the Western colonizers obtained their goods (their "cargo") seemingly through some mysterious Christian magic—it simply arrived on ships (later on planes) and the Western people merely gathered to pick it up.

The Cargo Cults that sprang up among native peoples were typically headed by a charismatic prophet who claimed that indigenous peoples would soon receive their own plentiful cargo of Western goods, that their long-dead ancestors would reappear with this cargo, and that the White colonizers would disappear. A new era of eternal utopian prosperity would ensue. To receive their cargo, indigenous peoples set up sites for the delivery, for example storehouses and landing strips. To further prepare for this new utopia, some would abandon their land and destroy their livestock. In some cases there was the belief that "cargo" goods were actually made by God for native peoples, but that the White people had removed this truth from the Bibles that missionaries had given them. During and shortly after World War II, Melanesian Cargo

Cults developed around the military supplies that were delivered first to Japanese occupiers and later to Allied forces.

Another classic example of a revitalization movement is the Native American **Ghost Dance**, a religious response to European invasion and loss of Indian land. The Ghost Dance movement started in the 1870s when a Paiute shaman declared that the world would soon be destroyed but then renewed through the return of dead Indian ancestors. To foster this return, followers were told to perform a circle dance at night. This movement spread through California and to tribes in Oregon and Idaho. Although the movement petered out, it was revived in 1889 by another Paiute Indian named **Wovoka**. Wovoka announced that he had had a spiritual vision: he had traveled to heaven where he met God and saw deceased Indians living their traditional life. God instructed him to return to earth and teach Indians to perform the ritual circle dance as a way to bring their dead ancestors back to life. This movement spread throughout the United States and Canada. In some versions of it, during the renewal of the world, the White colonists would be destroyed, the buffalo would return, and Indians would live as they had before the European invasion. Some Indian practitioners of the Ghost Dance, such as the Lakota, produced fear in government agents that the Ghost Dance could lead to open revolt. As a result, over 200 Lakota, including women and children, were killed by the United States Army at the massacre of Wounded Knee in 1890. This event put an end to the Ghost Dance.

In current times, expressions of religious fundamentalism can be seen as revitalization movements. One example is Islamic fundamentalism which holds that Muslims have abandoned the moral life prescribed for them in the Koran and need to return with piety to their true faith. Fundamentalists stress that decadent and secular Western influences account for much of the abandonment of Muslim faith and piety. Protestant fundamentalism in North America is another example. Many Protestant fundamentalists believe that the Bible is literally true and believe in the rapture—a divinely ordained time when the world will end (in the battle of Armageddon) and Christ will reign on earth for a thousand years. Similar to Islamic fundamentalists, Protestant fundamentalists decry Christian people's movement away from piety and faith; in place of decadent Western cultural influences, they largely blame "secular humanism" (ultimate reliance on human reason) for people's abandonment of divine guidance in their lives. Also like the Islamic fundamentalists, Protestant fundamentalists have developed political agendas and have become politically active. Both these types of fundamentalism also value family relationships and prescribe a subservient, domestic role for women, which they believe is prescribed by God, as represented in sacred scriptures.

Religious beliefs may be soothing, but it is clear that religion as an element of revitalization movements also serves as a cry of protest and a vehicle of rebellion. Even Marx seems to have understood this aspect of religion. In his likening of religion to opium, what he actually wrote was this:

> "Religious distress is at the same time the expression of real distress and religion is the protest against real distress. Religion is the sigh of the oppressed creature, the heart of a heartless world, and the soul of soulless conditions. It is the opium of the people (Marx 1970, orig. 1843)."

RELIGION AND ENVIRONMENTAL REGULATION

It is commonly thought that religious ritual addresses humans' *internal* states and emotional needs; it is symbolic in nature and has no real impact on the external world. Sociologist George Homans wrote that "Ritual actions do not produce a practical result on the external environment" (1941:172). Homans said that what religious ritual did was to address the "internal constitution of the society. It gives the members of the society confidence, it dispels their anxieties. It disciplines their social organization" (1941:172). In the mid-twentieth century, anthropologist Roy Rappoport (1967) presented an alternative view of religious ritual, showing how it often *did* have a material impact on the external environment. Since his classic work, anthropologists have come to see that religious ritual can do far more than symbolize ideas, enact mythology, and transform people's statuses and states of mind.

Rappoport studied ecological relationships among the Tsembaga people of New Guinea. The Tsembaga are a small group of horticulturalists, cultivating root crops and raising pigs. At the time of Rappoport's study, local groups of Tsembaga engaged in sporadic warfare with one another. Rappoport saw that their warfare, their use of their land, and their raising of pigs were all intertwined with Tsembaga religion and followed a "ritual cycle." At some point, hostilities would break out between two groups. At this point each side carried out religious rituals that officially categorized each other as "enemy." As the war began, the male warriors were religiously admonished to observe certain food taboos and refrain from sexual intercourse. Hostilities were ended when one group was driven from its territory or both groups simply gave up further struggle. At this point a group not driven away would establish a border to its territory (including the territory of an enemy they had driven off) and plant a *rumbim* (a ritual plant), addressing their sacred ancestors as follows:

> We thank you for helping us in the fight and permitting us to remain on our territory. We place our souls in this *rumbim* as we plant it on our ground. We ask you to care for this rumbim. We will kill pigs for you now, but they are few. In the future, when we have many pigs, we shall again give you pork and uproot the *rumbim* and stage a *kaiko* (pig festival). But until there are sufficient pigs to repay you, the *rumbim* will remain in the ground. (Rappoport 1967:191)

Pigs were at this point sacrificed to the ancestors, consumed, and given to allies who helped in the war. Then the Tsembaga waited for sufficient increase in the pig population for the *kaiko* pig festival they had promised. This took about five years. For as long as the rumbim was in the ground, open warfare could not take place. As the pig population increased, the pigs were initially beneficial to the Tsembaga: they wandered off on their own during the day, softening up garden soil and cleaning up human settlements by consuming garbage. They were easy to care for and feed; in the evening when they returned home they were given substandard tubers not needed by humans. During this time pigs were rarely slaughtered and consumed unless they needed to be ritually sacrificed to help cure an illness or ward off some other misfortune. But as their numbers grew, pigs became a problem: a large herd required more food and at some point the pigs needed to be given tubers that would otherwise be reserved for humans. Larger herds would also invade gardens, causing quarrels between neighbors. Eventually the pig population was more of a nuisance than a benefit, and everyone felt it was time to uproot the *rumbim*. Pigs were slaughtered and the ancestors ritually fed. Intergroup hostilities might then begin again, and the whole cycle would start all over. Enmeshed in religion, this Tsembaga ritual cycle regulated the environment and human action within it. Specifically, the ritual cycle redistributed land among people, controlled the pig population, and limited the frequency of fighting.

Another example of how religion works as an adaptation to the environment is provided with the sacred cow in India. In India cows are worshipped; Hindus should not eat beef; and the slaughter of cattle is forbidden in most states of India. Killing a cow would be a great sin. Cattle are numerous; in cities they wander about freely, sometimes snarling traffic and snatching pro-

Figure 8.4   A sacred cow in urban India.

Photo: John Hill. Wikimedia. CC BY-SA 3.0

duce from the open marketplace. Since cattle cannot be killed, India provides "old age homes" for elderly cattle, which are fed and cared for to their last days. Many outsiders have been critical of India for so protecting its cattle, or critical of Hinduism for forbidding beef consumption, while many Indians starve. These outsiders have seen the sacred cow as maladaptive. Anthropologist Marvin Harris (1966) has shown how, on the contrary, the sacred cow is very adaptive given India's particular agricultural economy. Here, castrated male bovines are used for plowing. Given the small size of fields, tractors would be impossible, to say nothing of the fact that small farmers could not afford them. Cows also provide people with milk, a crucial component of local Indian diets. And their dung is used for fuel and fertilizer. When they die of natural causes, cattle are given to untouchable castes, who are permitted to eat them, and who have few other sources of protein. The Indian economy is highly dependent on cattle and for this system to have continued over the centuries, cattle have needed to be protected. If India ate its cattle, the entire rural agrarian economy would collapse. Thus the Hindu concept of the sacred cow protects cattle and ensures the continuation of a particular ecological adaptation among humans.

Unfortunately, not all religious prescriptions are so adaptive and helpful. We will see a good example of this in Chapter 10.

SUMMARY

This chapter has looked at humankind's deepest concerns—creation, morality, the meaning of life and death—as expressed through religion. We have explored some fascinating ideas about the origin of religion, noting that most of these must for now remain speculative. We have looked at shamanism, witchcraft, and sorcery, which today exist alongside broader established religions. We have also examined religion as protest and resistance to domination and noted its connection to environmental adaptations.

We can summarize this chapter on religion by returning to the myths presented at the beginning:

Myth #1   Religiously based treatments of illness are ineffective quackery.

While this statement may apply to the dramatic performances of some televised "faith-healers," it would not apply to shamanism as widely practiced throughout the world. Most shamans are not fraudulent but rather believe in their experiences of the supernatural and their powers to intercede with them on the behalf of patients. Shamanic treatments are also often effective for psychological disorders and have the benefit of inspiring hope and a sense of well-being in many patients, which can itself be therapeutic.

Myth #2   People are emotionally attached to a religion primarily because of its set of beliefs.

Religious beliefs are important, and many people are strongly attached to the particular tenets of their religion. It appears, however, that it is ritual that gives religion its real power over people. Religious ritual may take us into liminal states and is thereby able to generate *communitas*, an abandonment of our ordinary status differences, and a merging with others. Humans seem to have a deep need for experiences of communitas.

Myth #3 Religion is the opiate of the masses.

Religious beliefs may be comforting, but religion does not seem to numb people into complacent acceptance of their lot. On the contrary, religions often arise in the first instance as protest movements. Religious movements are frequently frameworks for political activism and social change.

Myth #4 Religious ritual has no practical impact on the environment.

We are used to seeing religion as ephemeral, as largely symbolic and tending to our internal states and emotions. But religion in fact can regulate human behavior in such as way that it does have practical effects on the environment. The Tsembaga ritual cycle and the Hindu Indian protection of the sacred cow are examples.

QUESTIONS FOR THOUGHT AND REFLECTION

1. Religion, magic, myth, and ritual are all related phenomena. Explain these phenomena, showing how they are related to each other. Remember that anthropologists use some of these terms in ways that differ from how they are used in everyday discourse. Make sure you reflect the specific anthropological usage in your discussion.

2. What are some of the early speculations as to the origin of religion? Are there any features that unite them? How do they vary? Why can we still not come to a firm conclusion on this question?

3. Religion exists in all societies ever known. This does not, of course, mean that every person in these societies has followed the standard religious beliefs. Why do you think religion is a cultural universal?

4. What is a shaman, and how does a shaman differ from religious practitioners anthropologists refer to as priests? Although shamanic healing practices, like biomedical healing practices, do not always succeed, they often do. Why?

5. Very few people are members of religious groups because they have been convinced by arguments that appeal to reason. Most simply remain members of the religions into which they were born. Others have converted to a religion to follow a social or political strategy, or through

emotion, including attachment to a spouse. But many people are tied to a religion because of the appeal of ritual. Explain the power ritual has for religious believers, referring to arguments made by anthropologists of religion and providing ethnographic examples.

6. Religion seems to have two kinds of functions. The first is a spiritual/ psychological function, and the second is a practical/social function. Relying on the material in this chapter, describe some of the practical/ social functions of religion, providing specific examples.

ENDNOTES

[1] As preserved in Italian paintings and drawings, these confraternity members held a painted picture (*tavoletta*) of Christ in front of the faces of the condemned, to encourage them to seek salvation through remorse and to shield them from the scornful eyes of the pubic. Occasionally confraternities were given the privilege, especially at Christmas or Easter, to free a prisoner who had been condemned to die.

[2] Strictly speaking this is an archconfraternity, an aggregation of similar kinds of confraternities. Confraternities and archconfraternities have a long history in Italy with origins back to the ninth and tenth centuries (Black 1989). Their origin may go back even further to the funeral clubs of ancient Rome. By the 1500s, they extended all over Italy.

[3] *Miserere* is the first word of Psalm 50 of the Vulgate (Psalm 51 of the King James version) ["Have Mercy"] and refers to the psalm itself. This is King David's plea to God for forgiveness for his sin of adultery with Bethsabee.

REFERENCES CITED

Black, Christopher F.
    1989 *Italian Confraternities in the Sixteenth Century*. Cambridge: Cambridge University Press.

de Waal, Frans
    The Bonobo and the Atheist: In Search of Humanism among Primates. New York: W.W. Norton.

Douglass, Mary
    1966 *Purity and Danger*. London: Routledge and Kegan Paul.

Fos5ter, Lynn V.
    2002 *Handbook to Life in the Ancient Maya World*. New York: Facts on File.

Harris, Marvin
    1966 The Cultural Ecology of India's Sacred Cattle. *Current Anthropology* 7:51–63.
    Naure, People, Nature: An Introduction to General Anthropology. 7th ed. New York: Longman.

Hertz, Robert
    1960 *Death and the Right Hand* (Translated by Rodney and Claudis Needham). London: Cohen and West.

Homans, George C.
    1942 Anxiety and Ritual: The Theories of Malinowski and Radcliffe-Brown. *American Anthropologist* 43(2)164–172.

Leach, Edmund
　　Anthropological Aspects of Language: Animal Categories and Verbal Abuse. In Lenneberg, Eric H., ed., New *Directions in the Study of Language*. Cambridge, MA: Massachusetts Institute of Technology.

Marx, Karl
　　1844 *Deutsch-Französische Jahrbücher* (German-French Annals) Paris:

Karl Marx and Arnold Ruge
　　1970 [orig. 1843] *Critique of Hegel's Philosophy of Right*. Trans. by Annette Jolin and Joseph O'Malley. Cambridge: Cambridge University Press.

Rappoport, Roy
　　1967 The Ritual Regulation of Environmental Relations among a New Guinea People. *Ethnology* 6(1):17–30.

Robbins, Richard H.
　　2011 *Global Problems and the Culture of Capitalism*. 5th ed. Upper Saddle River, NJ: Prentice Hall.

Stone, Linda
　　2013 *Death, Confraternities and Communitas: Interpreting Good Friday Processions in Southern Italy*. Unpubl. Ms.

Torrey, E. Fuller
　　1897 *The Common Roots of Psychotherapy and Its Future.*.Lanham, MD: Roman & Littlefield..

Turner, Victor
　　1969 *The Ritual Process*. Chicago: Aldine.
　　1974 *Dramas, Fields and Metaphors*. Ithaca: Cornell University Press.

Tylor, Edward B.
　　Primitive Culture. New York: J.P. Putnam's Sons.

van Gennep, Arnold
　　1960 [orig. 1908] *The Rites of Passage*. London: Oxford University Press.

Wallace, Anthony F. C.
　　Religion: An Anthropological View. New York: Random House.

CHAPTER 9

ART

Culturally patterned forms of group and individual expression

Like religion (and a few other phenomena), art is a "cultural universal." As noted in Chapter 3, the precursors of what we recognize as art today originated with the ancestors of modern *Homo sapiens*. Today there is no society in the world that does not have art. One society's art may be very different from that of another society, but all human groups produce art of some kind, and usually of several kinds. As with other realms of life, anthropology does not attempt statements about *taste* in art, or render decisions about which art is "good" or "bad." Anthropology does, however, explore how art operates in a variety of different cultural systems, both now and in the past. Anthropology thus allows us to correct a number of myths and misconceptions that often distort the way people consider the structure and roles of art, and the cultural contexts that produce it. Here are a few myths this chapter will clear up:

Common Myths of Culture
Myth #1 People everywhere consider art a separate category of object or process that does not serve any practical function.
Myth #2 The goal of art is to produce beauty.
Myth #3 Artists are creative specialists who are likely to be peculiar or eccentric individuals.

| **Myth #4** | Art is fundamentally visual, primarily painting and sculpture. |
| **Myth #5** | All societies distinguish between high status art (fine art) and lower status art (folk art and craft). |

WHAT IS ART?

Most of us feel we know what art is. Even if we lack technical or historical information about art, we have an intuitive sense that we know it when we see it. Art is pleasing to the eye, and it is found in museums and galleries. It usually represents something, and it should look like what it represents, even though the artist may take some liberties with realism. Sometimes art is sculpture, but that is about as far as many of us are willing to go.

One important element of most North Americans' beliefs about art is that it is not useful. Even if you have an exceptionally beautiful silver gravy boat on your table, you probably would not consider it art. If that gravy boat was made by Paul Revere in 1776 (Paul Revere was a silversmith when he was not riding to warn his neighbors of imminent British attack), it might be worth many thousands of dollars, but still, few people would label it art.

Or consider the famous salt cellar, (a vessel to hold salt, and in this case, pepper, as well) made by the Italian sculptor, painter, and goldsmith, **Benvenuto Cellini** (1500–1571). This elaborate piece of tableware was made of gold, ivory and enamel; it includes a sculpture of Neptune, god of the sea (the source of salt), and Ceres, goddess of agriculture (the source of pepper) and held both condiments. Cellini made it for Francis I, the King of France, and it was intended as a showpiece; it is now in a museum in Vienna and is valued at more than $60,000,000. Cellini was and is considered an artist, but is this remarkable piece of tableware art? If we (contemporary North Americas) feel it is not art, this is likely because of the sharp boundary we draw between art and objects of utility or function, however beautiful or unique.

The point, here, is this: just as we have seen that the idea of religion in many societies is less bounded, less limited, than it is in our own society, the idea of art is also less bounded and less limited in many societies other than our own. Among the **Dogon** people of Mali, for example, blacksmiths used to form a special, caste-like category of people (Laude 1973). They had to marry within their own group, and they were the only people permitted to work iron, and to make agricultural implements like hoes and sickles. They were also the only people allowed to produce funerary sculptures, decorated granary

Figure 9.1   Cellini's salt shaker. Made in Paris 1540–1543. Wikimedia.
Source: Jerzy Strzelecki (1994). CC BY-SA 3.0

doors, and masks, all made out of wood. The Dogon considered all of these sculptures, doors, and masks to be as necessary to life and as in need of correct manufacture as the agricultural tools made by the same blacksmiths. Today, art galleries, museums, and the houses of wealthy Western collectors display Dogon wooden sculptures and masks, which their new owners consider "art." Few of these collectors own or collect Dogon tools, which they do not consider to be art. Though the Dogon recognized a difference in category between agricultural implements and funerary sculpture, they did not set one category apart from the other as ART. What we consider "art" was as thoroughly integrated into Dogon everyday life as was a shovel or a knife, and was considered just as useful.

People in the United States and participants in many other modern, metropolitan societies think of "good" art and "bad" art. For art to be considered good

Figure 9.2 Dogan masks.
Photo: Devriese. Wikimedia. CC BY-SA 3.0

or bad in such societies seems to depend primarily upon three considerations: 1) is it well made (or performed); 2) does it demonstrate originality, at least to some extent; and 3) does it have some significance or meaning. Well made or performed art requires a certain amount of information, education, training, or at least exposure to the medium (the material in which the art is produced) and type of art (painting, dance, architecture) on the part of the artist. Judgments about the quality of art also require certain information in the same areas in order to be credible. We have all seen many reproductions of famous paintings, and many of us have seen some of the actual paintings in museums. So we have a certain familiarity with what is officially supposed to be well done visual art. It is a little more complicated with performance art, like music and dance, which unfold over time. With this kind of art it is more difficult to figure out whether all the pieces are going together well unless we are very familiar with the medium. If the dancer skids and crashes to the ground, the performance is probably not a great one. If the horn screeches or the first violins do not all play the same notes, the orchestra is not doing a good job. In the same vein, it is a good idea if the spelling and the grammar in a novel are standard (unless there is an artistic reason for their not being so, as in Alice Walker's *The Color Purple)*. And it is also a good idea if the reader can follow what is going on in the novel, again, unless there is an artistic reason for confusion, as in James Joyce's *Finnegan's Wake.* But these characteristics are the bare minimum. Verbal art, like all other forms of art, involves much more than minimal technical competence to be considered "good."

In many nonindustrial societies, both in the past and today, technical competence has been considered the single most important element in assessing the quality of a work of art. Today, especially in the West, there is the additional, tremendously important criterion by which art is judged: originality. Generally, in nonindustrial societies, the goal has been to make art *correctly,* as it has been made by the ancestors since the beginning of time. In such societies, artistic innovation is seldom valued, because there is a general feeling that the ancestors got it right the first time. In fact, art, like all parts of culture, including language, and religion, as noted earlier in this text, changes over time. But in societies with simple technology for manufacture, transportation, and communication, change happens relatively slowly, and during an individual's lifetime there may appear to be no change at all. The stability of ancient Egyptian culture, for example, is legendary. It experienced remarkably little change in material culture throughout its roughly 3,000–year existence. This was especially true in state-sponsored Egyptian art, in which a major goal was to reflect the stability, dignity, and divine origin of the state. If we look at other state-based societies—such as China, for example—we see something similar: sculptures of **Mao Tse-tung** were produced in a style consciously based on sculpture that was made thousands of years earlier (modified by a dash of Soviet socialist realism). And even in the West, despite dramatic change and diversification in artistic styles in the last five hundred years, portraiture of official dignitaries has changed very little. Though costuming and hairstyles have changed in the last two hundred years, the style of official American presidential portraits has not changed much since the time of George Washington. This aside, for the past 150 years or so, art producers, critics, and collectors in the West (and more recently in such Asian countries as India and Japan) have preferred "originality" to conservative adherence to traditional artistic styles.

How much artistic originality a society can tolerate is an interesting question. The general public is usually fairly conservative, and tends to like art that people can recognize as such. Present-day art specialists in metropolitan societies, whether critics, collectors, or artists, are more likely to appreciate dramatically original forms and styles, but even they are likely to prefer art whose originality does not threaten contemporary notions of acceptability too vigorously. During his lifetime the Dutch painter **Vincent van Gogh** (1853–1890) sold almost none of his paintings, although his brother was an art dealer in Paris, because his paintings were considered depressing at first, and then wild and uncouth. Today they are worth millions. By contrast, **Richard Diebenkorn** (1922–1993), a California artist, became increasingly popular with art specialists as his work became more abstract and inaccessible to the majority of the population.

Along with the recent Western focus on originality, there is a slight preference for art that can in some way be considered "significant." Perhaps it is more accurate to say that there is a tendency for art specialists to devalue what they consider trite or superficial. But how to determine what is significant is not easy. Why would many art specialists consider a Dogon memorial portrait bust art, but a photographic portrait of someone's grandmother done by the local J.C. Penney's portrait studio trite and insignificant? The British poet, critic, and essayist, **Matthew Arnold** (1822–1888), argued in a very influential essay published in 1888 that to be considered art, a work must manifest both "high truth" and "high seriousness" of purpose. Arnold was specifically discussing poetry, and few people would take his claims literally today. Still, the influence of his argument lingers.

Many contemporary Westerners would consider the Dogon portrait sculpture to be art because they feel it captures the "essence" of the person it represents, and because in the culture that produces it, it is considered to be an essential component of funeral ceremonies and a required part of the periodic ritual feeding of the ancestors. In addition, the blacksmith who produced the sculpture is judged to have unusual skill. The Penney's portrait of a grandmother, by contrast, is mass produced through the medium of complex photographic technology, and most art specialists consider (consciously or unconsciously) the social status of Penney's shoppers to be lower than their own. The photograph consequently manifests neither "high truth" nor "high seriousness of purpose." It is therefore seen by most art specialists to be merely a cheap commercial product of no aesthetic merit and of interest only to family members. It is thus not art.

With abstract, or non-representational, art that does not depict any concrete phenomena, it is more difficult to describe the contemporary perception of "high truth" or "high seriousness." Because its content is abstract, the "truth" or "seriousness" has to come not from the *content* of the art, but from its *form*. This is clearly much more difficult to assess. Do ceramic vessels hand formed and painted by Zuni, Hopi, and other Pueblo Indian potters constitute art? What about hand-knotted rugs made for centuries in Western Asia, and known

Figure 9.3 An abstract painting. "Windows Open Simultaneously" (1912) by Robert Delauney.

to most Westerners as "Oriental rugs," or woven rugs and blankets made for the last couple of centuries by Navajo weavers?

It is clear that what constitutes art in one society may not qualify as art in another. Moreover, work that is considered "good" art in one society is not

Figure 9.4   William Holman Hunt's painting. "Awakening Conscience," 1853.

necessarily considered good in another. In recent times, what is considered acceptable or serious art, particularly by art specialists, can change rapidly. A dramatic illustration of this is **William Holman Hunt's** 1853 painting, *The Awakening Conscience.* Hunt (1823–1910) was British and a devout Christian, who in this painting depicted the moment in which a young man's mistress becomes aware of the sinful nature of her life as an unmarried "kept woman." In 1853 such a painting was taken seriously as art. Today the painting, though reproduced frequently, is used chiefly as an illustration, often condescending, of outmoded Victorian morality. It is no longer considered seriously as art, though no one questions the painter's technical skill.

A DEFINITION OF ART

How, then, shall we define art so that the term refers to a category broad enough to include all productions that are considered to be art by those who produce and consume them, and narrow enough to exclude what is not considered art by anyone (or nearly anyone)? A colorful sunset seen through urban pollution is beautiful, but it is not art. A hummingbird sucking nectar out of a fuchsia is beautiful, too, but it is not art, either. Hundreds of definitions of art have been proposed over the last 2,500 years or so, many of them having to do with beauty, morality, or imitation. For our purposes as students of anthropology, let us use the following definition:

> Art is the skilled **selection and arrangement of elements** in response to **specific cultural conventions** with the **intention** of producing an **intellectual or affective response in the expected audience.**

To clarify this definition, we will briefly discuss the terms in bold type.

skilled Art requires skill. In some societies (like the United States), artists are believed to have some kind of innate "gift" or capability, which needs only to be refined by training. In other societies it is assumed that anyone can be trained to produce art, though some people are better at it than others. In some societies, as in the case of the Dogon in times past, a particular category of person was designated to produce art. In other societies, only members of one sex produce a particular variety of art. For example, women were the basket makers among many Native American groups. Among the !Kung of Botswana, almost everyone will use his or her own person as a medium for artistic decoration, though adolescent girls are most adept at it.

selection and arrangement of elements   Whether the elements of art are specific motions of the body in dance, pitches produced by a sitar or a flute, words in a novel or traditional myth or legend, or colors painted on a canvas or knotted into a rug, the central act of artistic creation is choosing some elements over others and arranging them in a meaningful order. What is *not* selected is as important as what *is* selected. For example, in traditional Islamic visual art, especially religious art, representation of humans and animals have usually been avoided, on the grounds that makers of such images vaingloriously compete with the creation of God. In Western artistic traditions few painters or sculptors depict naked people who are old. And until very recently in the West, certain words could not be uttered in artistic performances or printed in books.

When it comes to issues of construction rather than content, certain artistic forms rely on rigid structures for their power. **Sonnets** (lyric poems in a specified number of lines and rhyme scheme), for example, must conform to a particular structure, and elements that fail to fit into this structure must be omitted. A particularly rigid poetic form is the Japanese *haiku,* which is limited to three lines of 5, 7, and 5 syllable-like entities respectively, and must contain certain additional structural and content elements, as well. Clearly, what is *excluded* in a work of art is as significant as what is *included.*

Once the elements are selected, they must be arranged, or organized in particular ways. In Shakespeare's sonnets, for example, the last two lines each have 5 pairs of two syllables, with the stress on the second syllable, and the last words in each of these two lines must rhyme, a structure referred to as the "heroic couplet": "For thy sweet love remembered such wealth brings/That then I scorn to change my state with kings" (the last two lines of Shakespeare's Sonnet #29).

Navajo Indian sand paintings have their own rules of arrangement to follow. They are made with colored sand or other materials on the floor of Navajo *hogans,* or houses, as part of healing rituals. Not only must the "Holy People," or Navajo supernatural beings, be depicted in specific ways, but the sand painting must be created according to a particular order of production, from the center outward, first to the east (the most auspicious direction), then to the south, then to the west, then to the north (the direction from which evil is likely to come), and back to the east again. There should be a border around three sides of the "painting," to protect its contents from evil, and it must face east, where there is an opening in the border. Thus the Holy People can enter the painting through the door of the hogan, which is always on the east, and complete the healing ceremony, which has been arranged for their arrival (Newcomb 1989). In all artistic productions, whether they are purely for aesthetic

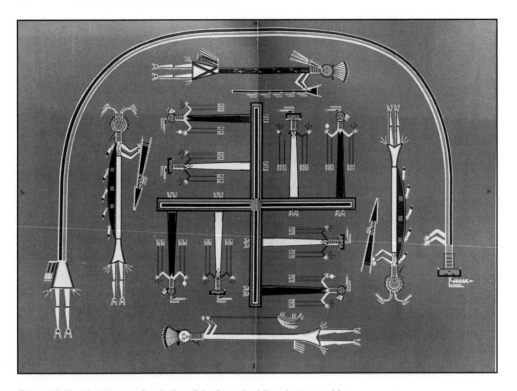

Figure 9.5   Navajo sand painting (black and white photograph).
Photo: H. S. Poley (between 1890 and 1908).

enjoyment, like sonnets, or for practical purposes, like Navajo sand paintings, it is the arrangement of the elements that is to a great extent responsible for the characteristic appearance or sound of the work. More than any other quality, it is the arrangement that makes art art.

specific cultural conventions   As we have already noted, all cultural systems have their own conventions, or agreed-upon notions about what is appropriate for art. These conventions include not only *how* art should be rendered (that is, style), but *what* should be rendered in art. In addition, there may be conventions dictating the purposes of art. That is, conventions cover both style (or form) and content, as well as function. As we have already pointed out, cultural conventions in the West have changed rapidly in the last two hundred years or so, but they have certainly not disappeared. It is just more difficult to keep up with them, and there are more subcultural variations in artistic conventions than there used to be.

Let us consider the question of artistic renderings looking like what they depict. In some societies a naturalistic or realistic depiction of people is considered desirable, while in other societies all persons are rendered in an idealized or conventionalized style, and few distinctive individualistic traits appear in portraits, whether sculptural or two-dimensional. We have already considered Dogon funerary busts and Western portraits of political leaders. Chinese ancestor portraits fall somewhere in between. They are more naturalistic than Dogon funerary sculpture, but they are almost as devoid of individual characteristics. Superficially, they look more like Western portraits of political elites, but they have fewer individual traits. What is important about these ancestor portraits is that the male and female ancestors are portrayed as honored elders in decorous clothing and a dignified pose. They should be luxuriously dressed and coiffed, but the details of their clothing and coiffure are not in themselves significant. They should be past middle age, because age is genuinely revered in China, but they should not look decrepit or lacking in physical or intellectual vigor. If Grandma had a wart on her nose or Grandpa was missing a finger, these personal characteristics should not be depicted. The point is not to represent one's ancestors as they might have appeared in an informal snapshot, but to create an image of them in such a way as to establish and maintain their importance as revered elders.

Of course, cultural conventions in art are not limited to painting and sculpture. Consider such varieties of art as music, dance, and theatre. From all the possible sounds of instruments and the possible pitches that can be made by the human voice, all societies select only certain collections of sounds in their music, and consider only certain pitch relationships harmonious. Some rhythms and collections of pitches may be considered to have specific links to particular human emotions in one culture but are completely insignificant in others or have quite different emotional values. Music involving drums and flutes that evokes religious awe in some parts of Africa and the Native New World, for example, may sound like secular dance music to contemporary Euro-Americans. These Euro-Americans are totally unfamiliar with the music, and their own religious music may never use whistles or drums.

The power of artistic conventions is culture-specific. For a striking illustration, a member of the audience at a performance of medieval (European) music remarked to an acquaintance that the music he had just heard was so inspiring it had moved him to tears. It is possible that the virtuosity of the performance had had this power, but it is more likely that the power was derived from the setting (a Catholic church), the language of the performance (Latin), and the fact that the sequences of pitches were characteristic of the thirteenth century. This collection of traits is usually found today in sacred music, so it had triggered an emotional, quasi-religious response in the audience member. If he had understood Latin (or read his program more carefully), he would have realized that he had just listened to a collection of medieval student drinking songs! Rather than singing about profound religious truth, the vocalists were singing about the need to drink as much as possible and have as much sex as possible while they were young, because life is short and they could die at any minute.

intention   Art is not produced by chance or mistake. That is, to qualify as art, someone (or several people) must have had the *intention* of producing a product. As we have already noted, many things are beautiful that do not qualify as art, and many artifacts and performances that few or no people consider beautiful may yet be considered art (we will take up the issue of beauty shortly). A beautiful rising moon over a village in New Mexico is not art. But **Ansel Adams**'s photograph, *Moonrise, Hernandez, New Mexico, 1941, is* art. Adams selected the image and arranged the elements (through the lens of his camera and later in the darkroom). He *intended* to produce the image, which then became art. The environmental elements were not intentional, and thus were not in themselves art.

intellectual or affective response   Art is usually created for others. Though many artists enjoy their own work, and many contemporary Western artists may even be said to be obsessed with their own work, they virtually always create their productions with others in mind. The intention is to have an effect upon an audience, whether the artist is a tattooist in the lowlands of Ecuador, beautifying the face of a young girl, or a sitar player in Mumbai, playing a classical Indian *raga*. Whether the desired response is produced or not cannot be entirely predicted, though the more traditional (that is, conservative or slow to change) the society, the more likely the intended response will be generated.

Today some Western artists intend to shock (and possibly awe) their audiences, and sometimes they succeed. They may even intend to enrage them. For example, **Andres Serrano**, a living American photographer, has been roundly reviled by the general public for some of his work, especially for *Piss Christ,* a photograph that depicts a plastic crucifix in a beaker of the photographer's own urine. Serrano's work is an extreme example of the virtually universal desire of artists to have an impact upon an audience; this is an essential ingredient in art. It can, however, be dangerous, as has been the case with Salman Rushdie's novel, *Satanic Verses,* which is critical of Islam; and with a depiction of the prophet Mohammed with a bomb in his turban drawn by Danish cartoonist, Kurt Westergaard. Both the novel and the cartoon have produced serious death

Figure 9.6   Man playing a sitar.

threats aimed at their authors. More successful revenge was caused by the cartoons and sarcastically critical articles in the French newspaper *Charlie Hebdo,* which resulted in the death of numerous people affiliated with the paper, and the wounding of others. The power of art should not be underestimated.

THE QUESTION OF BEAUTY

Art and beauty are clearly not the same thing. In Western societies intellectual discussion of art was often dominated by discussions and definitions of beauty, in a branch of philosophy known as *aesthetics*. Art was considered the human-created vehicle for beauty, and partly for that reason it has often been held to produce an ennobling effect on its audience. What is beautiful has long been associated with what is good, not only in Western cultures, but in others, as well. However, in non Western societies, as suggested earlier, the focus has tended to be on *correctness* rather than beauty, with an underlying assumption that what is correct is *ipso facto* beautiful.

Beauty, according to the above view, is thus the ultimate product of correct performance in art, and it may also be inextricably tied up with supernatural relationships. In Navajo culture, for example, one of the most powerful spiritual concepts governing the universe is ***hozho***, usually translated as "balance," "harmony," or "beauty" (Witherspoon 1977). When *hozho* exists, health, happiness, and prosperity prevail. Where there is no *hozho* there is pain and chaos. The correct performance of many everyday activities, like weaving, cooking, caring for sheep, and interacting with family, can be seen to some extent as *creating* beauty. More specifically, some artistic activities (including weaving and performing rituals requiring the singing of lengthy chants and the creation of sand paintings) must be accomplished correctly. If they are not carried out correctly the *hozho* of the work itself will be flawed, and the desired result will not be achieved. The rug will not fetch a good price. The patient will not be cured.

In the last century some contemporary artists in the post-industrial world have consciously avoided beauty in favor of what is interesting, exciting, shocking, or profound. In the past, some of these goals were considered incompatible with beauty, a position many artists continue to maintain. But some feel that the affective (emotional) power of beauty is so great, and conventional standards of beauty are so tied to other conservative cultural values, that they distract the audience from the significance of the new work itself. Artists with views like these are inclined to produce work that few nonspecialist audiences would consider beautiful, though later generations may consider them so. A classic example of a work that was not considered beautiful in its day is Russian composer Igor Stravinsky's *Rite of Spring,* a ballet first performed in 1913. The audience's objection was to both the music and the dancing, considering them to be ugly, harsh, discordant, and "primitive." Those present reacted violently, and the initial performance was a riotous failure. Today the *Rite of Spring* is considered a modernist classic, beautiful in its own way, though certainly different from such traditional romantic ballets as *Swan Lake.*

THE ROLES OF ART

The question of the roles played by art has been foreshadowed earlier in this chapter, when it was pointed out that art, like religion, is not only seen differently in different societies, but is often not thought of as a distinct, separable category. Instead, in many societies art is an integral element of a variety of activities and is important because it enhances them.

In the contemporary Western world there are many cases in which art enhances other activities. For example, there are many kinds of music, some popular (such as jazz, rock, and rap), some classical (including symphonies, chamber music, and opera), and some that might be described as functional (backgrounds to beer commercials, on one hand, and creators of a spiritual atmosphere in church services, on another). Though contemporary Westerners dance to music and drink, converse, and eat to some kinds of music, they also pay to attend concerts at which they simply sit as an audience and appreciate the music for its own sake.

Behavior at such artistic events varies somewhat, from genre to genre and also from culture to culture. Audiences at a rock concert are likely to be lively and to express their enthusiasm and appreciation by exclaiming and even singing along with the performers. If the performers are extremely popular, members of the audience sometimes scream, weep, and may try to rush onto the stage to gain personal access to them. This kind of behavior has occurred with a number of twentieth and twenty-first century rock performers, but was probably most extreme as a reaction to Elvis Presley and the Beatles. By contrast, audiences at classical concerts, especially in the United States, are totally silent until the performance is over, at which time they applaud and may even shout "Bravo" or stand while applauding to show their admiration and approval.

In some countries, notably Italy and Russia, where classical music has been more widely understood and appreciated than in the United States, audiences are more likely to express their reactions audibly and sometimes negatively, even while the concert is ongoing, by hissing, booing, and occasionally making insulting remarks. At the other end of Western classical concert behavior is the total silence that sometimes prevails when concerts are held in sacred spaces, generally churches. Here, there are often written signs reminding the audience that they are in a church, and that applause should be avoided after the performance.

In some non-Western societies, attitudes toward music are very different. An American Peace Corps Volunteer in Madagascar, trained as a classical violinist, discovered that the Malagasy people (as residents of Madagascar are called) not only found Western classical music alien to their sensibilities, but could not understand what the point of it was. They heard the Peace Corps Volunteer practicing her violin alone in her house and asked her what good her music was, because no one could dance to it. Young Malagasy people are very enthusiastic about Western (and South African) popular music, including rap, because such music involves active participation, mostly in the form of dancing, by the audience. In its traditional forms, Malagsy music was never passively absorbed by the audience; instead, the audience actively participated by dancing and by becoming involved in religious rituals that included entrance into a trance state. Or people participated by voicing opinions of the musical performers' skill and choice of repertoire in daylong performances. Hence the idea of music that serves no purpose other than to sound good strikes many Malagasy people as incomprehensible.

Having defined art earlier in this chapter, we may now understand it better. But what does art *do*? As a general category, art serves one very important function: it sets apart and distinguishes specific activities and spaces. When important ritual activities take place in most societies, not only do they often occur in special places, but these special places are often adorned with visual art (paintings, sculpture, sand paintings), and the construction or architecture of the location, itself, is often easily identified as a work of art (a cathedral or a temple). Special verbal art is often part of the event, including oratory, the recitation of prayers or poems, and sometimes the enactment of ritual drama. Music is often involved, and this music may be saved for these special ritual occasions and never performed in any other situations. Even the clothing worn by the participants may be special and can easily be considered art, especially because its function is to set its wearers apart from non performers, as well as to set the event apart from more mundane activities.

Another aspect of function, as discussed earlier, is the apparent *lack* of utilitarian purpose characteristic of fine art in the modern Western world. Of course, the lack of a utilitarian purpose does not mean that art in the contemporary Western world *really* has no function. For one thing, it gives pleasure to its audiences. Second, it serves as a medium of expression and communication for the artist and the community of which the artist is a part. Third, it serves as a social status marker for many art consumers, though this is often not an explicit or conscious function. Fourth, art in the modern Western world has a significant economic function. When a painting sells for $179.4 million, as Picasso's *Women of Algiers* did in May of 2015, then it is hard to ignore this function. In addition, the older functions of marking formal and ritual environments and occasions continue to be included in the role of art.

THE VARIETIES OF ART IN CULTURAL CONTEXTS

We now turn to an exploration of different varieties of art. It is possible to organize art into different kinds of groupings, and to include an almost infinite number of media and productions. Here we divide art into five primary varieties:

1. **Visual art**, both two dimensional (including painting, sand painting, drawing) and three dimensional (including carvings in wood and stone, cast and beaten metal, formation in clay, and assemblages in a variety of media, including basketry)

2. **Verbal art**, including poetry (organized by meter or rhythm) and prose

3. **Drama**, involving the enactment of both comedy and tragedy

4. **Dance**

5. **Music**, both vocal and instrumental

Visual art is what first comes to mind when most North Americans hear the term "art," and generally they think of two-dimensional pictures of something recognizable. Two-dimensional art is easy to produce with a wide variety of materials, available in most environments: a stick and some dirt or sand, for example, or a piece of charcoal and a flat stone or slab of rock. The artist may be any child or adult idly amusing himself or herself or a specialist decorating an important ritual site or a family home. The kind of paintings done on canvas or board, with which we are familiar today, fit into this category. Two-dimensional art may be intended to last indefinitely, like mosaics at the Minoan royal palace on the Greek island of Crete. Other varieties of two-dimensional art are ephemeral. That is, they are not intended to last beyond the specific purpose for which they were created. Navajo sand paintings fall into this category. At the end of the "sing," or curing ritual, the painting is destroyed, its function at an end.

All kinds of primarily decorative two-dimensional art exist throughout the world in infinite variety: decorated houses, tattooed skin, painted and incised ceramics, printed fabrics. These are all forms of two-dimensional art that serve primarily to embellish, entertain, and to identify people and groups. The tattoo on the arm of a Chicano activist in Texas differs in appearance from the tattoos on the face of a Maori man in New Zealand, but their purposes are similar: they enhance the wearer's appearance and establish his identity.

When thinking about art, three-dimensional forms are less likely to be in the forefront of American minds than two-dimensional art, but they have played an important role in many cultures. Among the earliest such art we know of are the small "Venus" figurines already discussed in Chapter 3. At the other end of the scale are enormous productions: Egyptian sculptures like the sphinx and the (badly named) "totem poles" of native peoples of the Northwest coast of the United States and the Southwest coast of Canada. These totem poles were carved and painted to depict ancestral and protective beings, important events,

Photo 9.7   Maori tattoos.

Photo: Stuartyeates. Wikimedia. CC BY-SA 3.0

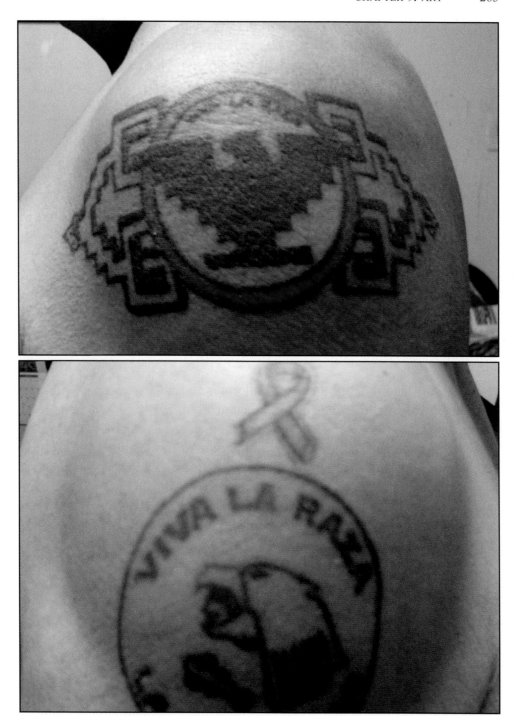

Figure 9.8 Two Chicano Power tattoos on the arms of a Mexican American political activist. The breast cancer awareness tattoo was added in solidarity with his wife's struggle with the disease. *Source:* Authors' collection

and mythological figures of particular importance to family groups. Enormous three-dimensional art of this kind always has a public function, and is almost always generated by stratified societies in which central coercive authority can organize the skilled labor required to produce it.

Smaller three-dimensional art, however, is often produced either by people for their own needs or by local specialists for other community members. We have already mentioned the masks and memorial sculptures once produced by Dogon blacksmiths as examples. Pottery is another example of three-dimensional art that in some communities is made by specialist potters, and in other communities is made by ordinary persons for their own households. Where pottery is made at home for domestic use, it is nearly always produced by women, who follow a traditional style, but usually embellish it according to their own tastes and family or ethnic conventions (Bowser 2000). If pottery is made on a wheel, and produced in large quantities for sale or trade, it is more likely to be made by men. These styles of painted, incised, or glazed decoration, as well as vessel shapes, change through time, and because pottery, usually in fragmentary form, often survives the ravages of time, it is often used by archaeologists to date other remnants of human life, and to note cultural linkages.

Verbal art is probably the most widespread of all varieties of art across the planet because it requires no special equipment. All normal humans come equipped with the tools for verbal art: a vocal tract and a brain. Because verbal art is so voluminous, anthropologists, folklorists, and students of comparative literature have used a number of different systems to divide it up for analysis. One of the most basic systems is a division by content, which was briefly mentioned in the preceding chapter: myth, **legend**, **tale**, and miscellaneous short pieces like riddles, jokes, bits of wisdom and moral sayings.

Myths, when the term is used in this sense, are narratives that deal with profound and fundamental issues of concern to humans. As noted both in the first chapter of this book, as well as in Chapter 8, there are two ways of using the term "myth." One is the common use of "myth" to refer to a false or erroneous belief. But in anthropological classification of verbal narratives, the term, "myth," has nothing to do with the truth or falsity of the narratives. Thus it is not insulting when anthropologists refer to various accounts of the creation of the universe as "myths." The term merely categorizes the narratives by content. In this context, myths deal with topics like the creation of the universe, the nature of supernatural forces, the obligations humans have toward each other and toward the supernatural, and the nature and significance of death.

Myths accounting for the creation of the world exist in all societies. One famous account of creation is that of the Quiche ethnic group of the **Maya** people of Guatemala. A sixteenth century Spanish translation of a collection of Mayan myths records how several supernatural beings made human proto-types using materials like dirt and wood that for various reasons did not work out well. Eventually humans of the kind we presently know were successfully created (Tedlock 1996).

After myths, in terms of cultural significance, come legends, which are usually the stories of important historical events involving characters anthropologists refer to as "**culture heroes**." These stories usually involve not only human superheroes but also supernatural beings. Often the superheroes are either themselves partly supernatural, or they have dedicated supernatural protectors who help them through their difficulties. **Cuchulain** (pronounced more or less "kuhulin") is one such superhero, who appears in legends especially in Ireland, but also in Scotland and Wales. His father was a supernatural warrior, and his mother was a mortal princess. Cuchulain, himself, was a famous warrior, whose battle frenzy was terrifying and showed elements of his supernatural father's prowess. Like other legends, those in which Cuchulain appears embody the values of nobility, bravery, and fortitude, values that **Celtic** peoples considered to be distinctively their own.

Tales, also referred to simply as stories, are told in all societies, and although they are known to everyone in the group, no one believes them to be actually true, except perhaps young children. Still, these tales embody important values of the cultures that produce them. They also often feature continuing characters, like Coyote, the clever and promiscuous old animal/man of many western Native American stories, or Tortoise, the wise and wily old animal/man of many West African (and subsequently African American) stories. Characters like Coyote are highly intelligent and understand the foibles of the animal/people with whom they live, but they are tricky, and often cheat or deceive those around them. For this reason people who study folklore refer to Coyote-like characters as "**tricksters**." Though not always virtuous, they are fascinating and much beloved by the people who have created and perpetuated stories that depict them.

Many different cultural systems have created trickster characters. In European folklore, there are other standard figures: the wicked stepmother is one of the best known, and appears in many traditional European fairy tales; the virtuous and beautiful but oppressed youngest daughter (and sometimes son) who wins in the end is another such character. These two stock personae are combined in what is probably the best-known fairy tale in the Western world,

"Cinderella." Though the Cinderella story we know best is derived from one written by the French author Charles Perrault (1628–1703), he adapted it from an earlier version. Indeed, the story has been known for thousands of years and in scores of countries. Over the last fifty years the story of Cinderella has been reshaped in the United States and elsewhere partly because of the influence of the Walt Disney feature-length animated version that appeared in 1950.

Though tales like "Cinderella" are now reserved for children, this was not originally the case. They were told to groups who included people of all ages, sometimes by family members and sometimes by community members who were known for their special narrative skills. It is easy to note the changes in Western fairy tales as they have shifted to all-child audiences. Early versions contained gory episodes of death and disaster, whereas more contemporary versions usually dispense with the blood and maiming. In Disney's version of Cinderella, the stepsisters did not slice off their toes trying to make the glass slipper fit them, nor did Snow White's wicked stepmother have to dance in red-hot shoes until she fell down dead.

Tales encode cultural values, fears, and concerns within them. In Western stories beauty, youth, and virtue are often allied. Stepmothers and step-siblings are sneaky, selfish, and evil, and try to manipulate the husband/father. But in the end the virtuous hero or heroine almost always triumphs, a satisfying result that most people cannot help but notice is not inevitable in real life.

As writing spread across the planet, and as more and more people began to read and write, stories and tales developed into what is now generally referred to as "literature," that is, narratives that appear in written form. Some of this literature has lasted for centuries or even millennia and is recognized as being of a philosophical and aesthetic quality that transcends the time and place in which it was written. Modern people are familiar with the plays of the fifth century (B.C.E.) Greek playwrights **Aeschylus** and **Euripides**, and the eleventh century (C.E.) Japanese work, *The Tale of Genji,* written by Murasaki Shikibu, the pen name of a widowed noblewoman who had lived at the Japanese imperial court. The plays of Shakespeare (1564–1616) certainly fall into this category, as do the works of Russian novelist Leo Tolstoy (1828–1910). But countless works of literature have been produced in the 5,000 years that at least some humans have been able to write that were momentary distractions, forgotten shortly after their creation.

A final grouping of verbal art is the well-known miscellaneous category, which includes riddles, proverbs, sayings, and brief rhymes. A variety of these pieces of verbal art exist in all cultures. Some of them are written down, but they are primarily transmitted orally, frequently by adults to children, but often by children to each other. How do English speakers remember how many days are in a month? Who does not know the rhyme "Thirty days have September, April, June, and November"? Of course, then we have to remember that the rest have thirty-one days, except for February, which has 28 except in leap year! Slightly less useful in the days of weather satellites is "Red sky in morning; sailors take warning. Red sky at night; sailor's delight." Or "A pint's a pound the world 'round," which had greater utility when the sun never set on the British Empire, and many countries employed the British, or Imperial, system of weights and measures. Not all of these rhymes and sayings are useful; some are just for fun, including rhymes for children's games, riddles, and nursery rhymes. One example of such a rhyme is given here:

> One misty, moisty morning, when cloudy was the weather,
> I chanced to meet an old man, dressed all in leather.
> And he began to compliment, and I began to grin:
> And how do you do, and how do you do,
> And how do you do again?

Though to some of today's readers this may seem like a sinister encounter between an aging and lascivious Hell's Angel and a little girl, it was composed purely for amusement two centuries ago.

Verbal art of all sorts is often grouped into either poetry or prose. Poetry is constructed so as to have a specific rhythmic or metric structure, while prose is not. At various times and in various places in the world one of the hallmarks of poetry has been rhyme. At other times and places rhyme has been considered crude and inelegant, suitable only for lewd or humorous purposes, or just seen as naïve and unsophisticated. Today few English speaking poets make much use of rhyme, but structure and rhythm in poetry continue to be important.

One element of structure that has been important in poetry in many of the world's cultures, especially in poetry that has been orally composed and transmitted, is the use of stock phrases, such as descriptive phrases characterizing important actors in the narrative. As was pointed out by Milman Parry (1987) and Albert Lord (2000) as early as the 1930s, orally composed poetry uses these devices to provide connectivity, establish familiarity, and buy the singer of these tales time, as he goes through narratives that are extremely long, and for which he has no written script, but only a remembered framework. Parry and Lord collected orally composed epic poetry from Yugoslavia, and discovered the same devices with which readers of the ***Iliad*** and the ***Odyssey*** are familiar. There, Athena, the protector of the hero Odysseus, is frequently referred to in the *Iliad* as "gray-eyed" or "glittering-eyed" (Homeric Greek, as we saw in Chapter 7, had no word for "gray"), and in the many violent battle scenes we hear that a soldier "fell to the ground, and his armor clattered about him."

Though most contemporary readers are far more familiar with prose than with poetry, a great deal of oral art in the past was composed as poetry, according to a regular metrical pattern. Before widespread literacy, these oral narratives, whether in prose or in poetry, would be narrated by storytellers, sometimes to the accompaniment of an instrument, and were performed for the benefit of a community audience. This was true in the eighth century B.C.E., when a poet we know as Homer sang the old stories of the Trojan War and the homecoming of Odysseus to the Greeks. And it is still true in some peasant and tribal societies, like those of the !Kung of Botswana, the Inuit peoples of the Arctic, and some of the rural villages of western Ireland.

Drama can be thought of as a special variety of verbal art, but it is often classified separately, as we are doing here. This is because drama, which includes both comedy and tragedy, is thought of primarily as *performance,* and nearly always involves multiple participants, as well as additional elements such as costumes, masks, scenery, and special effects. Today most people in the United States feel as though drama should be realistic, and are sometimes surprised that drama from other times and places does not aim at realism. Of course, we seem to accept without question the unusual physical beauty of characters in our plays, movies, and television programs, the choreographed fight scenes and love scenes, not to mention the idea that all telephone numbers have the prefix 555!

Even a contemporary American soap opera, where the amnesia rate approaches that of the common cold, and babies are routinely switched in the hospital nursery, is far more like daily life than the traditional dramas of the **Kwakiutl** people of the southwestern coastal area of Canada. In the ritual season of the year, the Kwakiutl performed elaborate dramas involving dance, drumming, verbal sound effects, props, and complicated carved and painted masks with moveable components. The dramas enacted important myths of the Kwakiutl people that served as vehicles to enhance family and personal status, as well as to reaffirm tribal values. The events and characters depicted (for example, a cannibalistic raven) are hardly likely to be encountered by the average Kwakiutl in daily life, but no Kwakiutl has ever expected art to imitate life in any naturalistic sense.

However distinct the traditional Kwakiutl forms may be from present day Western drama, it is interesting to note that one of the ancestral forms of Euro-American drama, that of the ancient Greeks, was also extremely stylized and

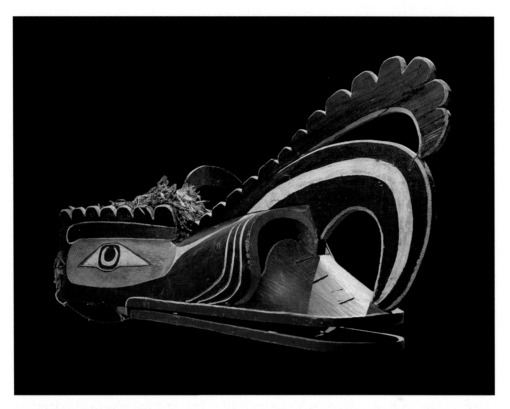

Figure 9.9 Kwakiutl mask.
Photo: PierreSelim. Wikimedia. CC BY-SA 3.0

even employed masks. The comedy and tragedy masks that are often painted or carved as decorations in Western theatres in recent centuries derive from the actual masks of wood and fabric worn by actors in classical Greek drama.

Contemporary emphasis on realism in drama has been facilitated by modern technology, not only in special effects, but in such modes of transmission as film and television. We want actors to resemble the characters they portray, and we usually want those characters to seem like real people (only better looking). But this has not always been the case, nor is it the case today in all forms of drama. Masks allow actors to portray idealized characters: a standard king, for example, or a standard princess, or a standard representation of a particular supernatural being like the Kwakiutl raven. What are important in these dramas are not idiosyncratic characteristics of a particular king, but the characteristics of kings, generally. Masks also allow a small and fixed group of actors to handle any of the roles in their repertoire. Since facial features are concealed, a young man can play an old woman, and a middle-aged man can portray a vigorous young warrior.

The stylistic expectations for drama vary widely from culture to culture, but the power of drama appears to be universal. Whether the subject matter is spiritual, like the drama of the Kwakiutl and the mystery and miracle plays of medieval Europe, or relatively secular, like the comedies and tragedies of classical Greece, the enactment of a story encodes and reaffirms the cultural values of a society and captures the imaginations and emotions of its audience.

Dance is another variety of art that takes dramatically different forms according to different cultural conventions. Though all dance involves moving the body in conventionalized ways, usually in response to music, the purposes of dance, as well as its styles, vary enormously. Today in the post industrial world, there are primarily two categories of dance: social dancing, in which largely untrained persons participate purely for their own entertainment, and dance performed by trained and paid dancers, as entertainment for an audience. There are many styles of dance in each category, but in the contemporary United States nearly all dance falls into one or the other of these two categories. One exception, however, does exist, a survival from ancient, precontact times: the ritual dancing of many Native American groups, sometimes done at powwows (large, fair-like tribal and intertribal gatherings), and sometimes at smaller, religious events. An example is the Snake Dance of the Hopi people, discussed in the previous chapter. The Snake Dance, performed in the summer, occurs at the end of a two-week ceremonial event, and involves men dancing with snakes in their hands. Though the dance is essential to this ceremony, what is important is not the artistry of the performance, nor the grace or athleticism of the performers. What is important is that the dance be conducted *correctly,* so that the snakes, released after the dance, will carry the Hopi people's prayers for rain to the supernaturals properly, and the supernaturals will be pleased and respond by sending rain.

On other continents dance has been equally important to non-industrial societies. The Dogon, whose traditional carved masks and funeral busts we have already discussed, have also been famed for their dancing. With their masks firmly tied on, adorned with their special fiber dance skirts, and with bracelets and anklets made of shell and beads, Dogon men danced vigorously and athletically in honor of their ancestors and the supernatural beings who control the universe. These were striking and dramatic performances that served to assure the continuation of Dogon religion and tradition, and in the view of the Dogon, also ensured adequate rain.

Music is fundamentally the production of sounds, vocal and/or instrumental, in a culturally recognized arrangement. Of all the arts discussed here, music is the most abstract, the least tied to specific representation of concrete

Figure 9.10 Hopi dance (1879). This dance was traditionally performed as part of a girl's puberty ceremony in the matrilineal, matrilocal Hopi society.

reality. Though it is possible to make music sound like the barking of a dog, the rumble of thunder, or the rhythmic marching of soldiers, very little music is actually like this. Instead, most music has only a conventional connection to specific significance, rather like the conventional connection between words and meanings in language. This does not mean that the power of music to create a mood or produce an emotional response in listeners is not real and powerful. It simply means that a significant component of this power is created by cultural experience. What makes music seem sad or jarring to a North American may have quite a different effect on someone from China, India, or Botswana. A good example of this phenomenon is the tradition of *raga* in the classical music of India. *Ragas* are sequences of tones upon which classical Indian music is composed. To educated Indian audiences different *ragas* are associated with particular times of day and sometimes particular seasons of the year. However natural this seems to musically sophisticated residents of India, the connection between a particular time and a particular *raga* is completely arbitrary; that is, it is culturally determined.

Common functions for music are celebrations of religious and secular events; enhancement of military events, from parades to charges of troops (in the past), to getting up and going to sleep; establishing the rhythm of work; and announcement of the arrival of an important person (like the playing of "Hail to the Chief" when the United States President arrives for a formal event). Modern warfare no longer signals an artillery charge with a flourish of trumpets or drums, but this did happen as late as the nineteenth century. And in some United States prisons, work crews still sing to make their tedious physical labor pass more pleasantly. When British troops lost the Battle of Yorktown (Virginia) in 1781 and surrendered to George Washington and his French allies, effectively ending the Revolutionary War, they marched off in defeat to the sound of their fife and drum military band playing a well-known English tune called "The World Turned Upside Down." The significance of that tune was clear to all who were present.

THE STRATIFICATION OF ART

In stratified societies, the nature of which we have already discussed at some length in previous chapters, not only are wealth and power differentially allocated, but so is the legitimacy of art. In addition to the higher status **fine art** that is produced for and sometimes by elites, and consumed primarily by them, there may be many other varieties of art that generally have lower status but much wider audiences. In this chapter, we will designate them as folk art, popular art, and outsider art.[1]

Folk art is a term usually applied to artwork that derives from peasant tradition. It is often mediated through a time, often multiple centuries, of peasant culture, during which these people are partly integrated into a state-level society but continue to retain many of their own traditional practices. Some practitioners of folk art are specialists in their artistic production, while others continue to be involved in subsistence activities, like farming and herding.

The term "folk art" is used differently by different people. It is sometimes reserved only for those items that are produced primarily for the community from which the producer comes. More commonly, especially recently, the term has been applied to any item or performance produced in ethnically or culturally distinctive communities by artists who have been trained locally, outside academies and schools of art. The term "folk art" is often applied to such mass produced items as ceramics that are turned out by the thousands,

Figure 9.11   Large alebrije in a shop in Oaxaca, Mexico. Alebrijes are fantastic carved animals (usually much smaller than this one) characteristic of Oaxacan folk art.

Photo: Alejandro Linares Garcia.   Wikimedia CC BY-SA 4.0

because they are painted by hnd and reflect elements of their peasant or tribal ancestry.

Many forms of folk art have grown out of traditional ceramic, weaving, carving, and metalwork production. For several decades, however, collectors in the post-industrial world outside the communities of production have become the primary consumers of folk art. They have become very influential in driving the styles, productions, and prices of folk art and have established canons of quality and "authenticity," mostly derived from the (ironically antithetical) values of capitalism and romantic aesthetics. Thus, Tiffany Tuttle (2005), in her master's thesis on the felted ***shyrdak*** rugs of Kyrgyzstan, points out that Western visitors, looking for "authentic" *shyrdaks* generally prefer smaller, more easily packable or shippable rugs in subdued colors, imagining that these are the "real" *shyrdaks* made by Kyrgyz women for their own use. In fact, Kyrgyz people generally prefer larger rugs, and for as long as they have had access to bright, aniline dyes, they have preferred *shyrdaks* in bright colors like acid green and hot pink. However, they rapidly realized that for the tourist market they would do better to produce smaller rugs, dyed with natural colors, making them look to tourist consumers like "authentic" pieces of Kyrgyz material culture. But which is really more "authentic"? Is it the small rugs dyed in hues that the Kyrgyz find profitable but boring, or the larger rugs dyed in lively colors that the Kyrgyz produce for their own use?

Popular art is not universal; like folk art, it exists only in stratified societies. In such societies art constructed for elites becomes inaccessible to the majority of the population. Elite "fine art," as we have seen, may require knowledge of a foreign or extinct language; it may require extensive education; or it may require knowledge about subject matter to which non-elites have no access. This does not happen in small scale, non-stratified societies. To most of the population in stratified societies, popular art offers diversion and satisfaction with much less investment in knowledge. In contemporary North American society, for example, vastly more people enjoy popular, formulaic fiction than those who read the novels, poetry, or essays that are considered "great literature" by literary critics. Formulaic fiction, including mysteries, science fiction, espionage thrillers, and romance novels, are usually simply constructed, easy to read, and lead the reader to a satisfying conclusion. Similarly, popular music is generally simply constructed and easy to follow, offering its audiences a rewarding experience without extensive preparation or education. In addition to pleasure derived from the popular arts, there is often a sense of group solidarity, especially in the case of contemporary popular music. Not only does this music offer a feeling of belonging to a group, but it also reinforces a defensive sense of *not* belonging to the group of older, elite members of the society.

The United States is not the only contemporary stratified society with a wealth of popular arts. Chromolithographs of religious subject matter, usually in bright colors, are ubiquitous in India and Mexico, found in many houses of the poor. These pictures are inexpensive, lively, stylistically accessible, and serve not only to intensify religious sentiments but also to brighten up the house. In Mexico, romance or "love" comic books are very popular with low income women, who may have limited education and difficult lives. For this audience the pictures help advance the story, while the difficult path of true love, always ending happily, is an antidote to the miseries of real life. And there are always the voluminous and pervasive popular arts of television and the movies, which seem to be among the most successful of all popular arts in transcending cultural barriers.

Outsider art is a third category of art that has emerged recently in Western, post-industrial societies. The term was originally coined by art critic Roger Cardinal, who used it in his book of the same name in 1972. Like folk art and popular art, outsider art cannot develop in small scale, face-to-face societies, where social stratification does not exist, and where there are no outsiders. But in large, stratified societies there are people who produce art who are not involved in any of the accustomed pathways, institutions, or social groupings that produce socially sanctioned art. Many of these "outsider artists" are self-taught, and many of them come from disadvantaged backgrounds. Some may be mentally ill; others are poor or members of ethnic minorities; while many are simply artists who have lived out of the mainstream of the official art world. A good example of the last category, often referred to as "naïve" artists, is Anna Mary Robertson Moses (1860–1961), better known as "Grandma Moses." A resident of rural New York State all her long life, Grandma Moses took up painting late in life, and her naïve (that is, artistically unsophisticated) portrayals of the rural world she had known since she was born made her work extremely popular with collectors. Not only was it simple and representational, but it also reflected an American past for which many people were nostalgic, especially if they had not experienced it!

Few outsider artists are as popular and as widely beloved as Grandma Moses, though there is now a lively market for outsider art. One interest-

ing variety of outsider art is often referred to as "ephemeral art," and refers to artistic productions that are made to be destroyed. Some art, like Navajo sand paintings, are intended to be destroyed after they have served their spiritual function in a curing ritual. But ephemeral art in the post-industrial world has no function other than to exist as a source of aesthetic interest or delight. British outsider artist Andy Goldsworthy constructs arrangements of sticks and stones, of dried flower petals stuck together with ice, or of patterns scratched in sand, all of which he knows will be destroyed in a matter of hours by the forces of nature. In modern capitalist societies such ephemeral art as Goldsworthy's presents a difficult dilemma for collectors. Because it has no lasting existence, collectors have nothing to show for their artistic investment other than a photograph. This tends to reinforce the status of ephemeral artists as outsiders, though the lure of high fees from collectors has persuaded some producers of ephemeral art to produce constructions that look temporary but are actually permanent.

Some outsider artists not only fail to conform to accepted conventions of productions, they actually antagonize them. Probably the most obvious example of this kind of outsider art is the graffiti now seen throughout many of the world's cities. Though many people consider graffiti a kind of vandalism or visual littering, some graffiti artists defend their work as a kind of anti-establishment public statement and a valid form of personal expression and social comment.

Outsider art, popular art and folk art all exist only in the world's stratified societies, where the population is large, the variation in subcultures great, and the distribution of wealth and power so inequitable, that the art created for elites is inaccessible to or lacks meaning for most others. Non-elite arts thus develop in response to the social and economic realities of stratified societies. Though in many respects they differ from elite fine arts and operate outside the fine arts world, they respond to the same kinds of social and economic pressures that shape elite fine arts. Consumers of many popular arts are drawn from all divisions of stratified societies, and great wealth is invested in and generated by the popular arts.

Folk art and outsider art have a much smaller following, but they, too, respond to the larger social and economic world. Collectors, galleries, and museums have a powerful impact on the form these schools of art follow and the prices their productions command. In stratified, state-level societies, then, while the traditional functions of art remain (self expression, enjoyment, reinforcement of group solidarity and cultural values), additional functions develop. These include economic benefits to the producers (or at least sellers) of art, and negotiation and reinforcement of socio-economic stratification. Popular and outsider categories of art frequently become permeated by the same market forces that control fine art; these same forces, then, ultimately drive the genesis of these stepchildren of art in stratified, post-industrial societies.

SUMMARY

Art is an element of culture about which many people feel they have an intuitive understanding, even if they have never given it much thought. This chapter has discussed art from an anthropological perspective. By providing a cross-culturally usable definition of art and by exploring a wide variety of artistic forms and media, we have made several discoveries: a) that art may function differently in different societies; b) that its functions and conventions can change over time; and c) that the very concept of art may mean different things in different cultural systems, and may mean nothing at all in some. Specifically, we have been able to explore and counter the following myths.

Myth #1   People everywhere consider art a specific category of object or process that does not serve any practical function.

As we have seen in this chapter, in many societies art is not considered a separate entity, set apart from other objects, performances, or activities. In many societies, particularly non-Western and small-scale societies, art is so thoroughly integrated into such activities as religious rituals or the manufacture of utilitarian items that it is not thought of apart from their context. In addition, the ornamentation of utilitarian objects like blankets, baskets, and ceramics, or the use of artistic productions like sand paintings in practical events such as healing ceremonies are now widely considered to be art by many outsiders.

Myth #2   The goal of art is to produce beauty.

In ancient and more recent non-Western societies, artistic production is considered beautiful if it is well made, according to the society's traditional aesthetic values and principles. In these societies beauty is seen less as the point or goal of art, and more as the natural result of art properly produced. A different perspective on the relation between art and beauty comes from some artists in recent post-industrial societies. Considering the pursuit of beauty to be trite or hackneyed, they aim for interest, originality, and shock value in their artistic productions.

Myth #3   Artists are creative specialists who are likely to be peculiar or eccentric individuals.

Although the notion of the idiosyncratic and moody artist at odds with his or her society became popular in the Western world in the nineteenth century, this idea is very far from universal. In earlier times even in the West, even fulltime artists, who depended for their livelihood on the patronage of wealthy elites, were considered normal members of society with a specific job to perform. In small-scale, non-metropolitan societies, artists—whether full time or part time producers—are well integrated into the group, and share their values and practices. The temperamental and eccentric artist is a cultural feature of a limited range in time and place.

Myth #4 Art is fundamentally visual, primarily painting and sculpture.

In all societies in the world, art is made up of a variety of different media. In addition to painting, drawing, and sculpture, art includes a wide range of verbal art, drama, dance, and music. Societies with the smallest populations, the simplest technology, and no fixed living space may not include all artistic media. But every group includes many media.

In addition to the varieties of art produced by human societies, there are numerous artistic styles. Some groups produce very little representational art, employing visual art primarily as abstract decoration or adornment. Other societies favor representational art of various styles, some realistic or naturalistic, and others more stylized and conventionalized. Whether a society produces realistic, representational art or not is not an indication of the society's skill or lack thereof. It has to do with the cultural values and principles the society believes should be embodied in art.

Myth #5 All societies distinguish between high status art (fine art) and lower status art (folk art, popular art, outsider art, and craft).

For a society to distinguish between high status art and low status art, it must distinguish between low status and high status group members. That is, the society must be stratified. In societies that lack social stratification in the form of social classes or castes, virtually all people share the group's dominant values and are likely to participate in the same rituals and other cultural practices. Though there may be a difference between men's art and women's art, even these differences are likely to be appreciated and understood by the whole group, because the entire population benefits from such gender-specific art as women's baskets and men's ceremonial dances.

Art is universal, and yet it is also unique to each culture. The urge to create art, to embellish, to express oneself, and to set some things, events, and persons apart from others appears to shared by at least some individuals in all human groups. But the specific forms, styles, and even functions of art vary according to culture through time and space.

ENDNOTE

¹**Craft** is an imprecise term that covers a variety of artistic productions, some of which may also be included at the margins of fine art, folk art, popular art, and outsider art. Hand thrown ceramics, hand-woven or hand-dyed textiles, jewelry produced by small, independent silversmiths and lapidaries, hand-blown glass, hand-made furniture and other wooden objects all come under the rubric of "craft." In general, to be included as a part of craft production, an item is likely to be made by a member of the majority culture of a stratified metropolitan society, usually has a utilitarian function beyond its aesthetic dimension, and is not included in the most commonly accepted forms of visual fine art: painting (or drawing, engraving, or serigraph) and sculpture. Because of the practical application of their artistry, their products are generally considered to be distinct from fine art.

QUESTIONS FOR THOUGHT AND REFECTION

1. Before you read this chapter, what would your definition of art have been? Has it changed now that you have read the chapter, and, if so, how? Would you alter the definition of art provided in the chapter? How? Why?

2. One of the points made in this chapter is that art is not synonymous with beauty. Further, different societies have different ideas of what constitutes beauty in art, and some contemporary artists try to avoid creating beauty. Judging from what you have read in this chapter and your general, informal information about art, what would you say is the relationship between art and beauty? Do you think that it is necessary to be an art specialist to have a legitimate opinion on this topic?

3. What does it mean to say that art is *integrated* into the rest of culture? What are some concrete examples? Why do anthropologists argue that art is not very integrated into contemporary North American culture? Can you explain how and why art was more integrated into these societies at an earlier time in history?

4. Though narrative myths continue to be important in the lives of most North Americans, legends, tales, and the smaller forms of verbal art seem to have declined. Do you agree this has happened? Why or why not? Provide examples. Can you recall riddles, sayings, proverbs, and game rhymes (like jump rope rhymes) from your childhood? What are some of them? (Of course, when we use the term "myth" in this question, we are talking about the myths as a significant form of verbal art, not to "myth" as false and unsubstantiated belief).

5. What has happened to poetry? Few North Americans read or memorize much poetry as children, and as college students many of them dislike having to read it. Why do you think this is the case? What has taken the place of traditional poetry in the US? What are some examples? Do you think these substitutes will be remembered twenty-five, fifty, or a hundred years from now, in the way that classic poetry is remembered? Why or why not?

6. Books continue to be produced that are reviewed in *The New York Times;* paintings and sculpture continue to be produced that are shown in galleries; and music, dance, and theatre performances continue to be pronounced "serious" or elite art. What, specifically, creates the gulf between this kind of art and folk, popular, and outsider art? Do you think elite fine art is doomed to extinction? Why or why not? If you think it is not, then who are likely to be the consumers of elite fine art in the future? What makes them different from the majority of the population who never develop a liking for elite fine art?

REFERENCES

Arnold, Matthew
  1880 "General Introduction" in *The English Poets* edited by Thomas Humphrey Ward. London: Macmillan and Company. Volume 1.

Bowser, Brenda
  2000 From Pottery to Politics: An Ethnoarchaeological Study of Political Factionalism, Ethnicity, and Domestic Pottery Styke in the Ecuadorian Amazon. *Journal of Archaeological Method and Theory* 7(3): 219–248.

Cardinal, Roger
  1972 *Outsider Art.* New York: Praeger.

Laude, Jean
  1978 *African Art of the Dogon: The Myths of the Cliff Dwellings.* New York: Studio Books.

Lord, Albert B.
  2000 *The Singer of Tales,* 2d edition. Edited by Stephen Mitchell and Gregory Nagy. Cambridge, Harvard University Press.

Newcomb, Franc J. and Gladys Amanda Reichard
  1989 *Sandpaintings of the Navajo Shooting Chant.* Minneola, New York: Dover Publications.

Parry, Milman
  1987 *The Making of Homeric Verse: The Collected Papers of Milman.* Edited by Adam Parry. New York: Oxford University Press.

Witherspoon, Gary
  1977 *Language and Art in the Navajo Universe.* Ann Arbor: University of Michigan Press.

Tedlock, Dennis
  1996 *Popul Vuh: The Definitive Edition of the Mayan Book of the Dawn of Life and The Glories of the Gods and Kings.* Revised edition. New York: Simon and Schuster.

Tuttle, Tiffany L.
  2005 *Old Designs for Young People: Art, Innovation, and Cultural Continuity in Kygyzstan.* Unpublished master's thesis, Washington State Universioty.

CHAPTER 10

APPLIED ANTHROPOLOGY

How anthropologists use anthropology in the world outside the university

The final chapter of this book takes a look at the practical applications of anthropological knowledge. Covering the main areas in which applied anthropologists work, this chapter develops a central point, namely that anthropological knowledge carries clear and specific benefits to those programs and plans seeking to assist human life or to alleviate poverty. Anthropologists, however, have also become aware that not all efforts to improve the human condition, usually referred to as "development," are beneficial to those in need. Some such efforts are harmful, even if well-intended, and many fail to address the root causes of world poverty. In the process of discussing these issues we will dispel the following myths:

Common Myths of Culture
Myth #1   However exotic and interesting it may be, anthropology has little relevance to the real world or to practical problems in human life.
Myth #2   There are no jobs in anthropology outside academia.
Myth #3   Many humans go hungry because the world can no longer produce enough food for all its people.
Myth #4   Some human groups suffer economic deprivation because of their particular cultural beliefs, practices or orientations.

In the popular imagination, anthropology—with its focus on the exotic, on far away peoples and places—has little relevance to the real world, to the practical problems and issues affecting many of us here and now. A corollary of this view is that there are few, if any, jobs for anthropologists outside the ivory tower of the academic world, and those jobs, themselves scarce, require advanced degrees. As a couple of anthropologists recently put it, "It is easy to imagine well-intentioned parents and friends advising students to steer clear of anthropology, out of fear that their long-term career prospects will amount to nothing more than a one-way ticket to flipping burgers" (Reyes-Foster and Matejowsky 2014:3).

True, jobs are hard to get everywhere these days, but this popular impression of anthropology is not accurate. Today about half of all anthropologists in the United States work as applied anthropologists in non-academic settings. President Barak Obama's mother was one of these, working for many years as an applied anthropologist in Indonesia.

Applied work draws on anthropological knowledge to address specific, here-and-now problems in the real world. Some applied anthropologists work for government foreign-aid agencies such as the United States Agency for International Development (USAID) or for international development organizations like Oxfam (originally called the Oxford Committee for Famine Relief), various United Nations (UN) agencies, the World Bank, or non-government agencies (NGOs) that implement projects in developing countries. Others work for similar agencies addressing the needs of marginalized groups in developed countries. Everywhere these projects may concern such issues as disease control, health care, agricultural productivity, environmental preservation, income generation, and education, among many other areas. One of the authors of this book (Stone) worked for several years in applied anthropology. One year she directed a United States Peace Corps training program in Nepal. For two years she worked for the Swiss Agency for Technical Assistance on a project to orient farming practices and livestock management toward environmental sustainability in rural Nepal. For shorter periods she worked for the World Health Organization (WHO) of the UN on projects to implement primary health care programs in Nepal, Thailand and Indonesia. While much of this kind of work does require advanced degrees, other applied anthropology work does not. For example, one of the authors' undergraduate students worked in a high level position for the resettlement of Hmong refugees in Colorado immediately after receiving her BA in anthropology.[1]

For cultural anthropologists, the major portion of applied work is with domestic or international development projects. At the same time, an increasing

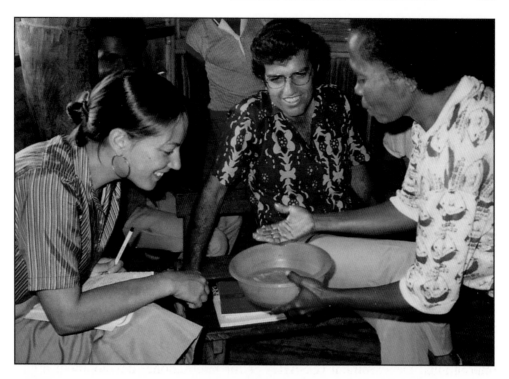

Figure 10.1 Author Linda Stone doing applied anthropology on Irian Jaya, Indonesia. She is collecting information about local healing practices.

Source: Authors' collection.

number of anthropologists are working in business (Jordon 2012). Here they may apply their cultural knowledge to marketing and product design. Hallmark, for example, has used anthropologists to design ethnically appropriate greeting cards (Elvin 2005). Others may work in personnel relations, where cultural differences among employees or between employees and employers create problematic work environments. Yet other anthropologists work as advocates for land claims and other rights of indigenous peoples. The range of applied anthropology is quite wide (and growing), covering, as we will see, forensic anthropology for physical anthropologists and applied branches of archaeology and linguistics. Today applied anthropologists appear to be cropping up everywhere, and sometimes in high positions. For example, anthropologist Jim Yong Kim, a Korean-American, became president of the World Bank in 2012.

One reason why applied anthropology is a diverse and growing field is simple: culture influences human behavior. To understand and change behavior (without the use of coercive force), cultural and cross-cultural knowledge is essential. This is seen perhaps most clearly in the area of medical anthropology.

APPLIED MEDICAL ANTHROPOLOGY

In the 1970s the Fore people of New Guinea were suffering high rates of death from a mysterious disease they called **kuru**. The Fore also referred to this ailment as "laughing sickness" because of the strange trembling and laughing sounds people made when afflicted. Outside investigators thought this must be a genetic disease because it tended to afflict family groups. But then an American physician, Daniel Carleton Gajdusek, made a discovery: Kuru was caused by the Fore cultural practice of honoring dead relatives by consuming a portion of their brains, internal organs, and limbs. Kuru, directly transmitted to relatives of the deceased through this religious practice, is similar to "mad cow" disease. For this discovery Gajdusek received the Nobel Prize in 1976. The Fore practice of consuming brain tissue of dead relatives stopped, but it had nearly exterminated the Fore.

From this stunning case of kuru and other examples from ethnography, it is now well understood that culture, health, and illness are closely interrelated. Many cultural beliefs and practices promote human health, but others go

Photo 10.2   Fore child suffering from kuru.
Source: D. Carleton Gajdusek's 1976 Nobel Lecture, fig. 13a. © The Nobel Foundation 1976. With permission.

against biomedical advice. We need only consider such conditions as anorexia and obesity in the United States against the cultural background of American cultural obsessions with food and super-slim bodies to see how culture impacts health. In some cases, changing behavior or introducing new behaviors is difficult because of entrenched cultural ideas. For example, throughout rural South Asia a common belief is that when an infant has diarrhea, this signals that its body contains too much water and so liquids should be restricted. In such areas many infants die of dehydration as a result. In rural South Asia, diarrhea is further seen as perfectly normal in infants; in fact it is considered a sign of growth. Thus when health development agencies sought to introduce Oral Rehydration Therapy (ORT, packets of a salt and sugar formula to be mixed with water) this was initially resisted in Nepal as the idea of infant rehydration conflicted with local beliefs about infant diarrhea. This problem was overcome when, at the advice of anthropologists, the ORT was simply called "medicine" and the idea of promoting "rehydration" by name was suspended.

Knowledge of local practices and local perceptions of health and illness is essential to attempts to lessen or control disease around the world. For this reason applied anthropologists are often a part of health intervention programs. One interesting case concerns the outbreak of **Ebola** hemorrhagic fever in northern Uganda in 2000 and 2001. Ebola is a zoonotic disease, that is, it is a contagious disease spread between animals and humans. It brings flu-like symptoms (fever, nausea, headache, diarrhea) and has a fatality rate that can be as high as 90 percent. In Uganda is it thought to have initially spread from infected bats to humans and later from humans to humans as one person came into contact with blood or other bodily fluids of another infected person. One area hit hard by Ebola was the region of the Acholi people. Here anthropologists were called in to assist an international health team (with the WHO) to control the disease (Hewlett & Amola, 2003; Hewlett & Hewlett, 2008). Right away in this case we can see how cultural factors influenced the nature of the Ebola epidemic. For example, Acholi women were far more affected than men because women act as caretakers of ill persons, and women (especially one's father's sister) wash and prepare corpses for burial.

Among the Acholi, the health team attempted to isolate victims, quickly dispose of the dead, and promote certain practices, such as avoidance of any sharing of bodily fluids. While these measures were helpful is some respects, they were undertaken without appropriate knowledge of Acholi culture. The result was that the Acholi often responded to this intervention with fear and anger. Ebola victims avoided the hospital and literally ran away from ambulances that had come to collect them. What went wrong? One problem was that the medical team banned the practice of traditional healers who used sha-manic treatments. The team mistakenly thought that one particular healer who eventually died from Ebola had spread it to many of her patients through body contacts. As it turned out, those deaths were not caused by the woman's heal-ing practice; rather, many people respected this woman highly and so closely cared for her when she was ill, strongly exposing themselves to the virus. Banning these traditional practitioners was not only an affront to these often respected community members, but these traditional practitioners initially had been interested in cooperating with the health team and helping with the dis-ease control efforts. Another problem was that the health team, in an effort to dispose of dead bodies very quickly, placed them in bags and took them to the airfield for burial without notifying relatives. The Acholi came to fear the hospital, not as a place of burial should they die, but from anxiety that once inside the hospital they would never see their families again. Among the Acholi rumors quickly spread that the medical team was snatching up bod-ies and hurrying them off because they were collecting body parts for sale in Europe!

Infectious diseases such as Ebola, malaria, West Nile virus, Middle East Respiratory Syndrome (MERS), and many others are major killers in the world today, a situation that is likely to get worse with increased movements of people and alterations of the environment. Where natural habitats are signif-icantly disrupted by human activity (for example, clearing forests for agricul-ture) new species of pathogens may emerge, and new modes of transmission of disease from insects or wildlife to humans may result (Inhorn & Brown, 1997; Sattenspiel, 2000). Over a quarter of all human deaths are due to infec-tious diseases (WHO, 2004); of these, about three-fourths are zoonotic. For this reason, many medical anthropologists and others are now looking closely at human interactions with animals, especially in disturbed ecological settings, to understand and control infectious diseases.

Interactions among humans, animals, and the environment, and the trans-missions of diseases that may result, are driven by a web of social, cultural, and economic factors. For example, the African country of Cameroon has seen the emergence of many new zoonotic pathogens, including Ebola, HIV/ AIDS, Marburg virus and Monkey pox (Wolfe et al. 2005). Here, new logging projects to extract rich timber resources have accelerated deforestation and brought new roads (funded by the World Bank and the European Economic Union) into the forested areas. Deforestation has increased the diversity of viruses, while the roads have increased the access of human hunters to forest wildlife which they poach for bushmeat or capture for sale. The new access to forests places bushmeat hunters at considerable risk of disease through contact with infected animals' blood or bodily fluids. Further risks are encountered by many people as infected bushmeat or live animals are transported and marketed. In Cameroon the urban demand for bushmeat is high among very poor households, while wealthy people show a strong demand for exotic pets. Some of these zoonotic diseases may later become transmissible from one human to another and, at a later stage still, may literally go global with increased human travel.

PHYSICAL ANTHROPOLOGY, ARCHAEOLOGY AND LINGUISTICS

Although most of applied anthropology in is the cultural wing of the discipline, each of the other subfields has an applied side, as well. For physical anthropologists this is the relatively new and growing field of forensic anthropology. Forensic anthropology assists criminal investigations through the examination of human remains. Given their special training in the examination and interpretation of skeletal and dental material, forensic anthropologists are often called upon to help solve murders. These professionals frequently appear on the popular television series "Forensic Files." Forensic anthropologists are able to tell the age, gender and often the ethnic origin of murder victims and can frequently determine the circumstances or causes of their deaths.

Applied archaeology is most often concerned with Cultural Resource Management (CRM). CRM is the assessment of the value of potential archaeological sites in areas where major construction is planned. Many countries such as the United States and Canada have laws specifying that construction of buildings, roads, dams, and so on must be delayed or even discontinued if land surveys show it would destroy valuable archaeological material. Perhaps the most striking case of CRM concerned the Aswan Dam in Egypt, built in the early 1960s. Here archaeologists had determined that the dam would create a lake that would destroy the temple of Ramses II along with other sites. Before the dam could be completed, this temple was taken apart piece by piece and reconstructed on higher ground to preserve this invaluable heritage of our ancient past. With the recent oil boom in North Dakota, CRM archaeologists are finding a "jobs bonanza" in surveying oil fields before digging and drilling can begin (Wood, 2014: A10). Also in the United States today., some archaeologists are doing applied work in transmitting their archaeology and CRM skills to Native American groups so that they can manage their own cultural heritage.

Applied linguists work in a number of areas. Forensic linguists are sometimes called upon to analyze the structure of written messages from anonymous criminals, to assess regional origin and education level of the message writers, and to assess whether particular messages are likely to have been produced by the same person. Anthropological linguists in the United States also assist in the development and administration of programs to teach English to speakers of other languages (ESL), both in schools and in other facilities. The advantages for immigrant children to learn English are obvious: they will gain more from their education and have a far greater chance of a successful future. But many immigrants to the United States are adults who speak little or no English. As we have already seen in Chapter 7, adults have a much more difficult time learning new languages than do children. Linguists, then, try to develop techniques and strategies that are specifically geared to adult learners. Anthropological linguists are particularly sensitized to cultural issues that may impact how adult immigrants approach the learning of English, ranging from issues of who in the immigrant culture normally speaks to whom about what to how to arrange ESL classes for women with small children and onerous household duties.

One special area of focus for applied anthropological linguists has to do with Native American languages. By the beginnings of American academic anthropology in the early twentieth century, anthropologists like Boas, Kroeber, and Sapir (all mentioned in earlier chapters) were actively involved in what is often referred to as "salvage anthropology," including salvage linguistics. That is, to preserve as much of the disappearing Native American languages as possible, anthropological linguists attempted to record as many of them as possible. One of the best known and most tragic cases of salvage linguistics is the case of Ishi, the last speaker of the native California language of Yana (see Theodora Kroeber 2011 for an account of Ishi's life and interaction with anthropologists). As time has gone on, American Indian peoples have increasingly taken charge of the preservation of their languages, sometimes seeking the assistance of linguists. For example, Jill Wagner, a former student of both authors of this text, who received her doctorate from Washington State University, has collaborated with members of the Coeur d'Alene tribe in Idaho to produce language textbooks for use in high schools serving Coeur d'Alene students. Though some Native American languages, especially Navajo and Cherokee, continue to have large numbers of native speakers, most Native American languages in the United States do not. They continue, however, to maintain significance as symbols of ethnic identity. They also provide a connection to the past and a source of historical information both for the descen-

Photo 10.3   Alfred Kroeber and Ishi.
Source: Wikimedia.

dants of their original speakers and for scholars, in much the same way as Latin, Sanskrit, or Old Church Slavonic do for other groups.

HUNGER, POVERTY AND POWER

Aside from, and sometimes along with, working for development agencies or within projects, many anthropologists have critically analyzed the development industry itself, or have examined global processes of development. Their work has thrown light on the root causes of the poverty and deprivation that lie behind development interventions. In this section we review a few of the major contributions of anthropologists and other scholars to this endeavor.

Moving, then, to the topic of human hunger, it is important first to dispel one basic and prevalent myth about it, namely that many people go hungry in the world today because the world can no longer produce enough food for all its people. A corollary myth, of course, is that the root problem here is global and regional overpopulation. In fact, however, the world has abundant food

(Lappé, Collins, & Rosset, 1998:8; Robbins, 2011:156). In fact, most of the malnourished children in the word live in countries with food surpluses—countries such as India—that export more agricultural food than they import. The problem is not one of growing food but rather that food has become a commodity. That is, it is produced, bought, and sold for profit. Over the course of centuries since the Neolithic Revolution, the world has moved from subsistence farming to mechanized, capital-intensive agro-business, producing a large nonagricultural work force whose access to food depends on wages and food prices, not on an ability to farm. As anthropologist Richard Robbins puts it, "In the culture of capitalism, access to food is determined almost entirely by the ability to pay, not by the need to eat" (Robbins 2011:156). People are hungry because they are poor.

Another common misconception about poverty and hunger is that these conditions arise from certain cultural beliefs, practices, or orientations. We may hear that a certain people "lack a work ethic" or that a people's religion "holds them back." By this point in the book we should certainly be alert to the fallacies of these ethnocentric, "blame the victim" approaches. It is true, as seen in this chapter, that some cultural beliefs and practices are harmful—for example, the Fore mourning practice that resulted in kuru disease. Among all cultures most such directly harmful beliefs or practices concern health and nutrition. For reasons not yet understood, while we do see these cases of bio-medically unsound cultural practices, we do not find much in the way of harmful beliefs regarding the environment and its exploitation, food production and so on (Chambers 1983). In any event, human culture is largely adaptive, and humans everywhere do whatever they can to avoid poverty and hunger. Why, then, are some people poor? And what can be done about it?

Victims of Progress

Among the very poor of the world are residents of Native American reservations in the United States. Many of their counterparts, both in the Unites States and around the world, exist as disadvantaged ethnic minorities in urban areas. These are indigenous persons, that is, descendants of the native people who once lived as autonomous foragers, pastoralists or small-scale horticulturalists in control of their own natural resources for subsistence. Today most of them live in poverty, in poor health, and suffer discrimination within the broader societies now dominant over their homelands. To anthropologist John Bodley, whose work is discussed extensively in Chapter 3, these indigenous people are "victims of progress." They have paid a heavy price for the global expansion over the past

400 years of a commercial culture that spread outward from Europe to colonize Africa, Australia, New Zealand, the Americas, and other regions.

As we saw in Chapter 1 and elsewhere throughout this book, this commercial European culture at the time of its expansion saw itself as highly advanced, civilized, the pinnacle of progress. Indigenous persons were regarded as "savages" in dire need of the benefits of civilization and, most important, as blocking access to forests, rivers, coastlines, ore deposits and potential farmland—all awaiting proper exploitation by the bearers of progress. Everywhere they were encountered, indigenous people were overcome—many were killed or forced into labor; all were deprived of their land and other natural resources. Bodley (2015: 38) sums up this process of the victimization of indigenous persons:

> There is certainly no mystery to be explained here. It has long been recognized that frontier violence, the dispossession of tribal people from their homelands, the destruction of their subsistence bases, the introduction of foreign diseases, the availability of guns and alcohol, and numerous forms of economic exploitation have all directly led to depopulation, apathy, dependence, and detribalization."

No mystery to explain here, but what Bodley notes as remarkable about this destruction of indigenous people was its sheer magnitude. He estimates that between 1780 and 1930 the world population of indigenous persons was reduced by 30 to 50 million people as a direct result of the steady encroachment of the new world culture bent on colonialism, market capitalism and industrialization. Clearly, this was "genocide on a grand scale" (2015:52). As late as 1820, indigenous persons controlled territories that covered over half the globe. Today they occupy only marginalized pockets of it or are dispersed in city slums.

Since the 1970s many indigenous people have joined various local, regional and international self-determination movements that are now meeting with some success. It is also now more widely appreciated that the treatment of indigenous people is a matter of human rights. In 2007 the United Nations General Assembly adopted the Declaration of the Rights of Indigenous People, supporting these peoples' rights to reject or approve the actions of outsiders with regard to their territories. Many anthropologists actively work to support the rights, claims, and self-determination efforts of indigenous people; virtually all anthropologists lend support by exposing the ethnocentrism behind the policies of many governments concerning indigenous peoples.

Also today, people generally are far more aware of the destructive impact of global-scale economies, of the global culture built on materialism, ever-expanding consumerism, and the defining of well-being as a perpetual growth of a nation's Gross Domestic Product. We see the effects in global warming and other environmental destruction, to say nothing of the ever-growing gap between rich and poor. In these ways, to John Bodley, we are all victims of progress. Indigenous people were the first victims and, so far, the hardest hit.

Hidden Hunger

Many people associate the problem of world hunger with periodic famines, often dramatically covered in the media when they occur. Most human hunger, however, is not due to famines but to endemic hunger caused by poverty. This hunger is largely hidden from view; one reason is that governments do not draw attention to poverty and hunger within their borders, seeking to safeguard their country's image or out of fear of criticism that they fail to provide for their citizens (Robins 2011:166). But there are other reasons, too, having to do with the powerlessness of the poor, the experience of poverty, itself, and what anthropologist Nancy Scheper-Hughes (1992) referred to as the "medicalization of hunger." Scheper-Hughes conducted her study in the 1980s in a shantytown near the city of Bom Jesus (a pseudonym) in Northeast Brazil, an area where she had previously worked as a United States Peace Corps volunteer. Here she documented conditions of abject poverty, acutely seen in extremely high rates of infant mortality. Poverty in this area has deep historical roots. For centuries it was an area of sugar cane plantations, first established by Portuguese colonists who imported slave labor. Later slavery ended, but the plantations expanded. As the mechanization of agriculture increased, plantation owners evicted most peasant sharecroppers from their land, forcing them to migrate to cities in search of jobs or work for poor wages on the plantations.

Scheper-Hughes found that while many infants were dying from hunger, their mothers, along with relatives, neighbors, and friends, perceived this as a medical problem and sought a medical solution. Many symptoms of starvation such as weakness, dizziness and diarrhea, were locally interpreted as signs of *nervos*, an illness that local people believed just happens, or develops in an innately weak or nervous body. They went to local clinics seeking medicines for these symptoms and received pain killers, rehydration therapy, and other medicines from doctors, only to return home to endure their illness-inducing poverty, unsanitary living conditions, and slow starvation all over again.

Meanwhile, government officials and politicians did not address their poverty but instead gave them slogans promising accessible health care. The hunger of their infants and the poverty behind it were in this way circumvented and no one was held accountable.

One result of the poverty and hunger in Bom Jesus was indirect infanticide. Because resources were extremely scarce among the poor, mothers unconsciously neglected weaker infants in favor of more robust ones who had a better chance of survival. Thus the weaker infants received less food and other care. Infant mortality in northeast Brazil was, and is, quite high. At the time of Scheper-Hughes' study, about 200 of every 1000 infants died within the first year of life, an extremely high infant mortality rate. For comparison, the infant mortality rate for the whole of Brazil at the same time was around 50 deaths for every 1000 live births; it is now 13. (Currently in Japan and Sweden the infant mortality rate is 2; in the United States it is 6 [WHO 2013]).

The poor of the Bom Jesus shantytown made grim cultural adaptations to their hunger, poverty, and high infant mortality, indirect infanticide being one. In addition, mothers did not usually bond with young infants until they were older and showing signs of a likely survival. There was also a prevalent belief in this Catholic area that dead infants were "angel babies" who would fly straight to heaven. Mothers reported that some of their dead infants had wanted to die or lacked the will to live, or that "It was a blessing that God decided to take them in their infancy" (1992:53). Grief over dead infants was minimized. It was said that mothers should not weep over their dead infants as their tears would fall on the baby's angel wings and stop them from flying to heaven; hence the title of Scheper-Hughes' moving book about Bom Jesus, *Death without Weeping*.

Scheper-Hughes' study illustrated how the very real conditions of hunger and poverty can be hidden and ignored. These conditions can also be hidden underneath official records and statistics. For example, in Bom Jesus not all infant deaths were even reported. To find an accurate count, Scheper-Hughes had to interview the local coffin maker! Also if one looks at the infant mortality rate for the country of Brazil as a whole, it hides the painful realities of people who live in places like Bom Jesus.

Following her early studies in Northeast Brazil, Nancy Scheper-Hughes became an activist in social movements in both Brazil and the United States, assisting such groups as rural workers, street children, and the homeless. In 2013 she received the first Anthropology in Public Policy Award from the American Anthropological Association.

Although the situation in North America is dramatically different from what Scheper-Hughes reported for Northeast Brazil, there is in the United States a variant of what she referred to as the medicalization of poverty. In the last twenty years, United States policy makers generally have become increasingly reluctant to provide relief for impoverished constituents. AFDC (Aid to Families with Dependent Children), which had no term limits, was replaced in 1996 with TANF (Temporary Assistance to Needy Families), which has a federal lifetime limit of five years, though some states have imposed shorter limits. SNAP (Supplemental Nutrition Assistance Program), the successor to Food Stamps, was significantly cut in 2014. And in spite of the introduction of the Affordable Care Act (aka "Obamacare"), many states refused to accept the extension of Medicaid that would have provided health care for the very poor. On the other hand, virtually no American policymaker is prepared to sweep the dead off the streets in the mornings, so solutions have been sought that allow some relief to reach the poor, without providing them with funds over which they have control. With this, policy makers also avoid appearing as though they are "coddling" the poor. So, instead of providing the poor with an adequate basic income or a means to secure one, TANF is subsidized by food aid such as SNAP; WIC (Women, Infants, Children, a feeding program for pregnant and nursing mothers, and children under five) and the federal school lunch program. Here, food aid plays a similar role to medicine in the Brazilian policies Scheper-Hughes describes: it provides some temporary relief but side-steps the underlying issue of poverty—the poverty to which the poor return day after day, no matter what food aid they receive. In this way government assistance remains inadequate, and though it provides some help, it does not open a way out of poverty.

Putting the Last First

Poverty may go unseen even when it is officially the focus of attention, as shown by Robert Chambers (1983), a development academic and practitioner from England. In contrast to the urban poverty discussed by Scheper-Hughes, Chambers' focus has been on the less visible *rural* poverty in the Third World, "on the hundreds of millions of largely unseen peoples in rural areas who are poor, weak, isolated, vulnerable and powerless" (1983:3). These five basic characteristics of the rural poor interact with one another to sustain their desperate condition. Thus lack of money to buy adequate food, medicine, health care, or sanitary living conditions will result in chronic illness and malnutrition that leave the poor physically weak, which in turn reduces their labor capacities and so lowers their possibilities for work and wages. These conditions all combine to make the poor especially vulnerable to periodic crises such as floods, crop failure, the death of livestock or a household earner, spiraling them into even deeper poverty and despair.

This kind of poverty is hidden from view because of biases in how outsiders encounter and approach the rural poor. Outsiders, to Chambers, are "people concerned with rural development who are themselves neither rural nor poor" (1983:5). Outsiders—who may be agricultural extension agents, volunteer aid workers, government officers, journalists, development consultants, and so on— engage in brief visits of "development tourism" that are conducted in such a way that they hide the truly poor, their conditions, their needs, and their perspectives. Development tourism takes outsiders to those rural areas that are closest to cities and most accessible to major roads or roads in better condition—in a word, to village areas that are better off by virtue of their greater access to urban cores. Outsiders tend to go to areas where there are development projects underway, atypical "model villages" and the like. In these areas outsiders are greeted and treated as VIPs by rural elites, village leaders, the "progressive farmers," and the local residents who have already adopted the new farming practice or are already sending their children to the new school. These biases then gear the attention of outsiders toward the better-off and effectively hide the poor who live further away or who, embarrassed by their poverty or intimidated by local elites, are unlikely to show up in the village square for outsider visits. In the tropics of the Third World, development tourism occurs nearly always in the dry season rather than the rainy season to avoid all kinds of discomfort and inconvenience brought by erosion of roads, the heat, and humidity. As a result, outsiders encounter rural people at a time when crops are in and people are more likely to be fed, not in the rainy season when both food and jobs are scarcer, disease and illness more prevalent, and poor people most desperate. Chambers further showed that biases similar to those in development tourism permeate the whole development enterprise. Here he refers to the world of the relatively wealthy, urban-oriented outsiders, their underlying values and perspectives as the "first," in opposition to the rural, poor "last." In research and development, "first" values prioritize, for example, capital-intensive in-puts over those that are labor-intensive; imported species of livestock and food crops over those that are indigenous; industrialization over agriculture; and within agriculture, cash crops over subsistence crops.

In particular, the world of the "first" favors scientific knowledge over the indigenous knowledge of the "last." As Chambers wrote, "The links of modern scientific knowledge with wealth, power, and prestige condition outsiders to despise and ignore rural people's own knowledge" (1983:25). The result is a paternalistic attempt to transfer knowledge and skills in one direction only—downward from first to last. A good example of how this approach is often counterproductive was seen in the case of mixed cropping in East and West Africa. Here, as in many tropical areas with small farms, the growing of two or more crops on the same land is widespread. In the earlier decades of international development, outsiders urged monocropping instead, as practiced in the Western world on large mechanized farms and as was consistent with the agricultural research that was geared to producing an increase in yield of a single crop. These outside developers eventually learned the hard way what local African farmers knew all along—that mixed cropping in the region carries a number of distinct advantages. To name only two, in mixed cropping, one crop may provide a favorable micro climate for another, and with mixed cropping, each crop is less vulnerable to pests.

There are many examples of the dominance of "first" orientations and values in development but perhaps Chamber's points are best illustrated with the so-called Green Revolution. The Green Revolution began in the 1940s and 1950s with agricultural research undertaken by United States scientists in Mexico. This research produced high-yielding varieties (HYVs) of grains such as rice and wheat. These HYVs exponentially increased crop production. They were then introduced and rapidly adopted throughout the Third World, often through projects sponsored by USAID. Here outsiders were at the helm, transferring "superior" scientific knowledge and technology downward to developing country peasants. But the problem with the Green Revolution was that the HYVs required significant inputs—water (irrigation), chemical pesticides, and herbicides. Only the better-off farmers could afford these requirements, leaving the smaller farmers at a disadvantage. Some smaller farmers obtained credit to buy the inputs but they could not compete with the larger farmers, and so gradually went into debt and ended up landless. As the Green Revolution expanded, more and more rural poor were forced to abandon farming and migrate into cities in search of wage labor (Robbins 2011). This development of larger capital-intensive farms in rural areas of the Third World thus widened the gap between the rich and the poor. There were other problems, too. For example, in the Philippines the use of pesticides for the HYVs killed off the fish that used to live inside rice paddies and that had been a valued source of food. In parts of India the introduction of chemical pesticides and herbicides may have increased human exposure to cancer-causing agents.

What Chambers suggested for rural development was a total reversal of orientations, values, and priorities that would genuinely put the "last first" in all stages and aspects of the development process. He advocated that outsiders encounter and relate to the poor as colleagues, rather than "recipients" of aid, that they listen to and learn from the poor and that they respect indigenous knowledge and perspectives. His first book, *Rural Development: Putting the Last First,* was very widely read and highly influential in development circles; many of his ideas were adopted (at least on paper) in development projects and proposals. He later wrote a number of sequels to this book, the most recent being *Into the Unknown: Explorations in Development Practice* (2014). Many of his books provide techniques for involving the rural poor in community needs-assessment and bottom-up development, such as the now widely used Participatory Rural Appraisal (PRA). PRA is a "reversal of learning" in Chambers' sense. It is a set of techniques for group discussions that encourages dialogue between outsiders and the poor and that incorporates local knowledge and perspectives into development planning, management, and monitoring. The goal of PRA is both to decentralize development and to empower the poor.

Figure 10.4 Development dialogues. Staff of a resource conservation development project use a PRA exercise to discuss development needs with villagers in rural Nepal.

Source: Authors' collection.

Chambers has initiated some much-needed reversals in development think-ing, policy, and planning. Meanwhile, there are signs of another kind of reversal in international development taking place quite recently. For instance, Portugal, now facing bankruptcy and World-Bank imposed austerity measures, is see-ing a reversal in its relationship with Angola, which was its colony for over 400 years. Independent since 1975, Angola now prospers with oil sales and achieves high rates of economic growth. Wealthy Angolans are buying up or heavily investing in Portuguese banking, media, and luxury seaside apartments to the point where Portugal is now economically dependent on its former Third World colony (Gatinois 2014). Unfortunately this kind of reversal does not alleviate poverty; the same global market forces behind the creation of poverty also work to make the poor become poorer in both Angola and Portugal.

Human Rights and Needless Deaths

The stark socio-economic inequalities in our current world become quite literally embodied in the differential patterns of human health and sickness. Life expectancy in Japan today is 83 years, and in Sweden it is 81. But in Afghanistan it is 45 and in Swaziland it is only 32.[2] Ninety-eight percent of all communicable diseases occur in developing countries. Every day about 800 women in the world die in childbirth, but nearly all of these deaths occur in the Third World. Within both rich countries and developing countries, the poor suffer disease and premature death from conditions that are preventable and treatable. Given the quality of current medical knowledge and technology, these are needless deaths.

Paul Farmer, an American anthropologist and a physician, has taken on this issue of needless deaths, and his work is making a difference. As Farmer notes, the poorest people suffer the highest rates of illness and premature death for two reasons. First, their life situations place them at greater risks to their health. Living in marginal areas, enduring unsanitary conditions, and already malnour-ished, the poor are far more vulnerable to pathogens than better-off people. Secondly, the poor lack access to adequate health care. Quite simply, they can-not afford it. Either it is present where they live, but they cannot pay for it, or it is not present where they live because there is too small a population with ade-quate wealth to support a community of biomedical health care practitioners.

Two diseases that clearly reveal the linkages among poverty, elevated health risks, and needless deaths are malaria and HIV/AIDS. With malaria, for example, over one million people die of this disease each year with 90 percent of these deaths occurring in sub-Saharan Africa (Bassett and Winter-Nelson

2010). Here, the poor lack resources to control malaria with drugs or preventive mosquito nets. Further, there is little outside employment-generating financial investment in malaria-ridden areas. And in these areas widespread malnutrition worsens the disease. As for HIV/AIDS, it is prevalent in both sub-Saharan Africa and the Caribbean island of Haiti, where dire poverty has propelled the prostitution and labor migration that serve to spread it.

To counter outsiders' ignorance of or apathy toward needless deaths, Famer has emphasized adequate health care as a basic human right. Poverty and the consequent high levels of illness are, in his view, cases of **structural violence**.[3] Structural violence is the deprivation brought about by social, political, or economic structures (including laws, conventions, cultural values, and practices) that prevent people from realizing their basic human needs. Slavery is a good example of structural violence; more common today are cases of institutionalized racism, classism, and sexism. These entrenched structures of inequality serve the interests of the wealthy and powerful and severely restrict the resources and opportunities of the poor. Structural violence is social injustice.

Opposing the realization of health as a basic human right is one form of structural violence—the commodification of medicine and health care. Market-oriented medical care favors the wealthy and excludes the poor. This situation does not just concern access to neuro-surgeons or expensive cancer treatments. For instance, globally today in the pharmaceutical industry, the greatest amount of research, financing, and marketing of drugs is devoted to those that treat high blood pressure, arthritis, high cholesterol, male baldness, and male impotence—all problems of the rich (and overfed) who can pay for the drugs.

Many have thought that the delivery of high-quality health care to the poor would be hopelessly unrealistic—too expensive, not cost-effective, and not sustainable. Proving this view incorrect, in 1987 Paul Farmer co-founded Partners in Health (PIH), a non-profit community-based health initiative that began in Haiti and has spread to Peru, Mexico, the United States (Boston), and other countries. PIH has developed innovative approaches to providing health care to the poor, free of charge and supplemented with food, water, education, and housing. PIH has without doubt met with success. In Haiti it has established clinics and hospitals, including a teaching hospital, in 12 locations. Also in Haiti it founded the world's first free program for AIDs treatment in a poor area. In Rwanda it introduced treatment for AIDs and in several countries it has trained cadres of community health workers who guide poor patients over the barriers of poverty, social intimidation, and discrimination to effective health care. In 1993, Farmer founded the Institute for Health and Social Justice to conduct research and advocacy for PIH. Most recently he has been working on the delivery of effective cancer treatments to the poor of developing countries such as Rwanda.

PROFESSIONAL AND ETHICAL ISSUES

Applied anthropologists have a different relationship to and position within the broader field of their profession from that of academic anthropologists. First, academic anthropologists are relatively independent; they are free to choose topics of research according to their own interests, constrained only by a topic's appeal to other anthropologists and to funding agencies. The kinds of questions they ask and the research methods they use are up to them. By contrast, applied anthropologists generally work for organizations where they are told what to investigate and what kinds of data to collect. Second, once they receive tenure, academic anthropologists have job security; that is, a tenured professor cannot lose his or her position unless he or she is found guilty of some dramatically dishonorable act. This ensures academic freedom and prevents retaliation against a faculty member for espousing an unpopular opinion or theoretical position. By contrast, there is no equivalent for applied anthropologists, who must continually demonstrate their worth to their employing agency (Ervin 2005). Third, academic anthropologists typically work on their own, whereas applied anthropologists usually work as part of an interdisciplinary team consisting, for example, of economists, agricultural experts, and medical professionals (Nolan 2002). Not all of these other team members will know much about anthropology or appreciate its contributions to a project. Stone recalls that while working on a health project in Nepal, another member of the team, a British management expert, asked her nearly every day what possible use anthropology could have for international development!

A fourth way in which the position of applied anthropologists is somewhat unique has to do with issues of professional objectivity and ethics. Some anthropologists feel that applied work is a direct intervention in a culture, and, however well-intentioned, it introduces a perspective biased in favor of change and "betterment." It inevitably reflects the implicit and explicit values and perspectives of the intervention program and, beyond it, the outside world in which it was devised and funded. In this way applied anthropology loses scientific objectivity. This criticism is often especially aimed at advocacy anthropology. Anthropologists working as advocates, critics say, are clearly "taking sides" and are thus heavily biased from the start.

Others question the ethics of applied anthropology, pointing out that a lot of so-called "development" ends up harming people, especially the very poor. We have discussed cases of this in the present chapter. Others add (a point also addressed in this chapter) that the roots of poverty and deprivation in the world lie in the larger world capitalist system of which development efforts are a part, so that applied or development anthropologists are merely serving the interests of a world order that produces and oppresses the poor in the first place (Escobar 1995).

Against these views, practicing anthropologists argue that inaction and the presumption of "objectivity" are themselves positions with a bias. Some also say that it is ethically better at least to try to make improvements in people's conditions, consistent with one's own conscience, than to stand aside and let the will of other, less culturally sensitive and informed agents guide human affairs or affect the lot of the poor and marginalized people of the world. As ever, the field of anthropology embraces controversial issues, and we can all only agree that we are a long way from answering the questions that the application of anthropological knowledge raises. Meanwhile, there are professional codes of ethics that have been devised to help guide practicing anthropologists along the way. The Society for Applied Anthropology, for example, has had a code of ethics since 1948. This code, among other things, specifies that practicing anthropologists "will avoid taking or recommending action on behalf of a sponsor which is harmful to the interests of the community."

SUMMARY

This chapter has given us a glimpse into the nature of applied anthropology and the work of some of its practitioners. This is an expanding branch of the field, and it is predictable that the diversity of careers in applied anthropology will increase in the years ahead. In applied work cultural anthropologists have maintained their traditional focus on marginalized peoples—indigenous groups, the rural and urban poor, along with other disadvantaged minorities— which has drawn them into critical awareness of the global problems of poverty, hunger, and injustice. Notice, too, that nearly all of the scholars covered in this chapter have called forth and "applied" a very distinctively anthropological concept, the *emic*. Again and again these scholars have demonstrated that an emic view, or understanding from within, is essential to the comprehension of human deprivation and any proposals for its elimination. We return, then, to the myths listed in the beginning of the chapter.

Myth #1 However exotic and interesting, anthropology has little relevance to the real world or to practical problems in human life.

The chapter has, we hope, thoroughly dispelled this notion. Today anthropologists assist not only with disease prevention in Papua New Guinea and limiting the spread of HIV/AIDS in sub Saharan Africa, but also the preservation of Native American languages and the link between income and health in rural Mississippi. What is significant about anthropology is not where it is done, but what questions are asked and how information is collected. When these questions and this information have a positive impact on human life, there is no question that anthropology is relevant and beneficial.

Myth #2 There are no jobs in anthropology outside academia.

Although this is a widespread myth, it is an easy one to refute: it just is not true. As we have seen, anthropologists are now actively engaged in domestic and international development projects, business, political advocacy, forensic science, contract archaeology and many other endeavors. Health, agriculture, education, and public administration are among the most common areas of concentration that call upon the expertise of anthropologists, some of whom are full-time applied practitioners, and some of whom also function as academics. Both governmental and non governmental agencies hire anthropologists, along with some commercial entities. You may recall from Chapter 7 that even linguists have found their way into commercial work, consulting for Hollywood on the construction of such communication systems as Klingon, the speech system devised for the *Star Wars* films by linguist Marc Okrand.

Myth #3 Many humans go hungry because the world can no longer produce enough food for all its people.

This myth is widely believed by many well-meaning people, and has been in circulation since at least the eighteenth century. In fact, however, as we have seen, world hunger is caused not by an absolute shortage of food existing on the planet. The problem has to do with one of three factors:

food not being adequately distributed to people who need it; food being too expensive for impoverished people to buy; or crops failing either because of natural calamities like drought or flood, or more commonly because of armed conflict that prevents planting, cultivation, or harvest. There *is* hunger in the world, but it is overwhelmingly caused by human agency, not by numbers of people.

Myth #4   Some human groups suffer economic deprivation because of their particular cultural beliefs, practices, or orientations.

There is no human group known to anthropologists whose culture has doomed them to poverty. Certainly, there are populations, even very large ones, who are desperately poor, but their poverty is not caused by a cultural system that values sloth over hard work or that irrationally refuses to adapt to changing circumstances. Instead, this poverty, as we have seen throughout the book, is based on the kinds of structural barriers to economic success and political voice that accompany the development of large nation states. To blame the poor for their own poverty is to misunderstand the structure of the modern world.

QUESTIONS FOR THOUGHT AND REFLECTION

1. Applied anthropologists work in many countries in the world, including the United States. What is it about anthropology that unites its approach in such a variety of different locations and cultural systems? What do you think makes anthropology uniquely productive in working to improve the lives of poor and oppressed peoples of the world?

2. Consider the cases of the two diseases of Kuru and Ebola, the former from Papua New Guinea, and the latter from sub-Saharan Africa. From an anthropological perspective, what is similar about the situations of the two diseases? How have applied anthropologists been useful in dealing with the two diseases? Can you come up with a medical/health situation in the contemporary United States that you think would benefit from investigation and intervention of an applied anthropologist?

3. As this chapter explains, applied anthropologists generally work for an agency that determines the policies under which they will collect data, as

well as the specific questions and issues they will explore. As they pursue their research, applied anthropologists often discover that there is some conflict between the goals of their employing agency and the interests and desires of the people whose lives they are exploring and trying to improve. What kinds of conflicts can you imagine may develop? How do you think an applied anthropologist might try to resolve the conflict?

NOTES

[1] For additional information on jobs and careers in anthropology, visit the following website: www.aaanet.org/profdev/careers/index.cfm

[2] In reading these figures it is important to keep in mind that they do not indicate that people in Afghanistan and Swaziland reach the age of 45 or 32 and then die. Although residents of those countries *do* routinely die at much earlier ages than inhabitants of much wealthier countries, the figures also take into account the very large numbers of infants and children who die in the first five years of life, as well as the disproportionate numbers of women who die in childbirth.

[3] Johan Galtung is usually credited with the introduction of the term "structural violence."

REFERENCES CITED

Bassett, Thomas J. and Alex Winter-Nelson
    2010 *The Atlas of World Hunger*. Chicago: University of Chicago Press.

Bodley, John H.
    2015 *Victims of Progress*, 6th ed. Lanham, MD: Roman & Littlefield.

Chambers, Robert
    1983 *Rural Development: Putting the Last First*. London" Routledge.
    2014 *Into the Unknown: Explorations in Development Practice*. Rugby, UK: Practical Action Publishing.

Ervin, Alexander M.
    2005 *Applied Anthropology: Tools and Perspectives for Contemporary Practice*. 2nd ed. Boston: Pearson.

Escobar, Arturo
    1995 *Encountering Development: The Making and Unmaking of the Third World*. Princeton: Princeton University Press.

Farmer, Paul
    2003 *Pathologies of Power: Health, Human Rights and the New War on the Poor*. Berkeley: University of California Press.

Gatinois, Clare
    2014 Lisbon's Desperate Need for Cash Leaves It under Angola's Thumb. *The Guardian Weekly* 190(26):9. Le Monde

Hewlett, Barry S. and Richard P. Amola
  2003 Cultural Contexts of Ebola in Northern Uganda. *Emerging Infectious Diseases* 9(10):1242-1248.

Hewlett, Barry S. and Bonnie L. Hewlett
  2008 *Ebola, Culture and Politics: The Anthropology of an Emerging Disease*. Boston: Wadsworth Cengage.

Inhorn, Marcia C. and Peter J. Brown, eds.
  1997 *The anthropology of Infectious Disease: International Health Perspectives.* Amsterdam: Gordon and Beach Publishers.

Jordon, Ann T.
  2012 *Business Anthropology*, 2nd ed. Prospect Heights, IL: Waveland.

Lappé, Francis Moore, Joswph Collins, and Peter Rosset
  1998 *World Hunger: 12 Myths*. Mew York: The Institute for Food and Develoment Policy.

Nolan, Riall W.
  2002 *Development Anthropology: Encounters in the Real World*. Boulder, CO: Westview Pres.

Reyes-Foster, Beatriz and Ty Matejowsky
  2014 Why Undergraduates, Why Now? *Anthropology News* 55:5-6:3.

Robbins, Richard H.
  2011 *Global Problems and the Culture of Capitalism*, 6th ed. Upper-Saddle River, NJ: Prentice Hall.

Sattenspiel, Lisa
  2000 Tropical Environments. Human Activities, and the Transmission of Infectious Diseases. *Yearbook of Physical Anthropology* 43:3-81.

Scheper-Hughes, Nancy
  1992 *Death Without Weeping: The Violence of Everyday Life in Brazil.*   Berkeley: University of California Press.

Wolfe, Nathan D., Peter Daszak, A. Marm Kilpatrick, and Donald S. Burke
  2005 Bushmeat Hunting, Deforestation and Prediction of Zoonotic Disease Emergence. *Emerging Infectious Diseases* 11 (12):1822-1827.

Wood, Josh
  2014 Archaeology Booms with Oil. *The Oregonian*, Thursday, June 17. Associated Press.

World Health Organization (WHO)
  2008 *The world Heath Report*. Geneva:WHO.
  2013 *The World Health report*. Geneva:WHO.

Glossary

Acculturation   The process of adopting the cultural practices of a new society. Usually the new society dominates one's original society.

Acephalous   Literally, "headless." Acephalous societies, which include bands and tribes, have no central, coercive authority.

Achieved status   Status that is derived from an individual's own achievements, as is characteristic of bands and tribes. Achieved status is contrasted with ascribed status.

Adams, Ansel   1902–1984. American photographer known especially for his large-format black and white landscape photographs.

Aeschylus   Ca. 525–455 B.C.E. Ancient Greek author of tragic plays.

Affinal   Referring to kin connected to an individual by marriage.

Age grade   A grouping, usually of males, based on age and characteristic of tribal societies. Membership in an age grade cuts across kin groups, such as lineages and clans, and serves to delineate age-determined obligations.

Age set   The members of a particular age grade. An age set, made up of members of different kinship groups, move together through age grades and usually experience a feeling of solidarity that transcends kinship boundaries.

Agriculture   Intensive production of domesticated plants on a large scale, involving such practices as irrigation, fertilization, and animal or fossil fuel traction. Agriculture is often accompanied by the raising of domesticated animals and is characteristic of state level societies.

Aka   A primarily foraging people of the Central African Republic and the Republic of the Congo, who refer to themselves as Baaka or Bayaka.

Animatism   The belief that a force animates the world and may become manifest in living or non-living things.

Animism   The belief that natural phenomena are endowed with spiritual features

Applied anthropology   The application of information derived from anthropology to local and global human problems. Applied anthropologists work both in the United States and in many other countries on problems such as health, hunger, income generation and agricultural production.

Archaeology   The study of past human groups and their environments, both natural and constructed, through investigation of their physical and cultural remains.

Arnold, Matthew   1822–1888. English poet, critic, and social philosopher, known for his erudition and Victorian sense of moral responsibility.

Ascribed status   Status that is determined by membership in a kinship group instead of by individual achievement, as is in the case of achieved status. Ascribed status is characteristic of chiefdoms and states.

Australopithecines   A member of one of the several species of the genus *Australopithecus,* the first bipedal hominid who flourished between 4 million and 2 million years ago in Africa.

Aymara   An indigenous ethnic group living primarily in the highlands of Bolivia, Peru, and Chile.

Aztec   A native ethnic group of central Mexico, whose state-based society flourished from the 14th to the early/mid sixteenth century, at which point it was destroyed by the Spaniards.

Band   A small, acephalous social/political group, usually made up of slightly extended families who live by foraging in a seasonal round and are linked to each other through kindreds.

Barbarian/Barbarism   An outmoded, ethnocentric term used in the nineteenth and early twentieth centuries to describe groupings now described as tribes or chiefdoms.

Big man   A term derived from Melanesian Pidgin English used to describe an influential, self appointed organizer. Big men have no formal, coercive authority and do not have access to a superior standard of living than other members in the group.

Bilateral descent   The tracing of kin connections over the generations through both males and females but without the formation of descent groups.

Bilateral kinship   The recognition of kin connections over the generations through both males and females, a characteristic of virtually all societies.

Boas, Franz   1858–1942. A German immigrant with a Ph.D. in physics, Boas established American anthropology as an academic discipline and stressed its values of cultural relativism and the avoidance of ethnocentrism.

Bonobo   A species of the genus *Pan,* closely related to the other species of *Pan,* the common chimpanzee. Bonobos were formerly referred to as "pygmy" chimpanzees.

Botswana   An independent country in southern Africa, formerly the British Protectorate of Bechuanaland. Botswana, independent since 1966, is the homeland of a large group of Ju/'hoansi (also called !Kung), who are a minority population there.

Bridewealth   Wealth transferred from the kin of the groom to the kin of the bride at marriage

Cargo cults   Millenarian movements in Melanesia in the early twentieth century. These movements were characterized by beliefs among native populations that European goods (cargo) would arrive for native people in the near future and usher in an era of prosperity.

Caste   A social grouping in which membership is set at birth, and cannot be altered during an individual's lifetime. Caste systems are highly stratified and are found today primarily in India and Nepal.

Cellini, Benvenuto   1500–1571. Italian sculptor, goldsmith, musician, public figure and autobiographer, an interesting and influential figure of the Italian Renaissance.

Celtic   The Celts are an ethnic group, originating in Central Europe roughly four thousand years ago, but eventually migrating as far west as Ireland. Today people of Celtic origin are most concentrated in Ireland, Scotland, Wales, and the tip of Normandy, where Celtic languages are still spoken by a minority of the population.

Chief   The central authority figure in a chiefdom. Chiefs have central, coercive authority, and their status is derived from their membership in a highly ranked lineage. Chiefs and their close kin enjoy a higher standard of living than members of lower ranked lineages.

Chiefdom   A social/political group characterized by ranked lineages and organized around a leader or chief, who comes from the most highly ranked lineage. Chiefdoms have little administrative infrastructure, and because they depend upon personal linkages, tend to be unstable.

Chomsky, Noam   Born 1928. An American linguist and social and political critic, best known for his development of the concept of transformational generative syntax.

Civilization   A social/political grouping centered upon an urban center. Since the middle of the twentieth century this term has been replaced in anthropological usage by the term "state."

Clan   A descent group in which the links to the founding ancestor (who or which may be supernatural) cannot be specified because of their great antiquity. Clans may contain multiple related lineages. Clans are characteristic of tribes and chiefdoms.

Class   A social grouping in which membership is ascribed at birth but can be altered through luck and personal achievement throughout an individual's lifetime. Social class systems are stratified, with members of the highest classes enjoying the most power, prestige, and wealth. Members of lower classes are poorer, have less prestige, less power, and are far more numerous.

Cognatic   A term describing descent group membership which is calculated through any combination of male and/or female links.

Communitas   A feeling of oneness, equality and unity with others, often brought about by religious ritual. This concept was developed by Victor Turner who opposed communitas to "structure" or the ordinary, everyday institutions, norms, rules and laws of society.

Comparative   In anthropology, a process involving the comparison of cultural practices, beliefs and/ or values of one culture with that of another or others.

Consanguineal   A term describing individuals who are linked through common biological heritage, or "blood," in contrast to affinal kin, who are joined by marriage, or fictive kin, who are joined by cultural convention.

Contagious magic   The principle that objects which have been in close contact with a person may continue to affect that person

Continuum   A collection of a elements that form a related group such that each element is slightly different from the ones preceding and succeeding it in a predictable and consistent way (e.g.: increased complexity or increased saturation).

Corporate descent group   A group of kin who collectively share rights, privileges and liabilities.

Corporate group   Any group of people who collectively share rights, privileges and liabilities.

Craft   A designation of a range of artistic production, such as ceramics, handweaving, quilting, woodworking, that is produced by noncorporate individuals. Crafts usually combine utility with personal attention to aesthetic value.

Creole   A language derived from a pidgin, but that has become the first language of a speech community.

Cross cousin   A cousin to whom one is related through parents of the opposite sex (mother's brother's child or father's sister's child).

Cross-cultural   Involving comparison and contrast between and among cultural systems.

Cuchulain   Irish culture hero of many legends known also in Scotland, Wales, and the Isle of Man. Like many other culture heroes, he was the son of a supernatural father and a mortal mother. He was known for his frenzied battle rage.

Cultural relativism   The notion that, as a rule, the values and practices of any given culture should be judged according to their own principles and not according to the values of other cultural systems.

Culture   The rules, values, practices, and productions shared by a group of people who live within a specific society. The "blueprint" for operating within that society.

Culture broker   A person who helps to explain a community, its members, and its cultural practices to an outsider.

Culture hero   A character appearing in myths and legends who embodies the noble and valorous virtues members of a society see as central to their culture and themselves.

Culture shock   A feeling, often experienced by anthropologists and others in an unfamiliar cultural situation, of being alienated, incompetent, depressed, and lonely.

Darwin, Charles   1809–1882. English naturalist who developed the idea of "natural selection" in his famous 1859 book, *On the Origin of Species.* Darwin is credited with being the prime mover in the now widely accepted principle of biological evolution of all organisms.

Descriptive linguistics   The branch of linguistics that explores the structure of the sound system, form, and grammar of language.

Dialect   A subset of a language that is mutually intelligible with other subsets of the same language, though they may vary to some extent in pronunciation, vocabulary, and/or grammar.

Dichotomous   Having to do with "dichotomy," or division into two parts.

Diebenkorn, Richard   1922–1993 American painter and printmaker, whose representational work evolved into progressively more abstract work over the course of his life.

Diffusion-   The spread of an idea, practice, or trait from one group to another.

Dinka   A cattle herding tribal population who live in Sudan, Africa.

Dogon   A Tribal group of horticulturists in Mali (Africa) widely known among anthropologists and many artists for their traditional sculpture and ceremonial masks.

Domestication   The process of modifying and producing organisms (plants and animals) to suit the needs of humans. Domesticated organisms always manifest some genetic differences that distinguish them from their wild ancestors.

Dominance hierarchy-   A ranking of power and prestige.

Dowry   Wealth from a bride's kin that accompanies the bride to her marriage

Durkheim, Emile   1858–1917. French sociologist whose work influenced the anthropology of religion and other topics. Durkheim proposed that religion arose as a collective worship of society and its power over individuals and groups.

Ebola   A contagious viral disease, most prevalent in sub Saharan Africa, that is transmitted from animals to humans and between persons. There is no cure for Ebola, and the death rate ranges from 50 percent to 90 percent.

Elite   Having high status, prestige, and privilege.

Emic   A term used. primarily by anthropologists, to refer to a point of view characteristic of people *inside* a particular culture. It stands in contrast to the *etic* (external) perspective.

Empirical   Relying on concrete observation and/or experimentation, rather than intuition or assumption.

Endogamy   Marriage within a social group to which an individual belongs.

Environmental niche   The complex of environmental characteristics that make up the environment of an organism or group of organisms.

Ethnic group/ethnicity   Members of an ethnic group share cultural values and practices; these shared cultural elements are what define ethnicity. Members of an ethnic group are often part of the same race, but this is not always true. Race is biological. Ethnicity is cultural.

Ethnocentrism   The notion that one's own culture is the best, ideal, normal, standard, and that all others are inferior to the extent that they diverge from one's own.

Ethnolinguistics   The study of the cultural values that are encoded in language and language use.

Ethnology   The comparative study of cultural systems.

Etic   A term used, primarily by anthropologists, to refer to a point of view characteristic of people *outside* a particular culture. It stands in contrast to the *emic* perspective, which is characteristic of the members of a culture being studied.

Euclid   Third century B.C.E. A Greek philosopher/mathematician working in the Greek city of Alexandria, Egypt, who established the discipline of geometry as a practical and intellectual discipline.

Euripides   Ca. 480–406 B.C.E. Ancient Greek author of tragic plays.

Exogamy   Marriage outside a social group to which an individual belongs.

Fallow   The uncultivated or "resting" stage of potential crop-producing land. The practice of leaving land fallow is essential for slash and burn horticulturalists.

Family parasitism   An ethnocentric term employed by some Western and colonial policy makers to describe the dependence of extended family members upon relatives who have become successful in the modern, metropolitan world. The term is frequently applied in Africa and represents the clash of traditional tribal values of mutual family support with urban, state level values of individualism.

Female register   A term used to describe what some linguists have identified as a distinctive style of language used by many women. The female register is usually described as involving an absence of aggressive expressions, pointed or direct remarks, and by the maintenance of standard usage and mitigating expressions.

Fictive kinship   Kinship based on cultural convention rather than biological relationship or marriage.

Field (in anthropology)   The location in which an anthropologist works. When they go to a place in which they collect data, anthropologists say they are "going into the fied," or that they are going to be "doing fieldwork."

Fine art   A term designating high status art of no immediate utilitarian function, especially painting, sculpture, and recently, photography.

Folk art   A term designating art produced by persons without formal/academic training, originally for their own use. Today, the term "folk art" often designates art produced by residents of peasant or tribal communities for consumption by members of the majority, metropolitan society.

Foraging   The practice of hunting for wild animal foods and gathering wild plant foods rather than *producing* domesticated plants or animals. Also know as "hunting and gathering."

Fraternal polyandry   The practice of two or more brothers sharing one or more wives.

Freud, Sigmund   1856–1939. Austrian physician, originally specializing in neurology, who was the predominant figure in the development of modern psychology, including the practice of psychoanalysis and the concept of the unconscious mind.

Friedl, Ernestine   American anthropologist known for her work on gender issues, especially her contention that a major determining factor in women's status is their participation in primary subsistence as owners or controllers of the means of subsistence.

Ghost Dance   A revitalization movement among Native Americans (especially Paiutes) in the late nineteenth century in the western United States.

Globalization   The accelerated movement of people, goods, ideas, and money throughout the world.

Goodall, Jane   Born 1934. Goodall is an English primatologist who is widely acclaimed both for her pioneering work in primate behavior in the wild, and for her efforts in conserving their populations and habitat. Before Goodall's work there was very little empirical information about the behavior of chimpanzees or other apes in their natural surroundings.

Habilines   Members of the species *Homo habilis,* who flourished roughly from 2.3 to 1.4 million years ago in Africa.

Haiku   An economical Japanese poetic form characterized by a rigid framework of three phrases of 5, 7, and 5 syllable-like structures, the juxtaposition of contrasting perspectives, and a seasonal theme.

Haplotype   A group of gene variants (alleles, for example the ABO blood groups are different alleles of the same gene) that are inherited together.

Herding   The practice of relying for subsistence primarily or exclusively on herds or flocks of domesticated animals. Also known as "pastoralism."

Heuristic   Helpful in learning, exploring, and/or discovery.

Hierarchy/hierarchical   Organization into a series of categories in which each category is considered superior to the one directly below it. In social hierarchies this superiority is reflected in higher social status, greater power, and access to more material wealth.

Historical linguistics   The study of the development, relationships, and change in languages and language families over time.

Holistic   Having to do with whole or complete phenomenon, rather than focusing on its constituent parts.

Homer   The traditionally assumed blind author of the ancient Greek epics, the *Iliad* and the *Odyssey.* Although there is no concrete evidence of Homer's existence, he is generally assumed to have lived in the eighth century B.C.E., and to have composed the two epics orally from preexisting traditional poetic accounts of conflicts that had occurred four hundred years earlier.

Hominin   Humans and their extinct ancestors after they diverged from the ancestral line with chimpanzees and other nonhuman primates roughly 5-7 million years ago.

Homo erectus   An extinct hominin species that flourished roughly from 1.8 million to 143,000 years ago. *Homo erectus* was the first hominin to move out of Africa and into Europe and Asia.

Homo sapiens   The scientific designation of the genus and species to which contemporary humans (*Homo sapiens sapiens*) belong, as well as Neanderthals (*Homo sapiens neanderthalensis*).

Hopi   A Native American group of Pueblo peoples who live primarily on the Hopi reservation in northern Arizona.

Horticulture The practice of relying for subsistence on small-scale growing of plant foods, without such practices as traction, irrigation, or intensive fertilization. Most horticultural plots must be periodically abandoned and left to lie fallow for a period of time.

Hozho A Navajo term for a central Navajo cultural value, usually translated as "beauty," "harmony," or "balance."

Human For most anthropologists, "human" refers to living or extinct members of the genus *Homo,* beginning with *Homo erectus*, and ending (so far) with us.

Hunt, William Holman 1823–1910. English Victorian painter, especially of religious themes, and a founder of the Pre Raphaelite movement that stressed a spiritual rather than a rationalist approach to art.

Hunting and gathering The practice of hunting for wild animal foods and gathering wild plant foods rather than *producing* domesticated plants or animals. Also know as "foraging."

Hypothesis (plural: hypotheses) A reasoned speculation about cause and effect based on limited evidence and subject to further data collection in such a way as to be validated or falsified.

Igbo An ethnic group of primarily farmers and traders in Nigeria (Africa), formerly referred to in English as "Ibo." They make up roughly a fifth of the Nigerian population.

Iliad Ancient Greek epic poem, attributed to Homer, that chronicled late battles in the Trojan War between the residents of the city of Troy and the allied forces of Greek city-states.

Imitative magic The principle that objects representing a person can be manipulated in such a way as to affect that person

Inca A native ethnic group of Peru, who from the mid fifteenth to the mid sixteenth century ruled an extensive empire centered in Cuzco, until it was conquered by the Spaniards.

Incest Sexual activity between individuals who are closely related by biological heritage or considered closely related by cultural convention.

Incest taboo The cultural prohibition of sexual relationships among certain kin.

Indigenous Native; originating in the place where a group, language or other cultural trait presently exist.

Inflected/inflection A characteristic of words (or of languages) in which the words are structurally marked to indicating their functions in a sentence. Latin and Sanskrit are highly inflected languages; English and Chinese languages are not.

Innovation Invention; creation of a novel object, process or practice.

International Phonetic Alphabet (IPA) A system of symbols that can be used to write any speech sound in any language.

Ju/'hoansi Also referred to (by outsiders) as !Kung. An indigenous population of sub-Saharan Africa, living primarily in Botswana, Namibia, and Angola. Until the middle of the twentieth century the Ju/'hoansi were primarily hunter-gatherers. The / and ' indicate implosive speech sounds in the Ju/'hoansi language.

Karma In Hindu theology, the cumulative effect of an individual's actions in all previous lives, considered to determine his/ her destiny.

Kazakhstan A central Asian country, formerly part of the Soviet Union, some of whose inhabitants are pastoralists relying on the herding of sheep, goats, and horses.

Kin selection The process whereby an individual enhances his/ her reproductive success by acts favoring the fitness of others who share some genes in common with the individual, namely close relatives.

Kindred A group that includes all persons to whom an individual is related by birth or marriage, through both male and female lines. Kindreds are large, unstable, and not organized, but they offer an individual a number of kin on which to draw in times of need.

Kinship The system of relationships established by blood (descent) and marriage and/ or cultural convention.

!Kung Also referred to (by themselves and some snthropologists) as Ju/'hoansi. An indigenous population of sub-Saharan Africa, living primarily in Botswana, Namibia, and Angola. Until the middle of the twentieth century the !Kung were primarily hunter-gatherers. The ! refers to an implosive speech sound in the !Kung language.

Kuru A fatal, progressive, neurological disease formerly prevalent in Papua New Guinea that was transmitted by mortuary or memorial cannibalism. Kuru is similar to "mad cow disease."

Kwakiutl A Native American tribal group, resident along the coast of British Columbia (Canada) and into Washington state. The Kwakiutl are known for their painted wooden sculptures and two dimensional wooden and fiber art.

Kyrgyzstan A central Asian country, formerly part of the Soviet Union, some of whose inhabitants are pastoralists relying on the herding of sheep, goats, and horses.

Labov, William Born 1927. An influential American linguist, known for his pioneering sociolinguistic research, including studies of Black English Vernacular and of cumulative change in the speech of the residents of Philadelphia.

Lapps Also known as Sami. A European ethnic group living mostly in Sweden and Norway, and to some extent in Finland and Russia. Traditionally the Lapps were a pastoral people, relying primarily on herding reindeer, but today only 10% of the population follows this practice.

Lee, Richard B. Born 1937. A Canadian anthropologist widely known for his extensive ethnographic accounts with the Ju/'hoansi people of Botswana nad Namibia.

Legend A narrative of past events, generally believed to be true by members of the cultural group in which it is relevant. Legends often involve both mortal and supernatural characters and embody important cultural values.

Lexicon Vocabulary; the stock of words in a language.

Limbic region An area of the human brain that is evolutionarily ancient, and that is involved with emotion, among other aspects of interpretation and response.

Liminality A ritual stage between a previous status and incorporation into a new status; a special state apart from everyday life and normal society.

Lineage   A kin group whose members trace their descent to a common ancestor through known links.

Linguist   Someone who undertakes the systematic study of language structure, origin change, and/or use. Though linguists may speak several languages, the specific term for such a person is *polyglot.*

Linguistic relativity   The principle that, despite variation in lexicon, no language is superior to or more advanced than any other. All languages are equally capable of expressing the entire range of human thought, feeling, and experience.

Linguistics   The systematic study of the structure, history, production, and functions of language and languages.

Lyell, Charles   1797–1875. British geologist and proponent of *uniformitarianism,* the notion, now very widely accepted, that the earth was formed over a long period of time by forces still in operation. This idea influenced similar notions in biology and spurred the development of the concept of natural selection.

Maasai   An indigenous population of Kenya and Tanzania (Africa). The Maasai have traditionally subsisted primarily on their large herds of cattle.

Macaque   A genus of Old World monkeys including several species.

Magic   A set of ritual actions intended to achieve a specific effect or outcome.

Malinowski, Bronislaw Kaspar   1884–1942. Polish born, British socio-cultural anthropologist, best known for his work in the Trobriand Islands, his development of the anthropological theory of functionalism, and as a pioneer of modern anthropological fieldwork.

Malthus, Thomas Robert   1766–1834. British social economist, best known for his view that it was in the nature of populations to increase more rapidly than the food supply. He then argued that the poor (who had less access to food) had an obligation to restrict the growth of their population through sexual abstinence. He also proposed that such natural disasters as war, flood, and famine would also disproportionately diminish their numbers.

Mana   A spiritual power or energy which can manifest itself in natural objects, persons and places. In Polynesian religious tradition, mana is an amorphous, intrinsic power inherent in some natural and human-generated phenomena. Some persons have greater abilities to control mana than others.

Mao Tse-tung   1893-1976 Chinese revolutionary, early member of the Chinese Communist Party, and first head of state of the People's Republic of China.

Maori   An indigenous ethnic group of New Zealand.

Marett, Robert R.   1866-1943. A British anthropologist who theorized about the origin of religion and developed the concept of animatism. Marett proposed animatism as humankind's earliest form of religion.

Matriarchy   A society dominated by women, as a group. Though some societies have near gender equality, and in some societies women may hold (or have held) extremely high status and great power, no matriarchal societies are known ever to have existed.

Material culture   The material/concrete objects produced and employed by members of a particular cultural system, including such elements as tools, houses, clothing, and art objects.

Matrilineage   A lineage in which membership is traced through the female line only.

Matrilineal   Having to do with descent calculated through the female line only, that is, from mothers through daughters, granddaughters, etc.

Matrilocal   Postmarital residence in which the married couple lives with or near the wife's family.

Maya   Indigenous ethnic population of southern Mexico, Guatemala, Belize, El Salvador, and Honduras. Mayan peoples are divided into multiple distinct subgroups, speaking a variety of related languages and dialects. The Mayan civilization, made up of loosely related city-states, flourished from roughly 200 B.C.E. to 900 C.E., and was ultimately destroyed by Spanish invaders in the sixteenth century. Alone among New World peoples, the Maya developed a fully elaborated writing system.

Mesopotamia   The area in western Asia centered between the Tigris and Euphrates Rivers, now occupied primarily by Iraq, in which many ancient civilizations existed, beginning with the Sumerian in the fourth millennium B.C.E.

Minoan   A stratified society that flourished on the island of Crete in the third and second millennia B.C.E.

Monogamy   The practice of marrying only one spouse at a time.

Morgan, Lewis Henry   1818–1881. An American ethnographer of American Indian cultures and theorist of the nature of cultural evolution. Though an advocate for Native American peoples, Morgan is today best known for his evolutionary sequence of savagery, barbarism, and civilization, which has been considered unacceptable by anthropologists at least since the middle of the twentieth century. Morgan also focused on kinship and social organization. He was himself married to his matrilateral cross cousin (mother's brother's daughter)!

Morpheme   The smallest word or part of a word with specific meaning. Thus, the word *ear* has one morpheme, *ear,* that refers to a part of the body. The word *arms* has two morphemes, *arm,* which refers to a body part, and *–s,* which indicates plurality.

Morphology   The study of the structure of words and the specific meanings of their constituents.

Myth   A narrative, believed within the societies that subscribed to it to be true, that presents an account of fundamental cosmic, human, and supernatural events and obligations. The term "myth," as used by anthropologists, does not have a negative connotation or imply inaccuracy. Myths commonly provide accounts of the creation of the world, the consequences of death, and the nature of the relationships among humans and between humans and others, natural and supernatural. A false or misguided belief.

Natolocal   Postmarital residence in which the married couple continue to live separately, each spouse with his/her family of origin.

Navajo   A Native American ethnic group many of whom occupy a reservation located in Arizona, New Mexico, and Utah. Artistically, the Navajo are known for their finely woven rugs, silver and turquoise jewelry, and their sand "paintings," originally made exclusively for curing rituals.

Neanderthal Extinct subspecies of *Homo sapiens,* who flourished in Europe roughly 135,000 to 35,000 B.C.E, characterized by a low cranial vault, heavy brown ridges, and often a knob, or "chignon" at the base of the skull.

Neolocal Postmarital residence in which the married couple moves to a new location that is the home of neither the wife's family nor the husband's family.

New World A term often used by anthropologist, especially archaeologists, to refer to North, Central, and South America, in contradistinction to the Old World (q.v.).

Nomadic Moving from place to place throughout the year, without having a fixed residence. Nomadic peoples, however, do not range aimlessly throughout the countryside. Instead, they follow a general pattern of seeking specific resources at times and places at which they are likely to be available.

Nuer A cattle herding tribal population who live in Sudan and Ethiopia, Africa.

Odyssey Ancient Greek epic poem, traditionally attributed to Homer, that chronicles the return of the hero Odysseus to his home in Greece after his victory in the Trojan War.

Old World A term used by anthropologists, especially archaeologists, to refer to Europe, Asia, and Africa, in contradistinction to the New World (q.v.).

Operationalize To render empirically workable within research. For example, an anthropologist who wants to explore the idea of "contentment" in a community must first render the term "contentment" empirically researchable by operationalizing it. This could entail dividing it into specific, concrete elements that can be systematically explored.

Outsider art A term coined in 1972 by Roger Cardinal to refer to art created outside the boundaries of work accepted by the mainstream artistic community. Outsider artists are often self taught and frequently have no connections with other, more widely accepted artists.

Parallel cousin A cousin to whom one is related through parents of the same sex: mother's sister's child or father's brother's child.

Participant observation A term coined by Bronislaw Malinowski to describe an overarching research method for anthropological fieldwork, now widely employed by anthropologists. Participant observation involves participating as much as possible in the life of the community under investigation, while also bringing one's anthropological frame of reference to bear upon one's observations and recordings of culture.

Pastoralism The practice of relying for subsistence primarily or exclusively on herds or flocks of domesticated animals. Also known as "herding."

Patriarchal Dominated by senior men.

Patricians In ancient Rome, a caste-like category of patrilineages who claimed descent from the founders of the Roman Republic, from whom most political and religious leaders were drawn, and who enjoyed more privileges and higher status than other free

Romans who were known as Plebeians. As time went on, Patrician membership was extended, and their exclusive privileges were lessened.

Patrilateral   Relating to the father's side of the family.

Patrilineage   A lineage in which membership is calculated through only male links.

Patrilocal   Postmarital residence in which the married couple lives with or near the husband's family.

Peonage   A system of subordination according to which labor is coerced and maintained through continuing debt, which can be inherited by the debtor's heirs. Peonage was characteristic of Mexico, Guatemala, and some South American countries after the Spanish conquest.

Phoneme   The smallest element of sound that is sufficient to alter meaning within a specific language.

Phonestheme   A component of a group of words that appears to have specific referential qualities, despite a lack of discernible genetic relationship. A classic example of a phonestheme is the "gl-" element in words such as "glow," "gleam," "glitter," "glisten," and "glint," that all concern low or unstable light.

Phonetic   Having to do with the sounds of language.

Phonology   The study of the sound system or structural patterns of language.

Physical anthropology   The branch of anthropology that concentrates on the biological aspects of humans and their close nonhuman relatives. Physical anthropologists examine such topics as evolution, human variation, and the order *Primates.*

Pidgin   A reduced linguistic system made up of constituents derived from three or more different languages. A pidgin is no speaker's native language, and usually develops in situations of trade or forced or voluntary migration. If a pidgin becomes the native language of a group, it will become a completely developed language, referred to by linguists as a "creole."

Piloerection   The erection of body hair as part of a strong affective response such as fear or aggression.

Plebeians   In ancient Rome, a caste-like category of patrilineages to which most free Romans belonged. Plebeians, roughly equivalent to commoners, originally had fewer rights and privileges and less political representation than Patricians, to whose status they aspired. As time progressed, Plebeians experienced greater equality and representation.

Polyandry   A form of plural marriage (polygamy) in which two or more men are married to (i.e., share) one or more wives.

Polygamy   A term that covers both kinds of plural marriage: polyandry and polygyny.

Polyglot   A speaker of multiple languages. This differs from a linguist, who is a person who studies language (though many linguists are also polyglots).

Polygyny   The practice of a man marrying more than one wife at a time. Polygyny is a variety of polygamy (plural marriage), which also includes polyandry, the practice of women being married to more than one husband at a time.

Popular art   An umbrella term referring to art not produced within elite art circles. Popular art may include folk art, outsider art, and art aimed at unsophisticatred consumers in stratified societies.

Precontact   Occurring before contact with another group. Anthropologists frequently refer to cultural systems as they were before contact with an invading colonial people, as with precontact Native American cultures in North, Central, and South America, before European invaders arrived.

Priest   A religious practitioner who operates within and derives authority from an institution.

Primate   A taxonomic order (*Primates* in scientific Latin) to which humans, apes, monkeys, prosimians, and their extinct ancestors belong.

Psycholinguistics   The study of the neurobiological aspects of language. Psycholinguistics includes studies of such phenomena as language acquisition, aphasia, and other impediments in language production.

Pueblo Indian   Term applied to Native North American groups who live in the U.S. Southwest originally and often still occupy "pueblos" (Spanish: towns) consisting of multifamily adobe dwellings. Some Pueblo groups include the Hopi, Zuni, and Acoma, and are known artistically for their hand built ceramic vessels.

Qualitative research methods   Research methods that are not based primarily upon the generation of quantitative data, and are thus likely to be more flexible, informal, and personal than quantitative methods.

Quantitative research methods   Research methods that are aimed primarily at generating quantifiable data. Quantitative methods are thus likely to be formal, rigidly structured, with an emphasis on consistency rather than personal interaction between the researcher and the informant.

Race   A social categorization of people based on subjectively perceived physical differences among them..

Raga   A form of Indian (that is, from India) classical music involving improvisation and related to particular times of day and seasons of the year.

Referent   The phenomenon to which a word or morpheme refers.

Register   In linguistics, oral style, conditioned by a variety of phenomena, including ethnicity, age, occupation, social status, and gender.

Revere, Paul   1734-1818. Massachusetts born silversmith and American patriot, active in the Revolutionary War.

Revitalization movement   A deliberate movement by some members of a society to construct a more satisfying culture, especially by reinvigorating perceived elements of of past cultural practices.

Rite of Spring   A ballet choreographed by Vaslav Nijinsky and with music composed by Igor Stravinsky, first performed in Paris in 1913. Though now acclaimed as a classic, the first performance of the ballet caused a riot on the grounds that its music and choreography were primitive, uncouth, and obscene.

Rites of passage   Rituals that accompany initiations or life-cycle stages such as birth, puberty, marriage, reproduction and death. Arnold van Gennep held that such rites typically follow a sequential pattern of separation, liminality and reincorporation.

Ritual   Prescribed, standardized ceremonial activity.

Sami   Also known as Lapps. A European ethnic group living mostly in Sweden and Norway, and to some extent in Finland and Russia. Traditionally the Lapps were a pastoral people, relying primarily on herding reindeer, but today only 10% of the population follows this practice.

Sapir-Whorf Hypothesis   A diffuse collection of statements and ideas about the relationships among language, thought, and culture, derived from the writings and lectures of Benjamin Lee Whorf and Edward Sapir. One useful summary of the Sapir-Whorf Hypothesis is that language encodes and reinforces habits of thought and thus affects culture.

Sapir, Edward   1884–1939. An American linguist (born in German Pomerania) most influential for his research on American Indian languages and his views on the influence of language on thought and culture.

Savage/Savagery   An outmoded, ethnocentric term formerly applied to band-based peoples.

Seasonal round   The organized nomadic circuit made by hunter-gatherers of their territory in search of seasonally available resources.

Sedentary   Having a fixed residence; not nomadic. In general, groups with a substantial investment in the land base on which they subsist tend to be sedentary.

Serfdom   An institution of subordination in which many agricultural workers are bound to their employers' land, though their persons are not usually subject to sale.

Serrano, Andres   1950– . American artist and photographer known for his controversial works, especially those involving bodily effluvia, such as urine and feces.

Service, Elman   1915–1996. An American anthropologist, best known for his classification of human groups according to their complexity of organization and integration. Service's categories, widely employed by anthropologists today, are band, tribe, chiefdom, and state.

Shaman   A religious practitioner, usually part time, who connects with supernatural entities, including the spirits of the dead, and often acts their mouthpiece. Shamans are most often involved with healing.

Sharecropping   A system of agricultural labor according to which agricultural workers receive a plot of land, often with a house, for their own use and a proportion of the crop they harvest, in exchange for their labor and the remainder of the harvested crop, which are owed to the landlord. Sharecroppers do not own the land they work, and few of them own even their house or garden plot.

Shifting horticulture   The practice of moving cultivation from one plot to another in order to maintain fertility and reduce weed infestation. Shifting horticulture is characteristic of slash-and-burn farmers.

Shostak, Marjorie   1945–1996. An American anthropologist best known for her exploration of the !Kung (or Ju/'hoansi) people of Botswana. Shostak is the author of

Nisa: The Life and Words of a !Kung Woman (Cambridge, MA: Harvard University Press, 2000) and its posthumous sequel, *Return to Nisa* (Cambridge, MA: Harvard University Press, 2002).

Shyrdak Traditional felted rugs produced in Kyrgyzstan.

Sitar A large stringed instrument used primarily in the classical music of India. During the 1970s, thanks to the influence of the Beatles, the sitar was sometimes employed in Western popular music, as well.

Slash and burn A form of horticulture in which the vegetation in a potential garden plot is cut down (slashed) and then burnt before planting occurs. Also called swidden cultivation. Slash and burn farming usually also involves shifting horticulture.

Sociolinguistics The study of the relationship between language and social life, especially with respect to social class, and ethnicity.

Sodality A non kin-based grouping or association of individuals organized for a specific purpose. In tribal societies sodalities, including age grades, cross-cut lineages; this helps to prevent lineages from fragmenting the group.

Sonnet A poetic form consisting of 14 lines. There are several varieties of sonnet structure, depending on time and place (notably France, Italy, and England), most of which conclude with a rhyming couplet.

Spencer, Herbert 1820-1903. English political philosopher, associate of Charles Darwin, and coiner of the term "survival of the fittest." Spence applied the term primarily to social and political contexts, though he also accepted its application to biological evolution.

State A social/political grouping with a large population; a stratified social system of castes or classes; central, coercive authority; and an elaborately organized system of integration. States have a wide range of occupational specialties and are inevitably marked by inequality of access to wealth and power.

Stratification Literally, "layering." The organization of a society into levels in which there is differential access to wealth status, and power according to social class or caste. Stratification is characteristic of urban based societies supported by agricultural subsistence systems.

Stratified Literally, "layered." Societies in which there is differential access to wealth status, and power according to social class or caste, are said to be stratified.

Structural violence Damage inflicted on people because of social, political, and economic institutions and practices. Racial, ethnic, sexual, and class-based discrimination are examples of structural violence.

Subdiscipline One of the four subdivisions of American anthropology: physical anthropology, archaeology linguistics, and cultural or social anthropology.

Subincision A form of body modification formerly practiced as part of puberty initiation among some indigenous communities of northwest Australia. It involved slitting the underside of the penis from the tip to the scrotum.

Subsistence Method of making a living. Though there are thousands of occupations by which the earth's inhabitants have made a living, anthropologists have long grouped these occupations in four categories: hunting and gathering, pastoralism, horticulture, and agriculture, all of which refer to the primary systems by which people acquire food. The greater the surplus provided by the subsistence system (and agriculture produces by far the greatest surplus), the greater diversity of actual subsistence activities within a society.

Swan Lake A romantic ballet with music completed in 1876 by Pyotr Ilyich Tchaikovsky

Swidden A form of horticulture in which the vegetation in a potential garden plot is cut down (slashed) and then burnt before planting occurs. Also called slash and burn cultivation. Swidden farming usually also involves shifting horticulture.

Symbol Something that stands for something else but that has no natural or necessary connection to it. Symbols are connected to what they refer to only because of cultural convention. In linguistics, the primary symbols are words and morphemes.

Syntax The arrangement of words in a meaningful sequence, such as a phrase or sentence. Syntax is often equated roughly with grammar.

Systematic Referring to phenomena in which the elements are related in a conscious, reliable, and predictable way.

Tajikistan A central Asian country, formerly part of the Soviet Union, some of whose inhabitants are pastoralists relying on the herding of sheep, goats, and horses.

Tale A story told for entertainment. Though tales usually contain elements that reflect important cultural values, they are intended primarily for amusement and are not considered to be factual accounts, except, perhaps, by children.

Terence (Publius Terentius Afer) Ca 190–159 B.C.E. A Roman playwright and freed slave of African origin. Today Terence's plays are seldom read, and he is best known for a single quote: "*Homo sum; humani nil a me alienum puto*" (I am a man; I think nothing human is foreign to me).

Totem A significant, supernatural entity, human, animal, natural or human made object that is emblematic of a human group, including a lineage or clan, and that is venerated and accorded ceremonial treatment.

Totemism The cultural practices, including religious and other rituals that accompany a group's veneration of its totem(s).

Transhumance A residential and subsistence pattern according to which a group maintains a primary residence in one location but moves (or part of the group moves) to another residence or to a series of temporary residences during another part of the year.

Tribe An acephalous, social/political grouping with a population larger than that of a band, organized primarily through kinship, often in the form of lineages. Tribes are egalitarian within age and gender groups and usually depend upon horticulture or herding for subsistence.

Trickster A character common in tales and legends, who is wily and clever, but who also violates cultural norms only to prosper in the end. In western Native American tales and legends, lascivious Coyote is a classic trickster figure.

Turkmenistan A central Asian country, formerly part of the Soviet Union, some of whose inhabitants are pastoralists relying on the herding of sheep, goats, and horses.

Uniformitarianism   The scientific theory that the physical processes that prevailed in the past are the same as those that have continued to operate throughout time, into the present. These processes have accounted for such phenomena as evolution and changes in geological and geographical features of the earth.

Unilineal descent   Descent traced through one line only, either the male line or the female line.

Uzbekistan   A central Asian country, formerly part of the Soviet Union, some of whose inhabitants are pastoralists relying on the herding of sheep, goats, and horses.

Van Gogh, Vincent   1853–1890. A Dutch artist, now revered by critics and the general public, but virtually unknown or dismissed by most members of the artistic community during his lifetime.

Washoe   1965–2007. An African born chimpanzee who was the first chimpanzee to be successfully taught to use American Sign Language.

Weltanshauung   A German term meaning "worldview," often used in intellectual circles in place of its English translation.

Whorf, Benjamin Lee   1890–1941. An American linguist and student and associate of Edward Sapir. Though originally trained as a chemical engineer, Whorf becme fascinated by linguistics and the influence of linguistic structure on thought and behavior.

Worldview   The philosophy of life or outlook on the world that is widespread within a given culture. Though different cultures may be said to have different worldviews, this does not mean that each participant in a culture shares every element of a worldview with every other participant in that culture. There are general similarities, but no absolute identities.

Zuni   A Native American Pueblo group whose traditional residence is in northwestern New Mexico. The Zuni are known artistically for their ceramics and silver jewelry.

Name Index

Subject Index

In this index, pages in bold type indicate a glossary entry; page numbers followed by "Fig." or "Table" indicate illustrative material.